Glossary of
Real Estate
Management
Terms

Glossary of Real Estate Management Terms

IREM Institute of Real Estate Management

CHICAGO

Library of Congress Cataloging-in-Publication Data

Glossary of real estate management terms
     p. cm.
  ISBN 1-57203-087-9 (pb)
   1. Real estate business—Dictionaries. 2. Real estate management—Dictionaries. 3. Real property—Dictionaries. 4. Real estate business—Law and legislation—Dictionaries.   I. Institute of Real Estate Management.
  HD1365.G55 2003
  333.33'03—dc21

                                                2002191335

Printed in the United States of America

1 2 3 4 5 6 7 8 9 10 Printing / Year 12 11 10 09 08 07 06 05 04 03

Contents

Publisher's Preface

As the leading source of real estate management information and education, the Institute of Real Estate Management has been defining terms used in its courses and textbooks for more than 70 years. This new *Glossary of Real Estate Management Terms* reflects the diversity of the interests and responsibilities of professionals who manage real property for others as well as the intricacies of operating a real estate management business. The focus of this *Glossary* is on the language of real estate management and the terminology that real estate managers use or are likely to encounter in their dealings with owner-clients, tenants/residents, and on-site employees they supervise. Definitions clearly identify differences in meaning and usage when they vary from one type of property to another.

The activities and responsibilities of real estate managers are wide-ranging. Their focus is on property operations and maintenance and the requisite accounting, record keeping, and reporting that are incumbent in property management. However, their day-to-day duties often require knowledge of a number of additional disciplines. Because purchasing real property is a major capital investment, real estate managers must understand the terms of mortgage loans used for financing and refinancing properties they manage. Rental properties and real estate management firms are operated as business enterprises, and these activities have a specialized vocabulary. Real estate managers work within a variety of contracts, including management agreements, leases, and service contracts so they need to understand the language of contracts. Definitions are also included for many types of lease clauses, in particular those whose meanings vary by property type.

Risk management is an important responsibility related to the safety and security of residents, tenants, and management employees. In particular, management personnel need to be trained in emergency procedures. Insurance claims must be filed when an accident on a managed property causes injury or property damage. Police reports must be filed when a crime is committed. Real estate managers and property owners may also be defendants in lawsuits arising out of such accidents or criminal incidents. All types of properties, but especially commercial properties, can have environmental problems related to hazardous materials. To facilitate real estate managers' understanding in these areas, the *Glossary* includes definitions of insurance coverages, types of crimes and their classification for punishment, and selected terms related to environmental compliance.

In addition, each type of property encompasses unique challenges. Managers of rental apartments must comply with fair housing laws. Government-assisted properties must comply with regulations administered by the U.S. Department of Housing and Urban Development (HUD). Managers of condominiums and similar types of properties work with the homeowners' association and its committees. Managers of mobile home parks and manufactured housing communities use specialized terminology regarding this type of housing and its installation. Office building managers work with space planners, architects, and construction contractors and must be able to communicate knowledgeably with them. To ensure the success of a shopping center, a manager of this type of property must be familiar with the terminology of retailing.

The goal in compiling this *Glossary* has been to provide definitions and sometimes context for the broad array of terms that are specific to real estate management or related to it. The *Glossary* is comprehensive but not all-inclusive. In particular, this book has excluded technical terms that have already been defined in the Institute publication, *The Real Estate Manager's Technical Glossary*. It is hoped that this small volume will be a helpful resource and reference for all those involved in the management of real property, both the career novice and the seasoned professional.

Some Notes on Usage

Listings are presented in alphabetical order following dictionary style (i.e., letter by letter). Thus, 'market' precedes 'marketing' but 'market research' follows 'marketing research.' Cross-references are indicated generally by the words 'see' or 'see also,' although there are sometimes instructions to 'compare' a definition to that of another term. Italic type is used to highlight words within definitions for specific purposes, as shown in the examples that follow.

> **promotional aid** A gift, usually marked with the name of the giver, used as part of a promotional campaign for a product or service; also called *handout* or *giveaway* and sometimes referred to as a *promotional item*. Used in real estate management to interest prospective tenants in leasing space at a particular property.

In the foregoing example, italics are used to identify alternate names. Someone looking up 'handout' or 'giveaway' would find a cross-reference to the primary definition.

> **giveaway** Another name for *promotional aid*.

Italics call out 'giveaway' when that searcher looks up 'promotional aid.' In the same example, 'promotional item' as an alternate name does not include a specific cross-reference because the entry would appear immediately after the definition of 'promotional aid.'

Some definitions include related subentries as a means of providing a clear explanation of the scope of a concept, even though the subentries are themselves defined separately. For example, the definition of 'maintenance' includes information about various types or categories of maintenance (e.g., corrective, preventive, routine, deferred). In some instances, however, the subentries are defined only within the definition of the main term. For example, 'standard specification' and 'nonstandard specification' are cross-referenced to 'specification' where they are defined.

Italic type is also used to highlight terms that a user may find instructive in understanding the definition of a particular term. For example, the definition of 'receiver' includes references to 'bankruptcy' and 'foreclosure' but does not provide any specific details. The italics indicate that those two terms are defined elsewhere in this *Glossary*.

> **receiver** An individual appointed by a court to manage a property that is the subject of a pending *bankruptcy* or *foreclosure*. A receiver's role is to preserve property that has been abandoned or for which there have been allegations of fraud or mismanagement by the owner. In some states, property is assigned to a receiver during the statutory redemption period after a foreclosure sale.

As an additional resource and reference, Acronyms and Abbreviations related to defined terms and Mathematical Formulas and Equations that appear in *Glossary* definitions are included as separate lists at the back of the book.

ACKNOWLEDGMENTS

The Institute gratefully acknowledges the contributions of the following individuals who served as Editorial Consultants on this project. By drawing on their knowledge and experiences in the field and sharing their insights regarding the selection of terms and the quality and accuracy of the definitions provided, they have enhanced the value of this reference publication.

Julia A. Banks, CPM®, CCIM, is CEO of Banks and Company, a Denver, Colorado, full-service real estate firm specializing in the sale, management, and leasing of apartments, office buildings, business parks, and industrial real estate. The firm also provides consulting services to income-property managers and owners. Prior to forming her own company, Ms. Banks was the chief operating officer and director of a real estate corporation. During her nearly 30 years in property management, she has been actively involved in the management of a real estate joint venture, limited partnerships, and several multi-state subchapter-S corporations. Her experience in multi-family and commercial real estate includes financing, development, renovation, sales, acquisition and property management. In addition to the CERTIFIED PROPERTY MANAGER® (CPM®) designation, which she achieved in 1978, she also earned the Certified Commercial Investment Member (CCIM) designation from the Commercial Investment Real Estate Institute (CIREA). A Senior Instructor on the IREM National Faculty, Ms. Banks also teaches property management courses for the University of Colorado and is an Adjunct Professor in the University of Denver Real Estate and Construction Management Department. She is the author of several articles published in the *Journal of Property Management,* has served as Editorial Consultant on numerous IREM books, and is a member of the IREM Academy of Authors.

Edward N. Kelley, CPM® Emeritus, has had executive management responsibilities for billions of dollars worth of investment real estate in a career spanning nearly 45 years. These include more than 100,000 apartments and several million square feet of office and other commercial space and hotels. His clientele includes major banks, financial institutions, branches of government, leading universities, and prominent investors. Mr. Kelley achieved the CERTIFIED PROPERTY MANAGER® (CPM®) designation in 1964 and was a long-time Senior

Instructor on the IREM National Faculty. Author of four editions of the IREM book, *Practical Apartment Management,* he has also written books on investment analysis and apartment marketing, and his articles on resident retention, rent setting, collections, staffing, and leasing techniques appear regularly in industry publications, including the *Journal of Property Management.* He has also written computer software programs designed to forecast optimum rents, schedule maintenance tasks, and track rental prospects.

David C. Nilges, CPM® Emeritus, is President of Nilges Commercial REAL-TORS® in Centennial, Colorado. He specializes in receivership, trusteeship, brokerage, and management for institutionally owned properties, including apartments, industrial, office buildings, shopping centers, residential, resort facilities, special-purpose properties, and hotels. Mr. Nilges was a long-time member of the IREM National Faculty, for which he earned Faculty Emeritus status, and he has presented seminars on all aspects of commercial and investment real estate for more than 30 years. He has also lectured at John Carroll University, Denver University School of Business, Colorado University, and Cuyahoga Community College. In addition to the CERTIFIED PROPERTY MAN-AGER® (CPM®) designation, which he achieved in 1969, Mr. Nilges is also a RE-ALTOR®. A member of the IREM Academy of Authors, he has been a contributing author and served as an Editorial Consultant for several IREM books. Mr. Nilges has the distinction of having been named "CPM® of the Year" by two different IREM Chapters, Cleveland Chapter in 1979 and Denver Chapter in 1995.

Robert D. Oliver, CPM®, CSM, was Executive Vice President, Property Management, for Urban Retail Properties Company, based in Boston, Massachusetts, where he continues to serve as a consultant. For more than 23 years, he directed the management of shopping centers in the northeastern United States. Previously, he served as President of First Eastern Management Corporation in Boston, where he directed management and leasing of a portfolio of apartment complexes, office buildings, regional malls, and community strip shopping centers. Mr. Oliver holds a Master of Business Administration degree from Boston College and is a licensed real estate broker. In addition to the CER-TIFIED PROPERTY MANAGER® (CPM®) designation, which he achieved in 1981, Mr. Oliver also holds the Certified Shopping Center Manager (CSM) designation from the International Council of Shopping Centers. He has served as an Editorial Consultant and provided content for a number of IREM books and courses.

About the Institute of Real Estate Management

The Institute of Real Estate Management (IREM®) was founded in 1933 with the goals of establishing a Code of Ethics and standards of practice in real estate management as well as fostering knowledge, integrity, and efficiency among its practitioners. The Institute confers the CERTIFIED PROPERTY MANAGER® (CPM®) designation on individuals who meet specified criteria of education and experience in real estate management and subscribe to an established Code of Ethics. Individuals who meet specified educational and professional requirements in residential site management and subscribe to a Code of Ethics are granted the ACCREDITED RESIDENTIAL MANAGER® (ARM®) certification. Real estate management firms that meet specific organizational and professional criteria are granted the ACCREDITED MANAGEMENT ORGANIZATION® (AMO®) accreditation.

Membership in the Institute of Real Estate Management accompanies the CPM®, ARM®, and AMO® professional certifications. The Institute also offers Associate Membership status to property managers and other real estate professionals who wish to establish an affiliation with IREM in order to increase their industry knowledge, enhance their skills, and network with other real estate management professionals. Recognizing that the real estate industry has a profound impact on every country in the world, IREM has taken a leadership role in developing and promoting global standards of property management practices through its international programs.

Since 1933, IREM has been enhancing the prestige of property management through its activities and publications. The Institute offers a wide selection of courses, seminars, periodicals, books, and other materials about real estate management and related topics. To receive current information about IREM programs, write to the Institute of Real Estate Management, 430 North Michigan Avenue, Chicago, Illinois 60611-4090, or telephone 1-800-837-0706. Also visit our web page on the Internet at www.irem.org.

Glossary of Real Estate Management Terms

A

AAA rating The highest credit rating given to businesses by credit reporting agencies such as Dun & Bradstreet; useful when determining a commercial rental prospect's financial status. Also used as a basis for credit underwriting.

abandonment A relinquishment or surrender of property or rights. In real estate management, abandonment of leased premises refers to the relinquishing of the premises by the tenant before the lease expires without consent of the owner/landlord. The term is also applied to personal property left behind by a tenant, a situation that has additional legal implications regarding the removal and storage or disposition of such property.

abate To reduce in value, as a tax or rental rate. To demolish or remove, as asbestos-containing material.

abatement In real estate, a reduction of rent, interest, or an amount due. Also an environmental term meaning partial or complete reduction of the intensity or concentration of a contaminant (e.g., removal of asbestos).

absorption rate The amount of space of a particular property type that is leased compared to the amount of that same type of space available for lease within a certain geographic area over a given period of time, accounting for both construction of new space and demolition or removal from the market of existing space. Also used in reference to the rate at which a market can absorb space designed for a specific use (e.g., office space). Absorption rate can be computed as follows:

	Units or square feet vacant at the beginning of the period
plus	units or square feet constructed new during the period
minus	units or square feet demolished during the period
minus	units or square feet vacant at the end of the period
equals	units or square feet absorbed during the period.

abstract of title A chronological summation from the public record of information concerning a parcel of real estate, including maps, plot plans, and other evidence of title, and encompassing all conveyances (deeds, mortgages, liens, judgments, estates, charges, or other liabilities) to which the land may be subject. Required to obtain *title insurance*.

access The right of an owner of a property (or the owner's agent) to enter leased premises in order to show the space to prospects, to make periodic inspections, and to perform needed repairs. This is usually noted in a lease by inclusion of a right of re-entry provision. See also *right of re-entry*. Also used in referring to vehicular or pedestrian approaches to a property (e.g., streets, sidewalks).

access control systems Security measures designed to limit access to (usually) commercial buildings and tenants' leased premises so only those who have a reason to be there can enter. Specifically, electronic locks on doors that are released by entering a code using pushbuttons or a numeric keypad or by presenting a magnetic encoded card to a reading device. Keypads or card readers are installed adjacent to the door jamb. They may also be installed at security desks for after-hours access. Used at commercial properties to limit access to a company's premises or to a specific area of the premises through limited distribution of numeric codes or selective coding of magnetic cards and readers. Electronic access control systems are also commonly used at parking lots and garages.

accessibility The quality or state of being reached, easily approached, or used as an entrance. An important component of the Americans with Disabilities Act is removal of barriers that limit or complicate access to buildings and areas of public accommodation by people with physical disabilities. More broadly, the law also requires accommodation to make facilities accessible for those who are hearing and vision impaired. See *Americans with Disabilities Act (ADA)*.

account A detailed statement of receipts and payments of money or of trade transactions which have taken place between two or more parties.

accountant One who is skilled in the discipline of accounting. A person who is charged with responsibility for public or private accounts.

accounting Classifying, recording, and summarizing financial transactions and analyzing, verifying, and reporting results.

accounts payable Monies due to others for services rendered or goods ordered and received.

accounts receivable Monies due from others for services rendered or goods ordered and delivered.

ACCREDITED MANAGEMENT ORGANIZATION® (AMO®) An accreditation conferred by the Institute of Real Estate Management (IREM) on real estate management firms that are under the direction of a CERTIFIED PROPERTY MANAGER® (CPM®) designee and comply with stipulated requirements as to accounting procedures, performance, and protection of funds entrusted to them.

ACCREDITED RESIDENTIAL MANAGER® (ARM®) A professional certification conferred by the Institute of Real Estate Management (IREM) on individuals who meet specific standards of experience, ethics, and education.

accrual-basis accounting The method of accounting that involves entering amounts of income when they are earned and amounts of expense when they are incurred, even though the cash may not be received or paid; also called *accrual accounting*. All certified audits must use accrual accounting. Compare *cash-basis accounting*.

accrued depreciation   In accounting, for tax purposes, the amount of depreciation expense claimed to date for a depreciable asset (i.e., the amount of the cost of such an asset that has been recovered); accumulated depreciation. In appraisal, the difference between an improvement's replacement (or reproduction) cost new and the present value of the improvement; sometimes referred to as diminished utility. See also *observed depreciation.*

acquisition marketing   The notion that potential customers are readily accessible in unending supply and that the essence of marketing is to attract new customers; also referred to as *conquest marketing.* The underlying strategy is to expand a company's client base by attracting first-time customers or a competitor's clientele.

active income   For tax purposes, income (and losses) from sources such as salaries, wages, tips, commissions, and other trade or business activities in which the taxed individual or entity is actively engaged.

actual authority   The authority expressly or implicitly conferred by a principal on an agent to act on his/her behalf.

actual cash value (ACV)   Insurance that pays a claim based on the purchase price of the item, minus an allowance for depreciation because of age and use. Compare *replacement cost coverage.*

actual damages   Monetary damages awarded to compensate for actual and real loss. See also *loss.*

actual fraud   Intentional misrepresentation of a material fact in order to induce another person to act on it and consequently to part with something of value or surrender some legal right. Differentiated from *constructive fraud.*

adaptive use   A process whereby a structurally sound older building is redeveloped for a new, economically viable use, as refitting an office building or warehouse space for use as rental apartments or condominium units; sometimes called *adaptive reuse* or *change of use.*

addendum   A legal document that adds to or amends the terms of a written agreement, as a lease or management agreement; also called *amendment* or *rider.*

additional insured endorsement   An endorsement to an insurance policy of an insured party that names another individual or entity as an additional insured party. In real estate management, an endorsement to the building owner's insurance policy or policies that names the manager or managing agent as an additional insured party; usually a requirement under a management agreement.

additional interest provision (AIP)   See *convertible loan; participation.*

additional living expense insurance   Coverage that reimburses the insured for costs in excess of normal living expenses if loss of or damage to property forced the insured to maintain temporary residence elsewhere; usually a component of a condominium owner's policy.

additional rent   Provision in a lease for payments to the owner/landlord by the tenant in addition to the unit rent or base rental rate. For example, at a residential property, a charge for parking space that is not included in the apartment rent may be stated in the lease as additional rent. At commercial properties, payments for pass-through charges for building operating expenses, excess cost of tenant improvements to be reimbursed to the landlord by the tenant, and retailers' percentage rent may be identified specifically as additional rent.

add-on factor   In commercial leasing, a multiplier that represents the amount of common area space that is factored into a tenant's rent. For example, a building may have an add-on factor of 0.10 (10%), which means that the rentable area is 1.10 times the usable area. The tenant's rent on the usable area of 1,000 square feet would be based on 1,100 square feet and would thus include a payment for 100 square feet of common area. See also *load factor; usable area.*

ad hoc committee   A special committee appointed to carry out a specific non-recurring task and disbanded when that task is completed. Often formed by the managing agent at condominium properties to encourage owner participation and educate new owners regarding association responsibilities. Such committees may also be formed to address specific financial and administrative issues that arise.

adjustable-rate mortgage (ARM)   A type of variable-rate mortgage loan for which the interest rate can be adjusted (raised or lowered) at specific intervals (e.g., semiannually or annually). The changes in the rate are included in the terms of the loan, or the adjustment may be based on a predetermined index or formula, such as the prime rate plus 2 percent. Compare *variable-rate mortgage.*

adjusted basis   An income tax term. See *basis.*

adjusted gross rental income   Another name for *effective gross income.*

adjusted sales price   Amount paid or payable for an item less actual sales costs and other expenses incurred to effect the sale; also called net sales proceeds or simply *net proceeds.*

adjuster   In insurance, an individual employed by a property and/or casualty insurer to settle loss claims filed by insured parties on behalf of the insurance company; also called *insurance adjuster.* The adjuster investigates individual claims and makes recommendations to the insurance company regarding their settlement. See also *independent adjuster; public adjuster.*

adjustment   A component of the *real estate cycle.* A period when demand declines, occupancy diminishes, and rent concessions become widespread, usually in conjunction with a period of recession or depression. In accounting, modification of account records to reflect actual conditions at the close of a given period (e.g., by adjustment of journal records for accruals, corrections, and depreciation). In employment, an increase (or decrease) of an individual's wages or salary. In insurance, agreement on the amount to be paid to the insured.

administration   Performance of executive duties such as management, direction, and supervision.

administrative expenses   Costs of goods or services that can be attributed to the management of a business entity or a property.

ad valorem tax   A tax levied on the basis of the value of the object taxed. Most often refers to taxes levied by municipalities and counties against real property and personal property.

adverse possession   A means of acquiring title to land by statutory limitation. The right of ownership of a parcel of land, which has been occupied without interference or permission from the title owner of record for a period of time, as defined by state statutes. Usually the time period is at least 15 years (time periods vary from an upper limit of 20 years to a lower limit of 5 years, depending on the nature of the possession and the specific state statute).

advertisement   Public notice; a paid notice or announcement that is published in some public print medium (e.g., a newspaper, magazine, or handbill; a billboard), broadcast over radio or television, or delivered online via the Internet.

advertising   The action of calling something to public attention, especially by means of paid announcements. An operating expense category in income property budgeting.

affidavit of service   A sworn statement that a legal document (e.g., an eviction notice) has been served properly.

affirmative action programs   Programs required by federal (and sometimes state) law designed to discourage, remedy, and eliminate discriminatory practices in the hiring of women and members of minority groups.

Affirmative Fair Housing Marketing Plan (AFHMP)   An outline of the marketing strategies that must be used at most assisted housing properties to attract applicants who are least likely to apply for an apartment at the property.

affordable housing   Often used in reference to housing in which the building or the tenants' rents are subsidized by some type of government program. Rents are lower than market rates for comparable properties, and there may be eligibility requirements regarding a person's income to qualify for residency.

after-tax cash flow   The money remaining for an investor after income taxes have been deducted; a real estate owner's *net profit.*

Age Discrimination in Employment Act (ADEA)   Federal law passed in 1967 that prohibits discrimination against older workers.

agency   The legal relationship between two parties in which one party represents the interest of the other in transactions with a third party. In real estate, when one person or entity (the agent) represents the interest of another person—a seller, lessor, or property owner (the principal)—in financial dealings with others, the agent is also called a *fiduciary.*

agency management   Management of property owned by another by an agent duly authorized to do so.

agent   A person (or business entity) who enters a legal, fiduciary, and confidential arrangement with a second party (the principal) and is authorized to act on behalf of that party. See also *fiduciary; leasing agent; managing agent.*

aggravated assault   See *assault.*

aggregate deductible   Another name for *cumulative deductible.*

aggregate rent   The total or gross rent amount for the lease term.

aging in place   Used in referring to retirement-age people (senior citizens) who prefer to remain in their own homes, whether owned or rented.

agreed amount insurance   A policy under which a coinsurance clause is waived if the insured carries insurance in an agreed amount. The insurer then agrees to pay the face amount on the policy in the event of total loss of property covered or upon occurrence of a stated contingency.

air space   Space above a property which may be sold or leased (air rights). In condominium ownership, the space of air or three-dimensional area located within the walls, floor, and ceiling of a condominium structure to which the condominium owner has title.

alarm system   A system of fire, burglar, and intrusion warning devices configured as an integral part of a building's security system.

all risk insurance   Insurance that covers losses caused by all perils except those specifically excluded in the policy contract; also called *special property coverage.*

alteration   Partial or superficial change to a building or property that preserves its original integrity and does not increase its exterior dimensions.

alteration provision   A lease provision that prohibits a tenant from making any alteration or improvement to the leased premises without ownership's express consent, usually required to be in writing.

Alternative Minimum Tax   Under U.S. tax law, a flat rate tax applicable to individuals who have certain types of income, including income derived from passive activities. The flat rate is applied to the individual's income without regard to exemptions. Affected taxpayers are obliged to compute their tax liability following both normal procedures and the Alternative Minimum Tax procedure and to pay the higher amount of tax.

amend   To modify or change. Under parliamentary procedure, to modify a motion by adding, deleting, or substituting words.

amendment   Revision of a legal document. A written revision of a contract specifying changes to the basic document that have been agreed to by the parties to the contract (e.g., a *lease amendment*). Also applies to revision of a governing document of a condominium. Under parliamentary procedure, revision of a motion.

amenities   Tangible and intangible features that enhance and add to a property's desirability and perceived value. Amenities at an apartment building might include a swimming pool or a fitness center. An office building might offer indoor parking, a conference room, or a cafeteria. Such amenities can result in higher rents than those at comparable properties and thus also increase property value.

amenity rental fee   In a condominium, a fixed charge paid by a unit owner or guest for use of a common facility and/or limited common area.

American Industrial Real Estate Association (AIR)   An organization of individuals and companies whose real estate and real estate-related business is specialized in industrial and commercial properties.

American Land Title Association (ALTA)   A national organization of title companies, abstractors, and attorneys that promotes quality and uniformity in title abstract forms and title insurance policies. Developer of standard forms for the *abstract of title* required to guarantee existence of a clear title for underwriting title insurance.

American Society of Heating, Refrigerating, and Air-Conditioning Engineers (ASHRAE)   Technical society of HVAC and refrigerating engineers that conducts research and publishes reference materials on HVAC systems, equipment, and applications, including engineering and *indoor air quality (IAQ)* standards.

Americans with Disabilities Act (ADA)   Enacted in 1990, the federal law that prohibits discrimination on the basis of disability. Of the five sections or titles, two are directly applicable to real estate managers: Title I (employment) prohibits discrimination in recruiting, hiring, promotions, compensation, training, and termination on the basis of physical or mental disability. If qualified applicants or employees who have a disability can perform the *essential functions* of a job, employers must make *reasonable accommodations* for them by improving access, restructuring jobs, adjusting work schedules, and the like. Title III requires all buildings that are open to public commerce to be made accessible to disabled people to the maximum extent possible by removal of architectural barriers in areas of public accommodation, provision of auxiliary aids and services to assist in communication, and modification of discriminatory policies, procedures, and practices. Title III affects all public areas of commercial properties and leasing offices and other areas of residential properties that are open to the public. See also *public accommodation*.

amortization   Gradual reduction of a debt by periodic payments which include interest and a portion of the principal over the term of the loan.

amortization schedule   A table showing the allocation between interest and principal repayment for each installment payment for a given loan as well as the unpaid balance of the loan after each payment; also called *loan amortization schedule*.

amortized mortgage   A mortgage loan in which the principal is paid back, with interest, in monthly (or other periodic) installments over the term of the loan; sometimes also called *amortizing mortgage*.

analysis of alternatives   A study of a property to determine its *highest and best use,* including tests of legal permissibility, physical possibility, economic feasibility, and potential profitability. Usually a component of a management plan.

anchor tenant   A major shopping center tenant that will draw the majority of customers to the site. Normally an anchor tenant occupies a large space in a desirable location in the shopping center. Often there are two or more anchor tenants, depending on the type of center.

ancillary income   A common term used to describe additional, *unscheduled income* such as receipts from coin-operated laundry or vending equipment and commissions; also called *miscellaneous income* or *sundry income*.

ancillary tenant   A shopping center tenant that occupies a smaller space and a location that is secondary in relation to the anchor tenant.

annual budget   A twelve-month estimate of income and expenses for a property. See also *operating budget*.

annual membership meeting   A once-a-year assemblage of unit owners to conduct condominium or homeowners' association business as required by the governing documents (e.g., electing a board of directors).

annual mortgage constant rate   The annual payment of a mortgage expressed as a percentage. A rate equal to the percentage derived by dividing the annual payment of principal and interest on a loan by the amount of the loan; used with level payment loans. Also called *constant.* See also *loan constant.*

annual report   A formal financial statement, issued once a year by a corporation (or other business entity) to its shareholders or investors, listing assets, liabilities, and earnings and indicating the company's standing and profits at the end of the business year. May also include events of the past year that have affected the corporation's worth.

annual statement   In real estate, a fully detailed and annotated statement of all income and expense items involving cash and covering a twelve-consecutive-month period of operation of an individual property. Variations in form and content are effected to conform with ownership directives.

annuity   An amount to be paid yearly or at other regular intervals, often on a guaranteed dollar basis. An insurance contract that provides a lump sum payout or makes a periodic payment for a specified period or for the life of the insured, beginning at a predetermined date. Money is paid into the fund in a lump sum or in the form of premiums until maturity. Payouts include a portion of the capital (premiums) plus accrued interest. The policy is designed to liquidate funds rather than accumulate them.

antidiscrimination laws   A broad category of federal, state, and local laws that provide for civil action against persons owning and operating real estate and business establishments by aggrieved persons claiming discrimination on the basis of some protected class. See also *Americans with Disabilities Act (ADA), Civil Rights Act of 1964/1968, fair housing laws,* and *protected class.*

apartment   An individual dwelling unit, usually on a single level and often contained in a multi-unit building or development.

apartment building   A building containing more than one dwelling unit.

apartment owner   See *unit owner.*

apportionment   In an insurance policy, a clause stipulating that all companies insuring a property will divide any loss in proportion to the amount of insurance on the particular property written by them.

appraisal   An opinion or estimate of the value of a property at a specific point in time. An estimate of value that is (usually) prepared by a certified or accredited appraiser and submitted as a written report. A real estate appraisal is based on information that includes data about competitive properties, market conditions, the national and local economies, and observed economic trends as well as an in-depth analysis of the property being appraised. Four methods of appraisal are common—the *cost approach,* based on the estimated value of the land plus the estimated cost of replacing the improvements on it less depreciation; the *market approach,* based on a comparison to similar properties in the market that have been sold recently; the *income capitalization approach,* based on the net operating income of the property; and the *discounted cash flow method,* which discounts all future fiscal benefits of an investment property over a predetermined holding period. All four are used to estimate value if sufficient information is gathered in each approach to do so.

Appraisal Institute (AI)   Membership organization formed in 1991 by the merger of the American Institute of Real Estate Appraisers and the Society of Real Estate Appraisers.

appraiser   One who performs a formal, detailed estimate of a property's value. An individual who is qualified to estimate the value of real property.

appreciation   An increase in exchangeable value, as of money, goods, or property. Compare *depreciation*.

appurtenances   Those things that pertain or attach to something else. Skirting, awnings, sheds, and porches attached to mobile/manufactured homes are appurtenances.

arbitration   A process of dispute resolution in which a neutral third party (arbitrator) renders a decision after a hearing at which both parties have an opportunity to be heard, often employed as a means of avoiding litigation. Arbitration provisions are common in collective bargaining (union) agreements and often required in commercial contracts. When arbitration is voluntary, the parties to the dispute select the arbitrator who has the power to render a decision, called an award, that is binding on the parties. Compare *mediation*.

architectural restrictions   Standards and restrictions that limit what common interest (e.g., condominium) unit owners can do to change the outward appearance of their units and outline procedures owners must follow to make changes to the exteriors of their units. The same types of restrictions may be imposed on other types of properties by outside entities (e.g., historical commissions).

arithmetic mean   The average of a set of values, found by dividing the sum of the values by the number of values in the set. See also *mean; weighted mean*.

arson   Starting a fire or causing an explosion for the purpose of damaging property or destroying a building or occupied structure. Arson is punishable as a felony. *Attempted arson* and *aggravated arson* in which there is danger to human life as well as property damage or destruction are also felonies.

articles of incorporation   The document that establishes a business as a corporation under state law, usually following a prescribed form as to required information and presentation; also called *certificate of incorporation*. A certificate that establishes a condominium or other homeowners' association as a corporation under the laws of the state.

artificial breakpoint   A negotiated breakpoint that requires a retail tenant to pay percentage rent before (or after) the natural breakpoint is reached. See also *breakpoint*.

asbestos   A fibrous mineral used to impart fireproofing characteristics to building materials, automobile brake linings, etc.; also used to provide insulation. Asbestos particles that become airborne (as *friable* asbestos) are a human health hazard.

asbestos-containing material (ACM)   Any material (e.g., insulation, flooring) that contains more than one percent asbestos by weight.

as-is value   The value of a property based on its current condition.

assault   An attempt or threat to inflict injury or a display of force that creates fear or apprehension of injury. An assault can exist without any actual injury resulting. *Simple assault* is usually classified as a misdemeanor while *aggravated assault,* including assault with a deadly weapon, is a felony. In addition to filing a police report, instances of assault are often documented in order to monitor the effectiveness of security at a managed property. Documenting crime is a critical component of *risk management.* All instances of assault should be documented and, in the event of any liability exposure, such documentation would be used to report a potential claim to the insurance company.

assessed value   The value of real property established by the local authority as the basis for taxation. The tax rate is applied to the assessed value to determine the amount of real estate tax. See also *millage rate.*

assessment   The imposition of a tax, charge, or levy, usually according to established rates; used in referring to local (municipal) taxes. In common interest real estate (e.g., condominium), an amount charged against each owner to fund its operation. See also *special assessment.*

asset   Any item that has monetary value and is owned by a person or business, such as real property, cash, land, stocks, bonds, or equipment. Usually used in plural, *assets,* to identify the collection of entries on a balance sheet that represent the book values of various categories of items owned (e.g., *capital assets, current assets*) as of a given date.

asset management   A specialized field of real estate management that involves the supervision of an owner's real estate assets at the investment level. See also *property management; real estate management.*

asset manager   One who is charged with supervising an owner's real estate assets at the investment level. In addition to real estate management responsibilities that include maximizing net operating income and property value, an asset manager may recommend or be responsible for or participate in property acquisition, development, and divestiture. An asset manager may have only superficial involvement with day-to-day operations at the site (e.g., supervision of personnel, property maintenance, tenant relations). Compare *property manager.*

assignee   One to whom some right or interest is transferred, either for the individual's own enjoyment or in trust. The person receiving an assignment.

assignment   The transfer, in writing, of an interest in a bond, mortgage, lease, or other instrument. The transfer of one person's interest or right in a property (e.g., a lease) to another. Also, the document by which such an interest or right is transferred. Specifically, the document used to convey a leasehold is called an *assignment of lease.* The assignor of a lease remains liable unless released by the landlord. Compare *sublease; sublet.*

assignment clause   A lease provision prohibiting the tenant from assigning its rights in the leasehold to another entity without the express (written) permission of the property owner. Often combined with subletting in a single clause; see also *sublet clause.*

assignor   One giving some right or interest. The person making an assignment.

assisted housing   Privately owned rental property that either receives government assistance in the form of mortgage insurance, a reduced mortgage interest rate, or tax incentives, or houses residents who receive some form of rental subsidy. Assistance may be property-based or resident-based.

assisted living facilities   Housing designed for senior citizens who need help with daily living activities but are not sick. Often developed by private companies; monthly fees include housing and services, and rents may be high.

association of co-owners   Another name for *condominium association.*

atrium   In building design, a central area of a building with a ceiling of translucent material that allows natural light to enter the interior.

attachment   Seizure or taking of property by legal writ to secure the debt or claim of a creditor in order to satisfy a judgment that has not yet been rendered.

attorney   A person licensed to practice law and authorized to perform civil and criminal legal functions for clients; an *attorney at law;* a *lawyer.*

audit   An official examination of accounting records and procedures conducted by a trained person, either a company employee or an independent third party (e.g., a *Certified Public Accountant*), to verify their accuracy, completeness, and reliability. Also, the report of such an examination; the process of conducting such an examination. See also *external audit; internal audit.* The term is also used in reference to nonaccounting inspections and evaluations. See *energy audit; security audit.*

auditor   A person trained to conduct an audit.

authority   Power or right conferred on a person, usually by another to act on his/her behalf, so that that person may perform the authorized activity without incurring liability. Delegated power over others conferred on a person, as on a property manager under a management agreement. See also *agent.*

automatic external defibrillator (AED)   A medical device used to provide electrical stimulation to the human heart in the event of cardiac arrest. Such devices are often installed in shopping centers and other commercial buildings to which the public is invited.

automatic renewal clause   A lease provision that automatically ensures renewal of the lease unless either tenant or landlord notifies the other party of a desire to terminate the agreement. Such a lease clause may be undesirable to a landlord unless it also includes provision for an increase in rent at renewal.

automobile insurance   A policy that insures automobiles and other motor vehicles against losses arising out of accidents and their consequences. It usually includes damage to the insured vehicle (comprehensive and collision) as well as bodily injury, property damage, and liability coverages.

average   In statistics, another name for *mean.*

avoidance   One of four methods of *risk management.* The act or practice of avoiding something, as a danger, or preventing its occurrence. When the choice exists, one can avoid a risk by not owning or operating something that is potentially dangerous (e.g., one can avoid the risk of a driving accident by not owning or driving an automobile).

B

back order   In manufacturing and retailing, part of an order that the vendor has not filled on time but still intends to ship.

balance sheet   A statement of the financial position of a person or a business (or investment property) at a particular time, indicating assets, liabilities, and owner equity.

balloon loan   A loan with a constant monthly rate of repayment and a much larger (balloon) payment at the end of the term to fully repay the outstanding principal balance; a *balloon mortgage.* Compare *fully amortized loan.*

balloon payment   The final payment of a mortgage loan that is considerably larger than the required periodic payments. This results from the fact that the loan was not fully amortized.

band-of-investment method   An approach to establishing a capitalization rate by weighting the return on investment required to cover mortgage interest and the return on investment required to provide a competitive return on equity.

bank   A business entity formed to hold monies of others in the form of savings and checking accounts, issue loans and extend credit, and deal in negotiable securities issued by corporations and government agencies. Banks are strictly regulated in the United States by the federal government. See also *Federal Deposit Insurance Corporation (FDIC).*

bankruptcy   A state of financial insolvency of an individual or organization (i.e., liabilities exceed assets); the inability to pay debts. Also used in referring to the legal proceeding whereby the affairs of a person or business unable to meet its obligations are turned over to a trustee in accordance with bankruptcy law. The objective of bankruptcy is a court action providing for the orderly and equitable settlement of obligations. In the United States, there are several federal bankruptcy acts.

base period   A selected period of time, frequently one year, against which changes in other years are calculated; used in constructing index numbers (e.g., the U.S. Consumer Price Index currently uses 1982–1984 as a base period). When used in a lease, often referred to as *base year.*

base rent   The minimum rent as set forth in a (usually commercial) lease, excluding pass-throughs, percentage rents, and other additional charges. See also *minimum rent.*

base tax rate   Usually defined in a single-family home lease as the current taxes and assessments imposed against the land, building, or improvements owned by the lessor at the subject property at a specified time or at a specific dollar amount.

base unit of value   The rent of a subject property arrived at by using the average of the rents of comparable properties. In comparison grid analysis, calculation of the average adjusted rent for the particular unit type at the comparable properties by (1) adding together the adjusted rents and dividing the sum by the number of competing properties involved or (2) adding together the adjusted rent per square foot for each of the comparable properties and dividing the sum by the number of comparables (the result is the average adjusted rent per square foot for the comparable properties). See also *comparison grid analysis.*

base-unit-rate approach   A method of establishing rental rates in which the typical unit within a specific submarket (either an actual unit or a perceived ideal) is used as a standard against which all similar units are measured.

base year   In a commercial (office, retail, industrial) lease, the stated year that is to be used as a standard in determining rent escalations. In subsequent years, operating costs are compared with the base year, and the difference determines the tenant's rent adjustment.

basis   The book value of a real estate investment. The *original basis* for tax purposes is the purchase price plus any other costs of acquisition that are capitalized. *Depreciable basis* (cost recovery) is the value of the improvements only, since land cannot be depreciated. Additions for capital improvements and subtractions for depreciation and partial sales produce the *adjusted basis.*

basis point   A hundredth of a percent, often used in relation to interest rates. A unit of measure for the change in interest rates for bonds and notes. When the Federal Reserve Bank raises or lowers interest rates, it often does so in one-quarter point increments (i.e., 25 basis points).

batch processing   A method of data processing in which information is accumulated over a period of time before being entered into a computer.

battery   The intentional and unjustified touching of another person. Battery requires some physical contact or resulting injury. Because the threat (assault) is inherent in the actual use of force (battery), the two are commonly classified together as *assault and battery,* which is considered a misdemeanor. In addition to filing a police report, instances of battery are often documented in order to monitor the effectiveness of security at a managed property. Documenting crime is a critical component of *risk management.* All instances of battery should be documented and, in the event of any liability exposure, such documentation would be used to report a potential claim to the insurance company.

bay depth   The distance from a corridor wall to the outside window or wall of an office, warehouse, or loft building.

bearing wall   Another name for *load-bearing wall.*

below market interest rate (BMIR) A rate offered by a government agency (e.g., HUD) for mortgage insurance on certain types of housing.

benchmarking In marketing, the theory that the best practices in place at one company or in an industry may be applied by another business, even if the second entity is not engaged in the same business as the first.

beneficiary A person designated to receive funds or other property under a trust, insurance policy, mortgage loan, etc. In financing, a lender holding a deed of trust or a promissory note as security for a loan.

best use In real estate, economically the most productive use in terms of net income or net return over a foreseeable period of time without prejudice to the total capital investment or fair market value of a property; also called *highest and best use.*

beta A measure of the degree of risk in an investment, used to establish a *risk premium;* also called *beta coefficient.*

beta value In financial analysis, a measure of the volatility of an asset's returns, which relates the asset's price to the market as a whole.

betterment Substantial improvement on real property. Improvement of a property, as by the addition of a building, that increases its value more than would result from simple repairs. Improvements to condominium and other owned units are often referred to and insured as betterments.

bid Offer of a price made by a supplier of goods or services; also called *quotation.* Often submitted in response to a *request for proposal (RFP).*

bid bond A guarantee or assurance provided by a third party (surety) that, if a contractor's bid is accepted, the contractor will furnish performance and payment bonds and enter into a contract with the property owner within a specified time period.

billback items Another name for *pass-through charges.*

billboard A large panel designed to carry outdoor advertising attached to a building or mounted on a roadside framework, often with lighting for visibility at night.

blanket fidelity bond Insurance to cover the loss of money or of real or personal property when such loss is due to dishonesty of any employee of the company. Otherwise, a *fidelity bond* is usually obtained on an individual basis.

blanket mortgage A mortgage that covers (encumbers) more than one property.

blanket policy A single insurance policy covering all of a specified quantity or class of property, or a variety of risks, or both. In real estate management, usual reference is to insurance written for owners of multiple sites that provides the same coverages at all locations. (Coverage may be for several kinds of property at one location or one kind of property at several locations.) Such a policy offers greater flexibility, reduces any limitations of value at a single site, and may lower premium costs (depending on property type, age and condition, deductibles that apply, coinsurance, and other factors); sometimes called *master policy.*

block grant   A federal revenue-sharing program that makes direct grants to local governments for development of urban communities.

block group   A subdivision of the census tract covering an urban population of 10,000 or more. See also *enumeration district.*

board of directors   The elected governing body of any corporation, including a condominium or other common interest realty association; also called *board of managers* or *board of trustees* in a condominium association. See also *corporation.*

bodily injury liability insurance   Protection against loss arising out of injury, illness, or death of another due to a negligent act by the insured party.

boiler   A pressure tank in which water is heated and from which it is circulated, either in the form of steam or as hot water.

boiler and machinery insurance   Property and liability coverage for loss or damage arising out of the operation of pressure, mechanical, and electrical equipment.

boilerplate lease   The owner's lease form containing clauses that are usually standard for all tenant-owner relationships; a *standard form lease.*

BOMA method of space measurement   A standardized method of measuring office space established by the Building Owners and Managers Association (BOMA) International.

BOMI Institute   An educational organization affiliated with the Building Owners and Managers Association (BOMA) International; formerly Building Owners and Managers Institute (BOMI) International.

bond   An interest-bearing instrument issued by a government entity or corporation as evidence of long-term debt, sometimes secured by a lien against property (mortgage) and designed to provide for a specific financial need. The issuer (borrower) promises to pay the bondholder (lender) a series of periodic interest payments and to return the principal at maturity. The term may also be used more broadly to refer to unsecured debt instruments and is also preferably used in naming different types of *sureties,* such as a fidelity bond. Also, an agreement stating that one party (surety or guarantor) will answer for the acts or omissions of a second party (principal) who has agreed to perform in some manner for a third party (obligee); the third party is indemnified in case the second party does not perform—a *surety bond;* also called *performance bond* or *contract bond.* A *fidelity bond* may be obtained by an employer to protect against the economic loss (money or property) due to dishonest acts of employees.

bonus   Any compensation to an employee over and above a regular wage or salary.

bookkeeper   One who records the financial accounts and transactions of a business in books of account.

bookkeeping   The systematic classification, recording, and summarizing of the financial transactions of a business. In real estate management, the same is done for individual managed properties.

book value   The value of an item, such as real property, as stated in books of account and differentiated from its market value. Calculated as the cost of a property, plus capital additions, less accrued depreciation (cost recovery) that has been charged off for income tax purposes and partial sales. Compare *market value*. Also, the value of capital stock (as of a corporation) based on the excess of assets over liabilities.

boundary energy   The total amount of energy from all sources that is consumed in operating a building.

breach of contract   Another name for *default*.

breakeven analysis   A financial technique used to determine when income will cover all operating costs. Calculation of breakeven may include or exclude debt service.

breakeven point   The point at which income covers all operating expenses plus debt service. In rental real estate, the number of units or the square footage that must be occupied by tenants (or the amount of income that must be generated) to cover a property's operating costs plus debt service. In retailing, the sales volume at which revenues and costs are equal.

breakpoint   In retail leases, the point at which the tenant's volume of sales multiplied by a predefined percentage rate is equal to the base rent stated in the lease and beyond which the tenant will begin to pay percentage (overage) rent; also called *natural breakpoint*. (Natural breakpoint is calculated by dividing the tenant's annual base or minimum rent by the established percentage rate.) Sometimes a tenant and owner will negotiate an *artificial breakpoint* that requires the tenant to begin paying percentage rent either before or after the natural breakpoint is reached.

bridge loan   A type of short-term, interim financing used to bridge the time gap between the end of one loan and the beginning of another, as between a construction loan and permanent financing.

British thermal unit (Btu)   The amount of heat required to raise the temperature of one pound of water one degree Fahrenheit.

broadcast media   Radio or television used for advertising. With the advent of streaming audio and video, the Internet has also become a means of delivering sounds and images.

brochure   A small printed booklet or pamphlet intended to provide complete information on a specific subject. In real estate management, a marketing tool using illustrations (e.g., photographs, floor plans) and narrative to provide specific information, as about a property and its rental space.

broker   An agent with a real estate license who acts as a representative for an owner or tenant, within specific limits of authority. Also, an agent who buys, sells, or leases for a principal on a commission basis without having title to the property.

brokerage firm   An agency operated by a licensed real estate broker that employs licensed real estate personnel who bring in business by canvassing the territory for prospective tenants or for listings on properties. A full-service real estate brokerage firm may also provide property management services in addition to handling real estate sales and rentals.

broker cooperation agreement   A document signed by broker, owner, and brokerage firm, stating that the broker is working for a particular owner on a particular property. It registers the names of prospective tenants and outlines terms of the broker's commission. It may also constitute an agreement between the listing broker and an *outside (cooperating) broker.*

bubble schematic   A simplified diagram that indicates activity centers, personnel interactions, and people circulation and is used in the early stages of space planning before a formal layout is prepared. See also *space planning.*

budget   An itemized estimate of income and expenses over a specific time period for a particular property, project, or institution. See also *capital budget; cash flow budget; operating budget.*

budget variance   The differences between projected and actual amounts of income and expenses. Higher income and lower expenditures than expected constitute favorable variances, while lower income and higher expenditures are reported as unfavorable variances. Usually a component of the monthly management report sent to ownership.

building and contents insurance   A form of insurance under which the insured obtains separate amounts of coverage on the building, its contents, and certain improvements to it.

building classification   See *office building classification.*

building code   A collection of regulations adopted by local governmental authorities to govern the construction of buildings or other permanent structures. Building codes regulate building size, setback requirements, construction methods and materials, use, and occupancy to preserve public health, safety, and welfare. They cover all aspects of construction, from foundations to roofing systems, including insulation and electrical, plumbing, and HVAC installations. See also *International Code Council (ICC).* Also, standards established by federal agencies that describe minimum structural requirements for manufactured housing. See *National Manufactured Home Construction and Safety Standards Act of 1974.*

building control system   A computerized system of controls that regulates building systems (HVAC, elevators, security).

building intelligence   The presence of special electrical or computer services that allow a building's operating costs to be reduced and technological services to be shared by tenants; see also *smart building.*

building module   A unit of length and width by which a building's plan is standardized, facilitating office space design and layout. Often determined by window size and placement, column spacing, and bay depths.

Building Officials and Code Administrators (BOCA) International   A nonprofit organization that set up a model building code used widely in U.S. municipalities. See also *International Code Council (ICC).*

building ordinance coverage   Insurance coverage purchased in addition to a fire and extended coverage policy to fully cover replacement cost of the structure (because rebuilding or repairs may have to conform with current building codes, increasing the cost of such work) and to meet any mortgage requirements that are in place.

Building Owners and Managers Association (BOMA) International
Membership organization of real estate professionals and others involved in all

facets of commercial real estate, primarily serving the interests of the office building industry.

building standard   A uniform specification that defines the quantity and quality of construction and finish elements a building owner will provide for build-out of space leased to commercial tenants. See also *tenant improvement allowance.*

build-to-suit   An arrangement in which a land owner constructs (or pays for constructing) a custom building on the land, and both land and building are leased to the tenant; a frequent arrangement in shopping centers (e.g., for pad or outlot spaces) and industrial properties.

bullet loan   A comparatively short-term (5–7 years) loan that has no provision for an extension or roll-over. Periodic payments cover interest only, and the loan amount is due at maturity *(balloon payment)*. Compare *roll-over loan.* Also used in referring to a financing agreement evidenced by a note or deed of trust with a very short due date, usually three years or less.

bundling   Combining of services or products. In securitization, bundling refers to assembling a number of products and services and offering shares of the resulting bundled financial product.

Bureau of the Census   A government agency within the U.S. Department of Commerce that is charged with counting and reporting the size and characteristics of the country's population every ten years. Many statistical compilations from the decennial census are updated and published in the annual *Statistical Abstract of the United States.*

burglary   Unlawful breaking into and entry of a building with the intent to commit a crime. In addition to filing a police report, instances of burglary are often documented in order to monitor the effectiveness of security at a managed property. Documenting crime is a critical component of *risk management.* All instances of burglary should be documented and, in the event of any liability exposure, such documentation would be used to report a potential claim to the insurance company.

business cycle   Recurring periods of high and low levels of business activity, often referred to sequentially as *prosperity, recession, depression,* and *recovery.* In reality, there are often recurring periods of recession and recovery without reaching the extremes of depression and full-blown prosperity.

business hours   See *store hours.*

business interruption insurance   A form of property insurance which provides coverage against the loss of profits (indirect loss) resulting from damage to the building or contents (direct loss), as by fire or other peril.

business owners policy program   Designed as an alternative to the Special Multiple Peril policy, a package insurance program for qualified small- and medium-sized businesses that includes property, crime, and liability insurance coverages.

buy-out   A form of concession whereby an owner or developer arranges to pay the rent for the rest of a tenant's lease term so that the tenant will relocate to the owner's property or move out of a space that the owner wants to use for another purpose.

bylaws Regulations that provide specific procedures for handling routine matters in an organization (e.g., a homeowners' association or a merchants' association). Secondary laws of a condominium association that govern its internal affairs and deal with routine operational and administrative matters; also called *code of regulations.*

C

cancel To render a contract void or inoperative.

cancellation Termination, as of a contract, before the time of expiration.

cannibalization To strip equipment or housing units of parts for use in other equipment or units to help keep the latter in service.

canvassing Contacting prospective tenants by telephone or in person in order to interest them in leasing commercial (office, retail) space. See also *cold calling.*

capital Money that can be invested; a capital good would be bought with capital and held as an investment. The total assets of a business. In finance, money or other property used in transacting business *(capital assets).* In economics, the man-made facilities or goods used to produce other goods *(capital goods);* the means of production.

capital appreciation Another name for *appreciation.*

capital asset pricing model A portfolio management technique that involves measuring portfolio risk using the weighted average of the individual risk values of the various assets.

capital assets *Long-term assets,* tangible or intangible (e.g., land, buildings, patents, trademarks, stocks), needed to generate income (profit) or to create a product or render a service and normally acquired to be retained rather than resold.

capital budget An estimate of costs of major improvements or replacements; generally a long-range plan for improvements to a property. Also used in referring to a long-range financial plan for acquiring and financing capital assets.

capital expenditure Spending on capital assets, such as major improvements, large equipment, additions to buildings, buildings themselves, and land.

capital gain The excess over market or book value at purchase that is or may be realized from the sale of a capital asset such as stocks or real property. Capital gain (loss) has income tax implications for the profit (loss) on securities or a capital acquisition held for a set period as defined in the U.S. Internal Revenue Code.

capital gains tax   A tax levied on profit realized on the sale of a capital asset, including an owner-occupied dwelling (e.g., a house or condominium unit) or land. Capital gains tax is calculated as a percentage of the gain, which is the difference between the asset's *adjusted basis* and its net sales price. The rate varies based on how long an investment is held.

capital goods   See *capital.*

capital improvement   A structural addition or betterment to real property that increases its useful life or productivity or extends the life of a building or its equipment. The improvement must have a life in excess of one year in order for the cost to be recovered (depreciated) for income tax purposes. See also *cost recovery; depreciation.* The use of capital for a betterment that did not exist before.

capital investment   Money invested or required to be invested in an enterprise or undertaking. Purchase of real estate is a capital investment.

capitalization   Treatment of future income as part of a firm's capital. In appraisal, the process employed in estimating the market value of real property by applying a proper investment rate of return to the annual net operating income expected to be produced by the property, the formula being: Income (I) divided by Rate (R) equals Value (V) or I ÷ R = V—the *IRV formula.*

capitalization method   See *capitalization.*

capitalization rate   A rate of return used to estimate a property's value based on that property's net operating income (NOI). This rate is based on the rates of return prevalent in the marketplace for similar properties and intended to reflect the investment risk associated with a particular property. It is derived from market data on similar, recent, sales (NOI ÷ property value/sales price = capitalization rate) or from calculations based on expected returns to debt and equity. Also called *cap rate* or *overall capitalization rate (OAR).*

capitalized value   The worth of assets expressed in terms of expected future earnings; the current worth of money expected to be earned (or received) calculated using a proper discount rate to accurately estimate current value. Also, the estimated value of income property based on the income capitalization approach under which value is estimated by dividing annual net operating income (NOI) by an appropriate capitalization rate; also called *capital value.*

capital loss   See *capital gain.*

capital reserves   Money set aside to pay for the cost of a major improvement to real estate or to fund replacement of major building components or equipment (e.g., a roof or HVAC system); see also *replacement reserves.*

cap rate   A shortened form for *capitalization rate.*

capricious value   A value determined by a user for real estate that is not based on an appraisal process. An arbitrary value based on sentiment, whim, or a fanciful idea. Also sometimes called *caprice value.* Not a *market value.*

cardiopulmonary resuscitation (CPR)   A basic emergency procedure for life support consisting of artificial respiration and manual external heart massage.

carport   A roofed, sideless shed for the storage of a motor vehicle.

carve outs   Items defined in loan agreements for *nonrecourse loans* that a borrower will be liable for in the event of default including, but not limited to, unpaid real estate taxes, costs for cleanup of environmental contamination, and security deposit balances.

cash   Ready money in the form of coins and paper currency. More broadly, an accounting category that includes currency, negotiable money orders, checks, and demand deposits.

cash accounting   Another name for *cash-basis accounting.*

cash-basis accounting   The method of accounting that recognizes income and expenses when money is actually received or paid; also called *cash accounting*. Compare *accrual-basis accounting.*

cash disbursements journal   An original-entry chronological record of payments made, usually in the form of checks, but the record may also reflect cash disbursements and wire or electronic transfers of funds.

cash flow   The amount of spendable income from a real estate investment. The amount of cash available after all payments have been made for operating expenses, debt service (mortgage principal and interest), and capital reserve funds; also called *pre-tax cash flow* to indicate that income taxes have not been deducted.

cash flow budget   Monthly or other projection of the cash position of a business (or investment property) accounting for all sources of income and all expected expenditures, including debt service and monies contributed to capital reserves as well as ordinary operating expenses, but excluding income taxes.

cash flow chart   The arithmetic steps used in calculating cash flow for a managed property:

	Gross potential rental income
minus	vacancy and collection loss
plus	miscellaneous income
equals	effective gross income
minus	operating expenses
equals	net operating income (NOI)
minus	debt service (interest and principal)
minus	reserves for replacement and capital expenditures (when applicable)
equals	pre-tax cash flow
minus	income tax
equals	after-tax cash flow.

A separate income category may be included for commercial properties where operating expense pass-throughs and/or percentage rent are collected as *other scheduled income*. The same may apply to utilities reimbursements at residential properties.

cash flow statement   A report of the actual inflow and outflow of cash and its related sources and uses in a given accounting period.

cash-on-cash return   A measure of the productivity of an investor's initial investment that compares the yearly cash flow of a property with its initial investment base: cash flow ÷ initial investment base. The result is given as a percentage. Also called *equity dividend ratio.*

cash receipts journal An original-entry chronological record of all cash taken in from all sources.

casualty loss A deductible loss of property resulting from disaster, accident, or theft. In insurance, any property loss from damage to buildings, their contents, and external equipment by fire, storm, theft, vandalism, or malicious mischief.

CCIM Institute Organization of commercial investment real estate brokers, developers, asset managers, and others involved in commercial investment properties; an affiliate of the National Association of REALTORS® (NAR). Formerly the Commercial Investment Real Estate Institute (CIREI).

C corporation See *corporation.*

ceiling loan See *floor-ceiling loan.*

ceiling rent In public housing, a cap on the amount of rent a family can be charged; sometimes called *maximum rent*. Ceiling rent caps the *total tenant payment (TTP),* which is the amount a family must pay to cover both shelter and a reasonable amount for utilities.

census The decennial enumeration of the U.S. population, reported by statistical areas and including demographic and economic profiles.

census block The smallest subdivision used by the U.S. Bureau of the Census to compile population data, usually by streets or roads in urban areas.

census tract A subdivision of the census data for a standard metropolitan statistical area (SMSA) which refers to an area that has a population not exceeding 4,000.

center court In an enclosed mall, a location midway between two department store anchors.

central business district (CBD) The central shopping or business area in an urban environment, usually the place where real estate values are highest; also called *downtown.*

certificate of incorporation Another name for *articles of incorporation.* In some jurisdictions, corporate existence begins after filing of articles of incorporation to which a formal certificate of incorporation is appended by the state.

certificate of occupancy A document issued by an appropriate governmental agency certifying that the premises (new construction, rehabilitation, alterations) complies with local building codes and/or zoning ordinances. Some jurisdictions require a certificate of occupancy for apartments based on inspection of units between each tenancy.

Certified Apartment Manager (CAM) A professional designation conferred by the National Apartment Association (NAA) on apartment managers who have demonstrated a level of experience and proficiency.

certified check A check of a depositor (individual or business) that has been stamped "certified" with the date and a signature of a bank officer, which makes the check an obligation of the bank. Such certification warrants that the signature is valid and that sufficient funds are on deposit and set aside to pay the check.

Certified Commercial Investment Member (CCIM) Professional designation conferred by the CCIM Institute.

certified copy A document signed and certified as true by the official in whose custody the original is held.

Certified Facility Manager (CFM) Professional designation granted by the International Facility Management Association (IFMA).

Certified Leasing Specialist (CLS) A professional designation granted by the International Council of Shopping Centers (ICSC).

Certified Manager of Community Associations (CMCA) A professional designation conferred by the Community Associations Institute (CAI).

Certified Marketing Director (CMD) A professional designation granted by the International Council of Shopping Centers (ICSC) to individuals who distinguish themselves in shopping center marketing.

Certified Occupancy Specialist (COS) A professional designation conferred by the National Center for Housing Management (NCHM) on professionals in the federally assisted housing industry who complete the necessary training and successfully pass the certification examination.

CERTIFIED PROPERTY MANAGER® (CPM®) The professional designation conferred by the Institute of Real Estate Management (IREM) on individuals who distinguish themselves in the areas of education, experience, and ethics in property management.

Certified Public Accountant (CPA) An accountant licensed by the state as meeting certain requirements for the public practice of accounting.

Certified Shopping Center Manager (CSM) A professional designation granted by the International Council of Shopping Centers (ICSC) to individuals who meet specific education and experience requirements and pass the qualifying examination.

chain store One of a group of retail stores operating under the same ownership that carries similar goods. National, regional, and local chains are defined in terms of the geographic areas they serve and the numbers of stores they operate.

change of use The process of changing the function of a structure without changing its exterior dimensions. See also *adaptive use.*

change order A change in the construction work specification.

Chartered Property Casualty Underwriter (CPCU) A professional designation for insurance agents granted by the American Institute for Chartered Property Casualty Underwriters.

chart of accounts A classification or arrangement of account items by type of income or expense (e.g., rent, advertising, insurance, maintenance), as well as assets and liabilities, accounts receivable, and accounts payable.

chattel Another name for *personal property.* The plural form, *chattels,* is also used in referring to equipment within a leased area that is owned or encumbered by someone other than the lessor or the landlord. Sometimes chattels are encumbered by a *Uniform Commercial Code (UCC)* filing regarding ownership.

chattel mortgage   A loan secured by personal property.

chlorofluorocarbons (CFCs)   A group of inert organic compounds containing halogen (chlorine and fluorine) atoms; once used as refrigerants in air-conditioning systems and other applications. Under the *Montreal Protocol,* CFC refrigerants are required to be replaced with nonhalogenated compounds.

Civil Rights Act of 1964   Federal law that prohibited discrimination in all federally funded programs, including housing programs assisted by federal funds (Title VI). The law also addressed employment (Title VII) and established the Equal Employment Opportunity Commission (EEOC). Title VII of this Act prohibits discrimination in employment—including hiring, compensation, promotion, termination, and other related activities—on the basis of race, color, religion, national origin, or sex. Title VI was superseded by Title VIII of the Civil Rights Act of 1968.

Civil Rights Act of 1968.   Federal law that prohibits discrimination based on race, color, religion, or national origin. Title VII is specific to employment practices; other protected classes were added under separate laws. See *Age Discrimination in Employment Act* and *Americans with Disabilities Act*. Title VIII, which is specific to housing, is also called the *Fair Housing Act*.

claim   In insurance, an insured party's demand for payment as rightfully due. In advertising, an assertion regarding quality, value, or effectiveness. Advertising claims are often made (or suspected of being made) without adequate justification.

classified advertising   Brief paid announcements, usually relegated to special sections of newspapers and magazines that are subdivided according to the types of items offered or sought; often referred to as *want ads*. A common form of advertising used for hiring employees and, in real estate, for leasing rental space.

class rate   In insurance, an average price applied to each exposure in a similar category or classification, a method of group rating; also called *class (or tariff) premium rate*.

Clean Air Act (CAA)   Enacted in 1970 and amended in 1977 and 1990, a federal law that sets forth air quality standards and determines administration of the same.

Clean Water Act (CWA)   A federal law that establishes standards for water quality and sets forth mechanisms for the administration of those standards. Originally enacted as the *Federal Water Pollution Control Act (FWPCA)* in 1972, it was renamed in 1977 and amended extensively in 1987.

client   One who engages the professional advice or services of another. One who consults or engages the professional services of an attorney. A patron or customer.

closed-circuit television (CCTV)   A system of surveillance and deterrence comprising a television camera, a monitor, and a time-lapse videotape recorder.

closed period   See *lock-in provision*.

closing   In salesmanship, persuading the customer to buy the product after the product has been explained and demonstrated; the last step in the sales process. The signing of a lease after negotiations have concluded. Used in apartment leasing to refer to the point at which the leasing agent's efforts have resulted in a prospective resident agreeing to sign a lease. More commonly in real estate, closing refers to the final transaction session at which the mortgage is secured (unless the sale is all cash), possession (title) of the real estate is transferred, and the money (consideration) changes hands.

closing ratio Another name for *conversion ratio.*

cluster anchors A group of smaller stores that sell similar or complementary merchandise and operate in the place of the traditional anchor tenant in certain specialty shopping centers.

cluster housing A type of planned subdivision in which detached houses are located in close proximity to one another and the residents share common open space (e.g., parking and recreational facilities). See also *zero lot line housing.*

code A systematic compilation of laws, rules, and regulations.

code of regulations In condominiums, another name for *bylaws.*

cognovit See *judgment clause.*

coinsurance An insurance option under which the insured (e.g., the property owner) is obligated to maintain insurance coverage at a stipulated level (e.g., 80 percent of the property's value) in order to receive the full value up to the limits of the policy in case of a loss, in exchange for a lowered premium rate. (Coverage is based on actual cash value of the improvements, which reflects a deduction for depreciation.) Failure to maintain that level of insurance coverage will reduce the amount reimbursed (in proportion to the property value). In the event of a loss, the insured shares in losses in proportion to the amount that the insurance coverage was *less* than the required percentage. See also *actual cash value.*

coinsurance clause A clause in an insurance policy that states a minimum percentage of value that must be carried in order to collect the full amount of the loss (up to the limit of the policy). This type of clause is no longer commonplace.

cold calling Calling on prospects with whom the representative has had no previous contact in order to interest them in leasing (commercial) space or employing property management services. See also *canvassing.*

collateral Security given as a pledge for the fulfillment of an obligation. Property pledged as security for a loan or debt.

collateralized mortgage obligation (CMO) A type of security made up of mortgage loans that may be separated into various classes (pools) offering investors a choice of maturities. See also *real estate mortgage investment conduit (REMIC).*

collateral materials As applied to advertising and promotion, printed items such as brochures, leaflets, floor plans, and posters as well as photographs, lapel pins, etc.

collection Securing payment of a check, bond, or other instrument by presenting it to the payer for cash. A sum of money collected, as rentals.

collections Monies collected. In real estate management, usually refers to rents paid or collected.

collections summary   In office building management, a report of monies collected from each tenant. It lists the tenant's name and suite number, rent due, and specific amounts received in payment of rent, pass-through charges, and other items. It may also include lease expiration dates and security deposits. Compare *rent roll; tenant roster.*

combination loan   A form of mortgage financing that combines characteristics of a variable-interest-rate loan with a roll-over loan.

commercial mortgage backed security (CMBS)   The secondary market for commercial mortgages, in which commercial mortgages are bundled and securitized.

commercial paper   Unsecured short-term (promissory) notes that are issued (sold) by reputable business firms to meet short-term capital needs; a form of *debt.*

commercial property   Real property developed or acquired for investment and designed for use by business entities such as retail, wholesale, office, industrial, hotel, or service users, as differentiated from *residential property* or housing. (Technically, all income-producing property is commercial property; however, residential rental property is not usually referred to in this category.) Also, real property used for the conduct of business that invites public patronage, as by advertising, merchandising, and display of signs.

commingle   To mix or combine; to combine the money of more than one person or entity into a common fund.

commission   A fee paid to an agent or employee for transacting a piece of business or performing a service. In real estate, the fee paid to the party or parties responsible for generating the business (e.g., the fee paid to an agent or broker for negotiating a sale or rental). The amount and payment of the fee is usually established via a written (commission) agreement. The fee may be a percentage of the transaction amount, an agreed-to fixed amount, or a rate per square foot. Real estate sales commissions are documented in a listing agreement; in real estate management, leasing commissions may be identified as separate compensation in the management agreement. See also *schedule of commissions.* The term is also used in referring to a group of individuals empowered by a government or other entity to exercise specific authority, as a state real estate commission that oversees real estate activity.

committee   A group of people officially delegated to perform a function (e.g., investigate, report, act on a matter). Committees are a common working tool of a condominium association.

common area   Areas of a property that are used by all tenants or owners. In commercial properties, the lobbies, public corridors, and service areas of office buildings and enclosed shopping malls. In a common interest development (e.g., condominium), the property owned jointly by all the unit owners, which ordinarily includes land and structure or portions of structure not otherwise described as units (e.g., lobbies, laundry rooms, recreation facilities, parking, roofs); also called *common elements.*

common area agreement   A separate agreement, usually between an anchor tenant and a shopping center owner, that sets standards for maintenance of the common area and states how the related expenses will be distributed between the parties. It may also prohibit the shopping center owner from making changes to the common areas (e.g., relocating entrances or adding a pad or out-lot building) without the written approval of each signatory to the agreement. (Often a shopping center common area agreement is incorporated in a *recipro-cal easement agreement.*) Such an agreement may also be established among multiple owners of a mixed-use development (MXD) or other similar property, in which case it may also address removal of the common area manager for non-performance.

common area maintenance (CAM) charges clause   Used in commercial leases to state the amount that a tenant will pay to maintain the common ar-eas of the property (e.g., landscaping, parking areas, sidewalks, roadways). In leases for office buildings and industrial properties, CAM costs may be paid along with other property operating expenses as *pass-through charges*. More specifically, a provision in a retail lease that stipulates how much the tenant will pay for maintaining the common area of a shopping center or mall (mall corridors and center court, courtyards, sidewalks, skyways, parking areas, landscaping, elevators, escalators, etc.).

common association   Another name for condominium *master association.*

common elements   Another name for the *common area* of a condominium.

common expenses   The costs of operating, managing, maintaining, and re-pairing a condominium's common areas and administering the condominium association.

common interest realty association (CIRA)   A term commonly used by accountants and real estate managers to describe real estate that is operated for the mutual benefit of the owners; also called *common interest development (CID)*. Condominiums, cooperatives, townhouses, zero-lot-line homes, and manor homes are the more popular examples.

common law   A system of laws, originating in England and based on court decisions (i.e., precedent) when no statute is in place. Compare *statute law.*

common stock   An equity security on which dividends are paid by the issu-ing company from its earnings. See also *stock.*

community association   A type of compulsory association membership in-cluding, but not limited to, condominiums, cooperatives, timeshare properties, planned unit developments (PUDs), and homeowners' associations.

Community Associations Institute (CAI)   Membership organization of condominium and homeowner associations, cooperatives, and association-gov-erned planned communities, individuals and firms that manage these types of properties, and other individuals and organizations who work with or provide services to community associations.

Community Development Block Grant (CDBG)   A federally funded pro-gram to rehabilitate inner-city and older neighborhoods. The CDBG entitle-ment program is used primarily in metropolitan areas; the nonentitlement pro-gram is applied mostly in smaller communities.

community shopping center   A shopping center commonly anchored by a junior department store, discount store, or variety store and having 100,000–500,000 square feet of gross leasable area (GLA), often configured as a large open-air strip with three or more anchors.

company   An association of individuals to conduct a commercial or industrial business or enterprise.

comparable sales approach   In appraisal, determining the price of a particular property based on the prices of recently sold properties with roughly the same uses and location as the subject property. See also *market approach.*

comparison goods   Merchandise that consumers will usually shop for at several stores before buying.

comparison grid   A form used to compare the features of a property with those of other properties in the same market that are similar in size and use. The form lists features and amenities of the properties in a column at the left and includes columns to identify the characteristics of the subject property and to evaluate those same characteristics in the comparable properties. The user usually also assigns a value to each item, an estimate of how much additional rent a tenant might willingly pay to have the feature. For rental apartments, a comparison grid should be completed for each different type and size of apartment. In commercial properties, the basis for comparison would be the square footage of an office suite or store space. Usual practice is to identify at least three comparable properties. The form is often used in determining a market rent for the subject property and usually included as part of a management plan.

comparison grid analysis   A method of price analysis in which the features of a subject property are compared to similar features in three or more comparable properties in the same market. The price (or rent) for each comparable property helps to determine an appropriate price (or rent) for the subject. This method involves assigning values for different attributes such as square footage, amenities, parking, floor and window treatments, age, location, and view. In making a rent comparison for rental apartments, features are compared for a specific type or size of unit (e.g., one-bedroom apartments). At commercial properties, the rent comparison includes base rents and additional charges; for shopping centers, percentage rent and sales potential of both similar and dissimilar centers would be additional comparison items. When using a comparison grid for mobile/manufactured home parks, the method of billing utilities must figure into the calculations; the proper adjustments must be made when comparing parks where monthly rent includes utilities to parks where utilities are billed separately.

The process should take market trends into consideration and is obviously subjective. Each comparable property is compared to the subject, feature by feature. When the feature being examined is superior in the comparable property, the comparable rent should be reduced by the amount that a particular feature is worth in the marketplace. When the feature being examined is superior in the subject property, the comparable rent should be appropriately increased. Rent for the subject property is determined by adding up the adjustments to the rent of each comparable and then either averaging the adjusted rents or using the final rent of the comparable that has had the fewest adjustments (because this comparable is most like the subject property).

compatibility   When used in reference to a mobile home or manufactured housing, general condition and overall appearance that is similar to other homes currently in a mobile home park or manufactured housing community (or in a neighborhood where zoning permits manufactured housing) or to the image being established for a new park or community (or neighborhood that will allow mobile homes).

compensation   Payment for services received, including salary and benefits. The compensation to a property manager may be a *management fee* rather than a salary. Leasing services may be compensated by a *commission*.

compensatory damages   Monetary damages awarded to compensate a plaintiff for the injury sustained and nothing more. See also *damages*.

competition   Two or more sellers vying to acquire buyers by offering more favorable terms. In real estate management, two or more buildings of the same type seeking tenants in the same market are considered competitors.

competitive space   Commonly used in referring to office space in the open market comparable to that in the subject building that will vie for the same tenant population; also called *competitive office space*. The term can also apply to retail, industrial, and flex space. Compare *noncompetitive space*.

complainant   The plaintiff in a lawsuit.

completed products liability   A type of insurance coverage purchased by contractors to protect themselves from liability arising from manufacturing defects after installation of fixtures, equipment, or mechanical items.

completion date   In a construction schedule, the date a rental space or unit is scheduled to be fully completed, inspected and certified, and ready for occupancy. Sometimes also called *delivery date* or *occupancy date*.

compliance   Fulfilling specified requirements as required by law or the terms of a lease agreement.

compounding   In banking, calculation and payment of interest on the principal and on any previous interest.

compound interest   Application of the rate of interest to both the principal amount and any previously earned (accrued) interest. Compare *simple interest*.

Comprehensive Environmental Response, Compensation, and Liability Act (CERCLA)   Enacted in 1980 and substantially revised through the *Superfund Amendments and Reauthorization Act (SARA)* in 1986, the collective law is often referred to as *Superfund*. Superfund provides funding and enforcement authority for cleaning up hazardous waste sites. Under CERCLA, liability, and therefore responsibility for remediation or cleanup costs, can be attributed to those who transported wastes to the particular site, those who arranged for wastes to be disposed of or treated at the site, and present and past owners or operators of the site.

comprehensive general liability (CGL) insurance   An inclusive policy that provides the broadest protection against liability claims.

comptroller   Another name for *controller*.

computer-aided design (CAD)   A computerized system used by architects, space planners, and building managers to facilitate space planning and building design; sometimes also called *computer-assisted design*. A CAD system makes it possible to create space plan drawings and make revisions to them much more quickly than can be done using traditional methods.

computer hardware   Programmable electronic devices used to store, retrieve, and process data.

computer program   A sequence of instructions which, when performed by a computer, allow specific types of data processing to occur; *software.*

computer software   Any of various programs, including procedures and documentation, that is associated with but differentiated from the hardware. Among other things, this includes operating systems and off-the-shelf accounting and word-processing programs as well as custom programming written for specific purposes to operate on specific hardware.

concession   An economic incentive granted by an owner to encourage the leasing of space or the renewal of a lease. Concessions are usually related specifically to the rental rate (e.g., a month's free rent). In office buildings, shopping centers, and industrial properties, they may also relate to the tenant improvement allowance. For retail tenants, a concession may be a lower percentage-of-sales requirement. Concessions usually affect the total economic value of a lease and, therefore, are subject to negotiation.

condemnation   A declaration that a structure is unfit for use. The taking of private property for public use by governmental power of eminent domain, including payment of just compensation. Also, the official act to terminate the use of real property for nonconformance with governmental regulations or because of hazards to public health and safety. See also *eminent domain.*

condemnation clause   A provision in a lease stating the agreed rights, privileges, and limitations of the owner and tenant, respectively, in the event of the taking of the subject property for public use.

conditional liability   Another name for *contingent liability.*

condo   Short for condominium.

condominium   A multiple-unit structure in which the units and pro rata shares of the common areas are owned individually; a unit in a condominium property. Also, the absolute ownership of an apartment or unit, generally in a multi-unit building, which is defined by a legal description of the air space the unit actually occupies plus an undivided interest in the common elements that are owned jointly with the other condominium unit owners. In mobile home parks or manufactured housing communities, outright ownership of an individual lot (including pad, utility connection, parking space, etc.) within a multiple lot park or community along with a prorated shared ownership of the common areas and common facilities.

condominium apartment   A type of *condominium unit.*

condominium association   A private, automatic, usually not-for-profit corporation comprised of the unit owners of a condominium that is responsible for the operation of the condominium community; a *homeowners' association (HOA).* Also called *council of owners, council,* or *association of co-owners.* The operation of a condominium association is governed by legal documents known as the declaration (also called *Covenants, Conditions, and Restrictions* or CC&Rs), bylaws, and articles of incorporation. See also *bylaws; declaration.*

condominium management agreement   A formal contract between a property management firm and a developer or an association board of directors to manage a condominium in exchange for a stated rate of compensation.

condominium unit   That part of a condominium development—a defined three-dimensional space located within the walls, floor, and ceiling of a condominium structure—that is privately owned and independently and exclusively used by a unit owner; also called *condominium apartment.* While residential condominiums are most common, there are also office, retail, medical office, flex space, and industrial condominiums.

conduit   An ownership vehicle that passes income tax benefits or liabilities directly through to individual investors; see *real estate mortgage investment conduit (REMIC).* In construction, a pipe or enclosed channel used to carry electrical wiring, water, or other fluids.

conflict of interest   A situation that arises when the private interests of an individual in a position of trust (e.g., a managing agent) conflict with his/her official duties. Such conflicts must always be disclosed to ownership.

congregate care   A type of housing for senior citizens that offers private living quarters (rented) with access to the services (transportation, housekeeping; for a fee) needed by persons who are not totally independent (i.e., need little or no assistance with daily tasks). Residents have individual apartments with kitchen facilities but may, through a central kitchen and dining room, share their meals with other residents. Congregate care, also called *congregate housing,* may be part of a larger development that includes *assisted living facilities.*

conquest marketing   Another name for *acquisition marketing.*

consequential loss insurance   Insurance that protects the insured against the consequences of a direct loss, such as indirect physical damage or loss of income.

consideration   Something of value exchanged for a promise or for performance of a service that makes an exchange legally binding, such as paying rent in exchange for use of a property.

consignment   In retailing, merchandise shipped to a seller (consignee) for future sale or other purpose for which title (ownership) remains with the shipper (consignor).

consolidated metropolitan statistical area (CMSA)   See *metropolitan area (MA).*

Consolidated Omnibus Budget Reconciliation Act (COBRA)   Federal law that requires employers to offer employees an opportunity to continue their group health care coverage for a period of time when they are terminated or leave their jobs by paying the premiums themselves.

constant   See *annual mortgage constant rate; loan constant.*

construction drawings   Architectural and mechanical specifications drawn to scale and in sufficient detail to guide workers in constructing tenant improvements in commercial buildings; also called *working drawings.*

construction loan   A short-term, usually interest-only loan made to finance the cost of new construction or rehabilitation (as opposed to permanent financing on a completed building), that may be funded by one or more commercial banks or other sources of capital (e.g., institutional investors such as insurance companies) or by the permanent lender. Money is normally released to the builder or borrower in stages as costs are incurred during construction.

construction management   The supervision of construction of tenant improvements to commercial space by a space-planning department or a firm specializing in this activity.

construction rider   That part of a lease listing in detail all work to be done for the tenant by the landlord; also called *workletter*.

constructive eviction   Inability of a tenant to obtain or maintain possession because of conditions of a property that make occupancy hazardous or the premises unfit for its intended use. To apply in a landlord-tenant dispute, the tenant must vacate the premises prematurely because of the conditions.

constructive fraud   Any action or omission that is contrary to one's legal or equitable duty, trust, or confidence and works to the injury of another. Any breach of duty, trust, or confidence that, without fraudulent intent, gains an advantage to the person by misleading another. Differentiated from *actual fraud,* which is intentional and successful deception used to cheat another.

constructive notice   Notice given to the world by recorded documents. All persons are charged with knowledge of such documents and their contents whether or not they have actually examined them. Possession of property is also considered notice that the person in possession has an interest in the property.

consultant   One who gives professional advice within a specialized field of knowledge or provides services based on specialized training.

consultation   A service offered by real estate managers or management companies to owners whose properties do not require ongoing management but who do need advice on specific problems such as marketing and leasing, rehabilitation, modernization, or property conversion. Common interest realty associations (CIRAs) may also seek such consultation services.

consumer goods   Products used directly to satisfy human needs or desires.

consumerism   A movement seeking to protect the rights of buyers through government action and controls.

Consumer Price Index (CPI)   A way of measuring consumer purchasing power by comparing the current costs of goods and services to those of a selected base period; formerly *cost-of-living index.* Sometimes used as a reference point for rent escalations in commercial leases (i.e., as a measure of inflation). The CPI is published monthly by the U.S. Department of Labor, Bureau of Labor Statistics. See also *base period.*

containment   A remedial method of isolating an environmental hazard, such as nonfriable asbestos, by enclosure or encapsulation. See also *friable.*

contingency   An event that may or may not occur within a designated time period or at all. In construction estimating, a contingency factor is commonly included to cover unexpected costs that arise as the job is in progress.

contingency reserves   Funds set aside to cover the cost of unanticipated emergencies or major expenditures not included in the current fiscal year operating budget.

contingent liability   Liability that can fall to one as an implied participant or contributor; *conditional liability.*

continuous occupancy clause   A lease clause that requires the tenant to occupy the space continuously throughout the lease term.

continuous operation   A shopping center lease provision that requires the retail tenant to operate the business throughout the term of the lease (sometimes including reference to established operating hours of the shopping center, but *store hours* are usually addressed in a separate lease provision); also called *operating covenant.* A continuous operation requirement may not be viable in jurisdictions where the courts will not enforce the lease provision but rather take the view that the landlord can recover money damages for a breach of the lease. In a shopping center, maintaining a continuously operating viable mix of retail businesses is key to the success of the center as a whole and that of all the individual tenants; money damages paid to the landlord are not adequate compensation in the event a tenant does not comply. A shop tenant will sometimes try to negotiate to have the continuous operation requirement apply contingent on a specific anchor remaining in operation; if the anchor is allowed to *go dark,* the continuous operation provision in the shop tenant's lease would not apply.

continuous operation clause   A retail lease clause that requires tenants to keep their stores fully stocked at inventory levels equal to (1) when they first opened for business, (2) their stores in other locations, or (3) stores offering similar merchandise in the area. There may also be requirements regarding store hours, staffing, and business name.

contract   An agreement entered into by two or more persons which creates an obligation to do (or not do) a particular thing. The document that serves as proof of such an obligation. The essentials of a contract are legally competent parties, the obligation created between them, consideration or compensation (e.g., a fee), and mutuality of agreement. Examples in real estate management include management agreements, leases, and maintenance service agreements related to building systems and equipment.

contract bond   See *payment bond; performance bond.*

contract of indemnity   Insurance coverage designed to compensate the insured for a loss in such a way that there is neither financial gain nor loss.

contractor   An individual or company that contracts to perform a service (e.g., construction, elevator or HVAC maintenance) or provide supplies (e.g., bulk cleaning chemicals).

contractor's liability insurance   Coverage that insures a contractor's employees against injuries that occur on the job.

contract rate   In newspaper or magazine advertising, a reduced rate provided when a contract is signed for a certain number of ad insertions.

contract rent   The rent stipulated in an existing lease, which may differ from the economic or market rent. In government-assisted housing, the total rent HUD (or the contract administrator) authorizes an owner to collect from all sources for a unit occupied by a family receiving assistance. See also *market rent; street rent.*

contractual liability insurance   Coverage for injury or property damage liability assumed under a contract.

control   One of four methods of *risk management*. Actions or practices undertaken to reduce the frequency or severity of loss.

controllable expense   An operating expense for which management has defined responsibility and over which it has control (e.g., advertising, energy consumption, maintenance and repairs, and purchase of supplies).

controller   The chief accounting officer of a business whose responsibilities usually include accounting, budgeting, and internal auditing functions, measuring financial performance against previously approved standards, and interpreting and reporting on these activities internally; also called *comptroller*. Duties may also include generating external financial reports, analyzing budget variances, preparing and filing tax returns, and countersigning checks.

convenience center   A small shopping center having up to 30,000 square feet of gross leasable area (GLA); often designed in a strip. Convenience centers are sometimes anchored by a quick-stop food store and usually occupied by service-oriented businesses.

convenience goods   Milk, soft drinks, chewing gum, candy, personal items, and similar goods that consumers will buy at stores closest to where they live or work, without making a special trip to purchase them.

conventional loan   A real estate bank loan that is not insured (FHA) or guaranteed (VA) by a governmental agency; also a *conventional mortgage*.

conversion   Transfer of a multifamily rental property to a condominium form of ownership through sale of individual living units; a multifamily dwelling whose ownership has been so transferred. Also, the unauthorized appropriation of another person's property or funds.

conversion ratio   The number of prospect contacts in a defined period compared to the number of leases that result from those contacts expressed as a percentage. Specifically, the number of telephone calls that lead to apartment showings and the number of showings that result in signed leases, usually tracked on a weekly basis. For example, if ten phone calls resulted in six showings, and three of those showings led to signed leases, six out of ten calls is a 60 percent conversion to showings; three out of six showings is a 50 percent conversion to leases. Conversion of showings to leases is sometimes also called a *closing ratio*.

convertible loan   A loan offered by a lender at a below-market interest rate in exchange for the possibility of changing the loan balance into an equity interest at any time during the term of the loan. A form of equity participation— sometimes called *additional interest provision (AIP)*—whereby the lender has the option for a specified period to convert the loan into a predetermined percentage of ownership in the project. See also *equity participation*.

conveyance   The instrument or document by which a transfer is made or title passed from one person to another.

cooling degree-day   See *degree-day*.

cooperating broker   An agent who brings a suitable prospect for a particular location to the broker who represents the owner of the site, or vice versa, thereby qualifying for a portion of the commission fee; also called an *outside broker*.

cooperative   Ownership of a share or shares of stock in a corporation that holds the title to a multiple-unit residential structure. A shareholder does not own a specific unit outright but has the right to occupy it as a co-owner of the cooperative association under a *proprietary lease.*

co-owner   Another name for condominium or cooperative *unit owner.* Also used when there are two or more (joint) owners of any real or personal property (e.g., real estate, an automobile). See also *joint tenancy.*

core space   The area in a high-rise office building, usually centrally located, that houses the building's systems and functional services, including elevator banks, stairwells, washrooms, and electrical and janitorial closets.

corporate income tax   Levy by the federal government and most states on the annual net earnings of a corporation.

corporation   A legal entity that is chartered by a state and treated by courts as an individual entity with the ability to buy, sell, sue, and be sued separate and distinct from the persons who own its stock. For purposes of taxation, the Internal Revenue Service differentiates regular corporations subject to corporate income tax under Subchapter C of the IRS Code from those whose taxable income is taxed to their shareholders per Subchapter S of the Code. See also *S corporation.*

corrective maintenance   Ordinary repairs that must be made to a building and its equipment on a day-to-day basis. See also *deferred maintenance; preventive maintenance.*

corridor   A hallway or passage in a building that provides a common means of travel to an exit or between apartments, office suites, or other defined spaces.

cosmetic maintenance   Work done on a building or property that enhances its appearance but does not contribute materially to its operation or preservation.

cost   Any expenditure of money, goods, or services for the purpose of acquiring goods or services. The price paid for something. An expense of doing business. In real estate, *reproduction cost* is the cost at current prices of creating an exact duplicate of a building. *Replacement cost* is the cost at current prices of replacing an existing building with one that fulfills the same function and is a factor considered during an appraisal.

cost accounting   Systematic classification, recording, analysis, and summarization of the cost elements for material, labor, and overhead incident to production of goods or rendering of services. The branch of accounting concerned with providing detailed information on the cost of producing a product or providing a service; a tool of *managerial accounting.*

cost approach   A method of appraising real property in which the value of the improvements is estimated on the basis of the cost to reproduce them minus accrued depreciation; also called *summation approach.* See also *appraisal.*

cost-benefit analysis   A method of measuring the benefits expected from a decision (e.g., to rehabilitate a building; to change an operating procedure) by calculating the impact of the change on net operating income (NOI) and cash flow, comparing that impact to the cost of making the change, and determining whether the benefits justify the costs. Also, a systematic evaluation of alternative ways to achieve the same objective by comparing costs and benefits of each alternative, as in developing a management plan.

cost center   Any department, process, or other component of a business for which cost records are maintained and to which fixed costs, along with direct labor and material costs, may be allocated.

cost-effective   Economical (i.e., when the results of an action are worth the money spent).

cost of living   The money cost of maintaining a particular standard of living in terms of purchased goods and services.

cost of living index   Former name for the *Consumer Price Index (CPI)*.

cost-plus pricing   A common method of setting prices by determining the cost of providing the good or service and adding to it a percentage (markup) to cover overhead expenses and profit; also called *cost-plus method* or *time-and-material method.*

cost recovery   A tax deduction allowed by the Internal Revenue Service to recover the cost of a depreciable asset. See also *depreciation; Modified Accelerated Cost Recovery System (MACRS)*.

council of co-owners   Also called *council*. Another name for a common interest or *condominium association*.

Counselor of Real Estate (CRE)   Professional designation conferred on members of the Counselors of Real Estate.

Counselors of Real Estate   Membership organization of real estate professionals with extensive experience in all phases of real estate who provide consulting services; an affiliate of the National Association of REALTORS® (NAR).

countersignature   A second or confirming signature, often required in issuing checks for a business when the amount exceeds a certain threshold.

covariance   As applied to business, the extent that an asset's returns vary in the same pattern as the market's average returns (i.e., the relationship of the change in two related variables).

covenant   An agreement written into deeds and other instruments promising performance or nonperformance of certain acts or stipulating certain uses or non-uses of the property.

Covenants, Conditions, and Restrictions (CC&Rs)   One of the documents that governs participation in a condominium or homeowners' association, CC&Rs are enforceable rules and regulations that protect the economic value, architectural uniformity, and long-term desirability of the property. See also *bylaws; condominium association.* In shopping centers, CC&Rs restrict the use of the property.

coverage ratio   The ratio of building to land, usually expressed in square feet (building sq ft ÷ land sq ft).

credit bureau   A firm that specializes in investigating consumers' credit ratings. Applied to establishments that collect information about the credit, character, responsibility, and reputation of businesses and individuals for the purpose of furnishing that information to others, usually for a fee.

credit check   An investigation of a person's capacity for and history of debt repayment.

credit investigating agency   A firm that prepares credit checks on prospective tenants for property owners or managers at a fixed fee per report; a *credit bureau.*

creditor   One to whom money or other compensation (e.g., goods) is owed.

credit rating   Evaluation of the current ability and past performance of individuals and businesses in paying debts. Also, an estimate of the amount of credit that can be safely extended to an individual or a business based on the person's or company's financial resources and record of debt payment. Such ratings are generally established by credit bureaus and used by others (bankers, merchants) to determine whether a loan should be granted or a line of credit given. Used in real estate management in qualifying a prospective tenant for a residential or commercial lease. Credit reporting practices are regulated under the federal *Fair Credit Reporting Act (FCRA).*

credit report   A report on the credit rating of an individual or business, usually made by a credit bureau.

credit score   A numerical value that measures the relative degree of risk of a potential borrower. A credit score takes into account payment history, amounts owed, length of time credit has been established, acquisition of new credit, and types of credit established (credit cards, installment loans, mortgage, etc.).

credit union   Savings and lending organization operated by businesses, labor unions, or community organizations for the benefit of their own employees or members.

crime prevention   The anticipation, recognition, and appraisal of a crime risk and the initiation of some action to remove or reduce it.

crime prevention through environmental design (CPTED)   The theory that proper design and effective use of the built environment can lead to a reduction in the fear of crime and the incidence of crime. Emphasis is on natural surveillance, natural access control, and territorial behavior supplemented with organized and mechanical methods of security, including guards and security devices and systems.

crisis public relations   See *emergency preparedness; public relations.*

cubicle   A usually square or rectangular shaped configuration of movable panels intended as a work space for a single employee. See also *workstation.*

cumulative deductible   A type of insurance deductible, the amount of which is determined by the total losses in a period, usually one year; also called *aggregate deductible.*

cumulative mark-on   In retailing, the difference between the total cost and the total original retail value of all goods handled to date.

curable obsolescence   Reversible deterioration of a building that is a result of deferred maintenance. Also, remediable loss of value due to a property becoming outmoded or noncompetitive.

curative maintenance   See *corrective maintenance.*

curb appeal   General cleanliness, neatness, and attractiveness of a building as exemplified by the appearance of the exterior and grounds and the general level of housekeeping. The aesthetic image and appearance projected by a property; the first impression it creates.

current assets   Assets of a short-term nature (e.g., cash on hand, accounts receivable, or merchandise that can be readily converted into cash, sold, or consumed in the near future through normal business operations); differentiated from *capital assets*.

current liabilities   Economic liabilities (e.g., accounts payable, accrued interest not yet due) that arise in the conduct of business activity and must be met in a comparatively short time.

current ratio   A measure of a company's ability to pay its current liabilities from its current assets; a measure of *liquidity*. Calculated by dividing the value of current assets by the value of current liabilities.

custodial maintenance   The day-to-day cleaning and other work that is essential to preserving the value of a property; also called *janitorial maintenance* or *housekeeping*.

D

damage To cause injury or harm to someone's person, property, or reputation; also used in referring to the injury or harm thus caused. The term includes bodily injury to human beings; physical damage to real estate caused by tenants, beyond normal wear and tear, as well as that caused by visitors, vendors, vandals, and others; and personal injury due to defamation of character, invasion of privacy, and similar acts. Differentiated from the plural form, *damages,* which has specific legal implications.

damages Money awarded by a court of law as compensation to a plaintiff (injured party). There are several categories: *Nominal damages,* awarded when actual injury or loss was very slight, may be as small as one dollar. *Compensatory or actual damages* are intended to compensate financially only for the loss sustained by a plaintiff, nothing more. *Punitive or exemplary damages* are awarded in addition to compensatory damages to punish defendants for conduct which showed a "conscious disregard" for the rights of others or was "outrageous," "willful," "wanton," or "malicious" in nature.

Compensatory damages are further differentiated: *General damages* cover injuries that are a natural result of the wrongful act and therefore common to all victims (e.g., "pain and suffering" and medical expenses). *Special damages* cover injuries that are unique to the victim (e.g., lost past and future wages, loss of affection, child care).

data Known information, including facts and figures. Information to be processed in a computer program; plural in form (the singular is *datum*).

database A collection of information organized for rapid search and retrieval as by a computer.

data processing Collection, interpretation, and transmission of data for reference as a basis for decision-making; see also *electronic data processing (EDP).*

death clause A special, rarely used lease clause that provides for termination of the lease before its expiration date in the event of the (usually residential) tenant's death.

debt Money, goods, or services owed by one person or organization to another. More specifically, a set amount of money owed by one person to another, including the debtor's obligation to pay and the creditor's right to receive and enforce payment (e.g., a mortgage loan against real property).

debt-coverage ratio   Used by lenders as a measure of financial risk. A measure of the amount of debt service that can be carried on a property pledged as collateral for a loan. The ratio is calculated: annual net operating income ÷ annual debt service payment (principal plus interest), and the result is written as a decimal (e.g., 1.55). The closer the resulting value approaches to one (1.0), the riskier the loan.

debt financing   Use of borrowed funds to invest in real estate. Compare *equity financing*.

debt security   A security issued by a company (or other entity) that obligates the company to pay investors periodic interest payments, which thus are a debt owed by the company. The best-known example of a debt security is a *bond*. Compare *equity security*.

debt service   Regular payments of the principal and interest on a loan as required under a loan agreement.

decentralization   Reorganization of a business entity into numerous autonomous entities (separate companies, subsidiaries, or divisions) that remain under central control.

declarant board   The first board of directors appointed by the developer of a condominium; also called *developer's board*.

declaration   A legal document that, when filed, commits land to condominium use, creates a condominium association and serves as its constitutional law, physically describes a condominium, defines the method of determining each unit owner's share of the common areas, and includes restrictions and covenants. Sometimes also called *declaration of codes, covenants, and restrictions*. See also *master deed*.

declining percentage rent   A negotiated percentage rent structure such that the retail tenant pays a smaller percentage of gross sales after a specified sales volume is reached.

deductible   In insurance, a specified amount the insured party must pay before the insurer pays on a claim.

deduction   Any expense or cost set off against revenue. For income tax purposes, any expense or cost that can be used to offset revenue, such as the operating costs of an investment rental property and the paper cost of depreciation or cost recovery.

deed   A legal document that transfers ownership (title) of a property.

deed of trust   The document used in some states in place of a mortgage. An instrument by which legal title to real property is held by a third party (trustee) as collateral to secure the repayment of a loan. Title is conveyed by the borrower (mortgagor) to the trustee to hold for the benefit of the lender (mortgagee) with the condition that title shall be reconveyed upon payment of the debt. The trustee is also empowered to sell the land and pay the debt in the event of a default by the debtor. (A deed of trust does not require a court order for foreclosure; a mortgage does.) In simpler terms, the deed pledges the property as collateral; title to the property is held by the buyer as a "warranty deed," and a note is executed as evidence of the debt.

deed restrictions   Clauses in a deed limiting the future uses of the property. Deed restrictions may limit the density of buildings, dictate the types of structures that can be erected, or prevent buildings from being used for specific purposes (or at all). Deed restrictions may impose numerous limitations and conditions.

deep subsidy   A government subsidy that directly assists residents. These may be both property-based and resident-based subsidies. They provide residents with assistance in paying rent and often utilities (e.g., rental assistance payments or rent supplements).

default   Failure to fulfill an obligation (as a mortgage or other contracted payment) when it is due. The nonperformance of a duty, such as those required in a lease or other contract. Sometimes called *breach of contract.*

defeasance clause   A mortgage provision that permits the borrower (mortgagor) to prepay the debt, thereby defeating the conditional, temporary conveyance to the lender (mortgagee) of title to real property.

defect of title   A claim, restricted use provision, or other imperfection that adversely affects the customary use and marketability of a property.

defendant   The person alleged to be at fault. The entity believed to be responsible for an injury for which legal relief is sought via a lawsuit. The entity that is sued.

deferred income   Current income (wages, salary) foregone to produce a higher income at a later time, as at retirement; also called *deferred compensation.*

deferred maintenance   Ordinary maintenance of a building that, because it has not been performed, negatively affects the use, occupancy, and value of the property. Also, an amount needed for repairs, restoration, or rehabilitation of an asset (e.g., real property) but not yet expended. See also *corrective maintenance; preventive maintenance.*

deficiency judgment   A personal judgment levied against the mortgagor when the foreclosure sale does not produce sufficient funds to pay the mortgage debt in full.

deflation   An economic condition occurring when the money supply declines in relation to the amount of goods available, resulting in lower prices. Compare *inflation.*

degree-day   A unit that represents one degree difference in the mean outdoor temperature for one day. Temperatures above 65° F represent *cooling degree-days;* those below 65° F represent *heating degree-days.*

delegation   Assignment of a task, including related responsibility, as by a manager to a subordinate employee.

delinquency   Failure to make payment on a debt or obligation when due. A state of being overdue. A debt on which payment is in arrears, as of mortgage principal or interest or rent under a lease.

delinquent   Past due. In real estate, delinquency is commonly used in reference to rent or other payments not paid as agreed under a lease or a loan.

delivery date   Another name for *completion date*. However, in some situations, a developer may agree to a specific "delivery date" (separate from the building construction completion date) so that a commercial tenant may perform its own work in time to meet an occupancy or opening date. Also, a delivery date may (or may not) be the commencement date of a lease or the closing date of a sale.

demand   In economic terms, a need or request for a good or service. Willingness to purchase a good or service. The amount spent on a good or service or the quantity that is purchased. Compare *supply*. In engineering, the load on a building system. Also, the electricity load (as of a power plant or an individual consumer) expressed in kilowatts and averaged over a specified period of time.

demand analysis   An analysis of *energy demand*.

demand for compliance or possession   Another name for *eviction notice*.

demand meter   An instrument that measures *energy demand*.

demand to pay or quit   Another name for *eviction notice*.

demised premises   That portion of a property conveyed by a lease agreement, usually defined by the walls and other structures that separate one tenant's space from that of another and further identified by a unit or space (suite) number.

demising wall   A partition or wall separating the leased space of one tenant from that of another tenant and from common areas.

demographic profile   A compilation of social and economic statistics of a specific population, such as size, density, growth and decline, and vital statistics (e.g., age, birth and death rates, family/household size, education, income), usually within a geographic area (as a neighborhood or region).

demographics   The statistical analysis of populations, using information derived primarily from census records, including overall population size, density, and distribution, birth and death rates, and the impact of inmigration and outmigration. Also included are age, gender, nationality, religion, education, occupation, and income characteristics of people who live in a geographically defined area. Used to characterize discrete markets. Residential property owners and managers are also interested in such concurrent data as household size, numbers of children and their ages, and levels of homeownership because they relate to requirements for living space in the form of rental apartments. Retail tenants are interested in population and household data within a prescribed *trade area* to help establish price points, merchandise mix, and marketing focus. A tool of *marketing research*.

demography   The statistical study of populations, which examines sets of characteristics about people that relate to their behavior as consumers. The most frequently analyzed demographic factors are age, sex, race, marital status, education, and income; however, household size and composition (e.g., number of children and their ages) are other factors that directly impact housing choices. Demographers use data from a variety of sources, including censuses, surveys, and birth and death records.

demotion   A lowering in job rank.

density   In housing, the number of dwelling units constructed per acre.

Department of Housing and Urban Development (HUD)   A department of the U.S. government that supervises the *Federal Housing Administration (FHA)* and a number of other agencies that administer various housing programs.

Department of Veterans Affairs (VA)   An agency of the U.S. government that administers benefit programs for veterans, including the guarantee of loans to purchase housing; formerly the *Veterans Administration.*

deposit   Money placed in a bank or in someone else's safekeeping by an individual or business, which is credited to the depositor's account and subject to orders for withdrawal, thereby creating a relationship of creditor and debtor. Also, money given to bind a transaction, as an application deposit for a rental or as a damage or security deposit (held in escrow). See also *security deposit.*

depreciable basis   An income tax term. See *basis.*

depreciation   Loss of value. In real estate, decline in value of a property resulting from physical deterioration (ordinary wear and tear), functional obsolescence (out-of-date systems and/or equipment), and/or economic obsolescence (market changes). See also *obsolescence.* In accounting, the gradual process of converting a fixed asset into an expense. Also, the tax deduction that allows for recovery of the investment in certain types of property by allocation of the cost over the estimated useful life of the property; also called *cost recovery.* In real estate, depreciation (and cost recovery) applies to the cost of improvements to land; the land itself is not depreciated.

depreciation reserve   In accounting, the accumulated loss of value charged against all productive assets as stated on the *balance sheet.*

depression   Part of the *business cycle,* a period of low economic activity characterized by high unemployment, low levels of investment, falling prices (including rents), reduced purchasing power, decreasing use of resources, and currency deflation.

depth   In retail properties, the distance between the front window of a store and its back wall. In retailing, the variety of goods stocked for sale.

destination tenants   Used in referring to ancillary or shop tenants in a shopping center because the merchandise or services they offer are specifically sought out by consumers (e.g., beauty salons, barber shops, shoe repair services); also sometimes referred to as *destination uses.* Compare *impulse tenants.*

destruction provision   A lease provision stating the applicable procedure and rights of the parties in the event the leased premises are damaged or destroyed by fire or other mishap. As a rule, the lessee will be held financially liable if deemed responsible for the mishap. In leases at a multitenant commercial property, such a provision may refer to the extent of casualty damage to the building, landlord's responsibility to repair/rebuild to prior condition with possible abatement of rent, and/or termination of the lease in the event the damage cannot be repaired.

deteriorating neighborhood   An area in which buildings are in disrepair and occupants are mostly transients.

developer   The individual or entity that invests in building a property and is responsible for construction and, when the development is a rental property, may also engage in marketing and leasing. The developer may also be the owner of the land, or the developer's investment may consist solely of time and expertise. Real estate development is often done on a speculative basis.

developer's board   Another name for a condominium *declarant board.*

developing neighborhood   A growing area with new construction and stable occupancies.

development   A component of the *real estate cycle.* A period when occupancy is high, rents are rising, and absorption levels are high, usually coincident with increasing prosperity and leading to new construction to meet demand for housing and commercial space that exceeds the available supply. Also used in referring to developed real estate, as a large-scale or multi-building residential or commercial project that may be built in phases.

development loan   An interim loan characterized by a short term and a higher, risk-related interest rate that is used to finance construction of improvements on vacant land. It usually provides for continuous funding throughout the construction period.

different impact   Under fair housing law, an action or policy that affects members of a protected class differently even though it is applied equally—e.g., refusing to rent to applicants who receive Aid to Families with Dependent Children (AFDC). Even though applied to all applicants, single mothers may be adversely affected since they comprise the majority of AFDC recipients.

different treatment   In fair housing law, a type of discrimination that may arise when members of a protected class are treated differently than others who are not members of that class (e.g., charged a higher security deposit or a higher rental rate).

dignified use clause   The provision in a retail lease that the merchant will not use the property in a way that will damage the image or reputation of the shopping center as a whole.

dioxin   A family of chemical compounds (known as dibenzo-*p*-dioxins) that are often found in conjunction with chlorinated hydrocarbons (e.g., pesticides). Concern about dioxins arises out of their potential toxicity to humans and animals.

direct capitalization   Use of an income projection divided by a cap rate to give an estimate of a property's value. See also *capitalization.*

direct costs   In construction estimating, labor (wages and benefits for the contractors' personnel), materials (building parts, permanently installed equipment, etc.), and heavy equipment to be used in the process (cranes, bulldozers). Subcontracted work is also a direct cost.

direct deposit   A procedure whereby funds (usually a check) are mailed to a bank to be deposited directly into a particular account. This type of transaction may also be done via electronic transfer.

direct housing subsidy   A financial grant that increases the housing supply available to specified (e.g., low- and moderate-income, disabled, elderly) households.

direct loss   Economic loss due to physical damage caused by an insured peril such as fire; see also *indirect loss.*

direct mail A form of advertising that relies on printed matter (letters, brochures, cards, etc.) sent to potential customers by mail, often utilizing specialized mailing lists.

directors' and officers' liability insurance Protection against financial loss arising out of alleged errors in judgment, breaches of duty, and wrongful acts of a board of directors and/or officers in carrying out their prescribed duties. A recommended coverage for condominium associations.

direct-reduction loan A loan in which payments are equal amounts, with a portion applied first to the current interest and the remainder applied to reduction of the principal; also called *level-payment* or *self-amortizing loan.*

direct solicitation A procedure in which a property manager or management firm specifically asks an owner for property management business.

disability With respect to a person, a physical or mental impairment that substantially limits one or more major life activities, a record of such an impairment, or being regarded as having such an impairment. Further defined as such a condition which is expected to be of long, continued, and indefinite duration.

disability clause A special, rarely used lease covenant that provides for the alteration of the lease terms, or the termination of the lease before expiration, in the event that the tenant is physically disabled and unable to continue his/her use of the leased premises; most often included in leases for residential property.

disbursement Money paid out by cash or check.

discount A reduction in price, usually as a reward for paying a charge prior to the date of delinquency or for buying in quantity.

discounted cash flow (DCF) Financial analysis using the time value of money to determine how much an investment held for several years into the future would be worth in present dollars.

discounted cash flow (DCF) method A method of valuation that discounts all future fiscal benefits of an investment property over a predetermined holding period. See also *appraisal.*

discounting Calculating how much a future sum of money would be worth at present.

discount point An amount equal to one percent of a loan charged by a lender for the use of capital in order to balance (offset) a submarket interest rate. Also, the discount on a loan that is bought or sold.

discount rate Any rate used to translate a future dollar amount into an equivalent present value. Also, the interest rate the Federal Reserve Bank charges commercial banks.

discretionary income Money available for spending after physical needs (food, clothing, shelter) have been met and taxes have been paid.

discrimination Unfair treatment or denial of normal services or privileges to a person or persons because of their skin color, race, national origin, or religion. Sex, disability, and familial status are also protected classes in regard to some types of discrimination. See also *Americans with Disabilities Act (ADA); Civil Rights Act of 1964/1968; fair housing laws.*

disk   In computers, a magnetic storage medium offering random access to information. This may be either a rigid magnetic disk or a flexible (floppy) disk or *diskette.*

disorderly conduct   Any behavior that is contrary to law and, in particular, disturbs the public peace or safety.

display advertising   Large paid notices that use display techniques (large print, graphics, color) and generally are not presented in newspapers and magazines under classified headings. Display ads are usually more than one column in width, and they may have a border and include a headline and/or an illustration or logo.

disposable income   The amount of personal income (i.e., wages) left over after all statutory deductions such as federal, state, and local income taxes and Social Security benefits. The amount of money that consumers actually have available to spend or save. This take-home or net income is the basis of an individual's or a household's ability to purchase goods and services, including housing.

distressed property   Income property that is in foreclosure or for which foreclosure is imminent due to a lack of sufficient income. Also, real estate that yields an insufficient return.

diversification   Expansion of the scope of business activity, usually into related areas of business. In investment, reducing risk by investing capital in different types of instruments such as real estate, precious metals, stocks, bonds, and mutual funds.

dividend   Corporate earnings (profits) allocated for distribution to individual shareholders in proportion to their shares of ownership.

documentation   A written record of an act, event, or incident for purposes of supporting a claim (legal, insurance) or action.

doing business as   More commonly seen as the abbreviation *dba* or *d/b/a,* it represents the business name assumed by a sole proprietor or the trade name of a business as opposed to its legal name. In regard to the latter, a retailer may use a name for a store site (e.g., XYZ Shoe Store) that is different from the name under which the business is legally established (e.g., XYZ Limited Partnership) in order to ensure that customers know the retailer's type of business.

double-net lease   Also called net-net lease. See *net lease.*

double-section   In the manufactured housing industry, another name for *double-wide.*

double taxation   A disadvantage of the corporate form of ownership because the business entity is required to pay income taxes on its profits, and the individual shareholders must also pay income taxes on the dividends they receive.

double-wide   A mobile or manufactured home consisting of two individual sections, each on a separate chassis, that are assembled on site. *Single-wide* mobile homes are generally twelve to fourteen feet wide (although there are sixteen-foot single-wides). Double-wide (or multiwide) homes are usually twenty-four to twenty-eight feet wide. Also called *double-section.*

downpayment   An initial incremental payment to secure the delivery of property or goods upon payment of the total price in accordance with a specific agreement.

downtime   A period when equipment or employees are idle because of breakdowns, adjustments, or other interruptions.

downtown   See *central business district (CBD)*.

downtown retail space   A mall, freestanding store, or space in a mixed-use development in an urban environment, primarily the *central business district (CBD)*, but not limited to it.

downzoning   A type of rezoning in which the prevailing *zoning ordinances* are changed to allow for less intensive use. Downzoning may involve reducing the allowable density for development (e.g., fewer housing units, fewer stores) or changing the allowable character from high use to low use (e.g., from multi-family to single-family). See also *zoning*.

Drug-Free Workplace Act   Federal law that requires employers who contract with the U.S. government to certify that they maintain a drug-free workplace and have a published statement notifying employees that drug activity is prohibited in their workplace and specifying the actions that will be taken against those who violate the prohibition. Employees must abide by the terms of the employer's drug-free workplace policy as a condition of their employment.

dual agency   A situation in which a single agent, with disclosure to each party, represents both parties to a transaction (e.g., buyer and seller in real estate sales).

due diligence   The duty of a seller to ensure that the offering statement does not misstate or omit pertinent information. The appropriate or sufficient level of care and attention that should be given during the examination or evaluation of a property, either as preparation for financing or refinancing or in an effort to identify environmental problems that must be addressed.

duly authorized   Properly authorized to act for another in accordance with legal requirements and in conformance with a written series of conditions and covenants (e.g., power of attorney). The status of one who has legal authority to bind a corporate or other business entity in a lease or other contract.

Dumpster   Trademark for a type of large trash receptacle used for accumulating waste materials, generally over two cubic yards in capacity, which must be emptied by hydraulically lifting the container and dumping the contents into a truck or removed from the site using a specialized truck.

E

earnings   The operating profits of a business. Wages or dividends as compensation for labor or the use of capital.

easement   An interest in or right to land that is owned by another person. A legal right to use land owned by another person or business for a specific purpose. An easement may be granted by a deed or created as a result of actual use that was not prohibited *(easement by prescription)*. See also *adverse possession*.

economic   Pertaining to the economy; economically advantageous.

economic analysis   Part of the appraisal of income-producing properties, a method that focuses on determining the present value of future economic benefits by using capitalization rates.

economic base   The businesses or industries that provide an area with the basis for its economy.

economic life   The period during which an economic good (e.g., real estate) remains useful. The number of years during which a building will continue to produce a high percentage yield (i.e., generate income).

economic obsolescence   Impairment of desirability or useful life of property, or its loss in use and value, arising from economic forces outside of the building or property, such as changes in optimum land use, legislative enactments that restrict or impair property rights, and changes in market conditions (e.g., supply-demand relationships). See also *obsolescence*.

economic oversupply   Vacancy that occurs entirely because of tenants' inability to pay current rents.

economic rent   Another name for *market rent.*

economic rent increase   An increase in rent based on market shortage and general consumer income level.

economics   The science that deals with the production, distribution, exchange, and consumption of goods and services.

economic shortage   A condition that arises when there are more prospective tenants who are able to pay market rental rates than there are available rental spaces.

economic turnover   A type of turnover that involves tenants moving from a rented apartment to either a purchased single-family home, townhouse, or condominium or another part of the country. See also *lateral turnover; turnover.*

economic vacancy   Commonly used in rental housing to mean all vacant units that are not producing income. In addition to physical vacancies, this includes units that are not available for lease (e.g., apartments used as models or offices, staff apartments, cannibalized units) as well as leased units that are not yet occupied and occupied units that are not producing rent (i.e., delinquencies); usually expressed as a percentage of the total number of units. (In other words, the number of unoccupied units may not always be an accurate reflection of the impact of vacancies.) A similar determination may be made for commercial properties based on unoccupied square footage. In economic terms, the rent dollars lost from such vacancies, expressed as a percentage of the gross potential income of the property. See also *physical vacancy.*

economy   The structure of economic life in a nation or region. Thrifty (economical) use and management of material resources.

effective gross income   The total amount of income actually collected during a reporting period; the gross receipts of a property. Gross potential rental income *less* vacancy and collection losses *plus* miscellaneous or unscheduled income.

effective interest rate   The actual rate of interest paid on a loan, which may include adjustments.

effectiveness   Ability to bring about results.

effective rent   In residential property management, the rent per month reduced by the monthly value of any leasing concessions computed on a per-month basis for that unit. The cumulative rental amount collected over the full term of a lease. Also, the amount of rent a commercial tenant actually pays after base rent is adjusted for concessions, pass-through charges, and tenant improvements. The effective rent differs from the quoted base rent set forth in the lease. See also *base rent.*

effective space   The amount of retail space in a given trade area that is capable of drawing consumers.

efficiency   Ability to produce desired results with a minimum expenditure of time, money, energy, and/or materials. The ratio of work done to energy expended.

efficiency apartment   A small, bedroomless apartment usually with a less-than-standard-size kitchen. See also *studio apartment.*

efficiency factor   The percentage of gross building area that is actually rentable: net rentable area ÷ gross building area.

efficiency ratio   In office buildings, the relationship of net rentable area (space used and occupied exclusively by tenants) to gross area, which includes the building core space, expressed as a fraction: net rentable area ÷ gross area.

elderly housing Housing with design features and facilities intended for use by elderly families. A specialized type of residential property that includes services and amenities as an adjunct to independent living (e.g., congregate housing) and may be owned and operated by nonprofit entities. See also *assisted living facilities; congregate care; lifecare facilities.*

electric spectacular A large illuminated sign with special lighting and action effects, sometimes used by free-standing retail establishments.

electronic data processing (EDP) The conversion of raw information (facts, figures) to machine-readable form and its subsequent processing (storing, updating, combining, rearranging, printing) by a computer.

electronic transfer of funds Movement of funds between banking institutions and between individual accounts via computer transfer of credits rather than using a check or other payment instrument. Direct deposit is commonly handled electronically. Individual consumers can also use computer software to "bank online," transferring money from their personal accounts to the accounts of various creditors (e.g., utility, credit card, and rent payments).

elevation A drawing or design representing a vertical side or portion of a building. The height of a building from ground level. A place above the level of the surrounding ground.

Ellwood tables Computations of capitalization rates that take into account equity buildup resulting from regular amortization payments as well as loan terms.

e-mail Short for electronic mail. Communication via the *Internet.*

embezzlement Fraudulent appropriation of money or personal property by a person to whom it was lawfully entrusted, either by or for the owner. See also *conversion.*

emergency An unforeseen combination of events or circumstances, or the result of such events or circumstances, that requires immediate action. A usually distressing event (e.g., fire, flood, earthquake; explosion, civil disorder) that can be planned or prepared for but not necessarily foreseen.

emergency maintenance Unscheduled repairs that must be done immediately to prevent further damage or to minimize danger to life or property.

emergency preparedness Having in place established procedures for addressing various types of distressing incidents or events and ensuring that building occupants are trained to follow them.

emergency procedures Procedures developed in order to minimize injury to people and damage to property in the event of natural or manmade disasters, usually including specific procedures for evacuating buildings.

emergency response team A group of individuals, usually at a commercial property and comprising members of the management staff and representatives of the tenants, who are trained to respond to various types of emergencies and to expedite *evacuation* of the building.

eminent domain The right of a government or municipal quasi-public body to acquire private property for public use through a court action called condemnation in which the court determines that the use is a public use and determines the price or compensation to be paid to the owner. (The owner of the property must be fairly compensated, usually based on an appraisal of the fair market value.) See also *condemnation.*

emission   In environmental terms, pollution discharged into the atmosphere.

employee handbook   A compilation of a company's employment policies and procedures. It is advisable to include a notice that such handbook does not constitute a set of promises or an employment contract. Depending on state law, it might include a statement that employment is at the will of the company, and that the company or the employee may terminate the employment at any time for any reason. To protect the employer's interests, the contents of such a handbook should be reviewed by an attorney.

Employee Polygraph Protection Act (EPPA)   Federal law that prohibits the use of lie detector tests in most business situations. However, in the event of an economic loss, polygraph tests may be used subject to notification and other restrictions.

Employee Retirement Income Security Act (ERISA)   Federal law that safeguards employees' rights to benefits under a company's pension. Passed in 1974, the law sets up structures and regulations for pension plans offered by employers.

employee turnover   An estimate of the number of employees who are likely to leave a company in a given period based on an evaluation of past trends, usually expressed as a percentage of the total number employees in the firm. Also, the number of employees who actually leave compared to the total number of employees in the firm.

employment agency   A firm in the business of finding employees to fill vacant positions and jobs for individuals seeking employment.

employment contract   A formal (preferably written) agreement between an employer and an employee outlining conditions and terms of employment.

employment practices liability   A form of liability insurance to protect against employee claims arising from sexual harassment, wrongful discharge, discrimination, and disability suits.

empty nester   A demographic category referring to someone whose children have grown up and left home permanently.

encapsulation   In regard to environmental hazards, a method of *containment.*

enclosure   The conversion of part of the common area of an open shopping center to a fully enclosed mall by addition of a roof and walls. Also, in regard to environmental hazards, a method of *containment.*

encroachment   A building or some portion of it, or a wall or fence, that illegally extends beyond the owner's land onto another's land or a street or alley. See also *adverse possession; easement.*

encumbrance   Any lien, such as a mortgage, tax lien, or judgment lien; also, an easement, a restriction on the use of land, or an outstanding dower right which may diminish the value of property. See also *easement; judgment lien; mortgage; tax lien.*

endorse To approve or guarantee payment. To alter a document by adding a covenant.

endorsement Signature placed on the back of a check transferring the amount of that instrument to someone else. An attachment to an insurance policy that provides or excludes a specific coverage for a specific portion or element of a property or makes additions or changes to the existing terms of a policy; also called a *rider.*

endowment policy See *life insurance.*

end report In accounting, the final summation of a building's financial operations.

energy audit A careful examination of a property's energy use.

energy conservation A program designed and implemented to reduce energy waste.

energy demand A building's total requirement for power during a given period.

energy efficiency ratio (EER) A measure of the efficiency of an HVAC device or system expressed as the ratio of output (Btu/hour) to energy input (watts).

energy management Programs designed to reduce energy consumption and lower utility costs without jeopardizing tenant comfort or shortening the maximum engineered lives of building systems.

energy management system A computerized mechanical system designed to monitor and control energy usage in order to maximize efficiency and minimize fuel consumption. See also *building control system.*

enhance To increase the value of, as real estate.

enthalpy A measure of the heat content of a substance, such as air, quantified as a unit of heat per unit of weight (Btu/lb).

entity Something that has separate or independent existence, as a human being or a corporation.

entrepreneur One who organizes, owns, and operates a new enterprise and undertakes the attendant economic risks.

enumeration district A subdivision of a census tract in a rural area with a population of 10,000 or more. See also *block group.*

environmental audit A formal study of the impact of a property or business on the environment, including its effect on air and water quality and its treatment of emissions and wastes, often required for the sale of a property or as a periodic filing with a state or local environmental agency.

environmental impact legislation Laws aimed at regulating construction in regard to its effects on the environment.

environmental impact statement (EIS) An analysis of the anticipated effects of a development or action on its surroundings. Such an analysis may be required prior to development under federal or state law (e.g., under the National Environmental Policy Act of 1969, an EIS is required for federally supported developments). An EIS can reveal impediments to development (e.g., the presence of underground tanks or toxic waste).

Environmental Protection Agency (EPA)   An independent agency of the U.S. government established in 1970 to enforce laws that preserve and protect the environment.

Equal Employment Opportunity Commission (EEOC)   A U.S. governmental body that enforces Title VII of the Civil Rights Act of 1964, which prohibits discrimination in the workplace.

equalization   The raising or lowering of assessed values of properties in a particular county or taxing district for the purpose of making them equal to assessments in other counties or districts.

Equal Opportunity in Employment Act   Title VII of the Civil Rights Act of 1964, which prohibits employers with fifteen or more employees from discrimination in hiring, firing, or terms of employment on the basis of an individual's race, color, religion, sex, or national origin.

Equal Pay Act   An amendment to the *Fair Labor Standards Act (FLSA)* that guarantees equal pay for equal work regardless of one's gender.

equity   The value of real property in excess of debt. The interest or value that an owner has in real estate over and above the mortgage and other financial liens against it; outright ownership. In accounting, the excess of a firm's assets over its liabilities. See also *balance sheet*.

equity accrual   Buildup of an owner's interest in a property because of mortgage loan amortization or appreciation in its total value.

equity dividend ratio   A measure of the productivity of an investor's initial investment that compares the yearly cash flow of a property with its initial investment base: cash flow ÷ initial investment base. The result is given as a percentage. Also called *cash-on-cash return*.

equity financing   Capitalization of a project through partnerships or other investment entities that acquire an interest in the project. Equity financing contrasts with financing through debt.

equity participation   A share in the cash flow from an investment property, sometimes offered by developers to major tenants in new buildings. A similar arrangement may be made with lenders who make participating loans.

equity participation loan   Mortgage financing that, in addition to a fixed interest return, gives the lender the right to share in whatever benefits the equity investor/borrower receives.

equity residual model   A method of computing an investment's value that relies on capitalizing cash flow and adding to that figure the balance of the mortgage at that point.

equity security   A security that represents ownership in a company and that pays periodic dividends to investors from the company's earnings. The best-known kind of equity security is a *stock*. Compare *debt security*.

ergonomics   An applied science related to the design (and arrangement) of such things as tools, equipment, and office furnishings so the people who use them can interact with them most effectively.

errors and omissions (E&O) insurance   A form of liability insurance. In the case of the property manager, E&O insurance protects against liabilities resulting from honest mistakes and oversights (but provides no protection in cases of gross negligence). See also *professional liability insurance.*

escalation clause   In a lease, a provision for increases in rent based on increases in operating costs, changes in a standard economic index such as the *Consumer Price Index (CPI),* or an agreed-upon schedule stated in the lease, commonly used to account for inflation over the lease term or to maintain the rent at market levels. Also called *rent escalation clause.* A provision in a mortgage or loan agreement under which the entire amount of the debt becomes due immediately in the event of a specified occurrence such as missing a set number of monthly payments or other default. (A similar provision in a lease that would make the full amount of rent for the remainder of the lease term due under specified circumstances such as default. Most courts will not allow the remaining rent to be escalated in this fashion.)

escalator clause   A clause in a contract, lease, or mortgage providing for increases in wages, rent, or interest based on fluctuations in certain economic indexes, costs, or taxes. Also called *rent escalator clause.*

escrow   An agreement that something (a deed or bond, money) should be held in trust by a third party until certain conditions are met. The transfer is effected by one party to a contract, and the money or other item in escrow is returned upon fulfillment of the specified conditions. Also, the process of handling these types of agreements.

escrow account   A fund or deposit that serves as an escrow. A bank account used to hold funds of another party (e.g., security deposits) separate from the personal funds of the depositor. See also *trust account.*

essential functions   The skills required to qualify for a particular job. See *Americans with Disabilities Act (ADA).*

estimate   To judge the value or worth of something. A value judgment (opinion) that is often approximate, tentative, or incomplete; the judgment itself. A statement of the anticipated cost of services or products to be provided.

estoppel certificate   A document by which the tenant states the terms of the lease and the full amount of rent to be paid for the entire term of the lease, commonly requested by the landlord in conjunction with a transfer of ownership or in relation to financing or refinancing.

ethics   The discipline dealing with what is right or wrong, good or bad, often related to duty or obligation. The rules of conduct or code of principles recognized in respect to a particular class of human activity.

evacuation   An organized withdrawal or removal of people from a building or a geographic area. An evacuation plan is a vital component of an emergency preparedness program to ensure the safe removal of building occupants, usually developed in consultation with the local fire department.

eviction   A legal process to reclaim real estate from a tenant or someone holding a mortgage who has not performed under the agreed-upon terms of the lease or mortgage.

eviction notice   A written notice to a tenant to cure a breach of the lease immediately or vacate the premises within a specified period. Also called *demand to pay or quit* or *demand for compliance or possession.*

exchange rate   The rate at which one currency can be traded for another currency, as the value of the U.S. dollar versus the euro or the Japanese yen.

exclusion   A provision in an insurance contract detailing perils that are not covered.

exclusive   A right granted to the tenant that restricts the owner from leasing space in the same shopping center to other retailers that sell similar merchandise or provide similar services, usually defined in an *exclusive use clause.* Care must be taken in granting exclusives because limitation of competition violates antitrust regulations. When granted, exclusives must be taken into account when prospecting for and leasing to additional retail tenants.

exclusive agent   An agent with exclusive rights for a fixed period of time to sell or lease property owned by another.

exclusive authorization to lease   A document stating that the agent will receive a commission for any prospect who signs a lease within a certain time period, regardless of who actually negotiated the transaction.

exclusive right to sell   The appointment of a broker as the exclusive agent for the sale of a property for a specified period of time. The broker receives a commission whether the property is sold by the owner, the broker, or any other agent during the specific period. The management contract for a rental property may guarantee the managing agent the exclusive right to sell, but a separate listing agreement should always be used when the property is placed on the market.

exclusive use clause   A clause preventing the owner of a shopping center from leasing space to other retailers who sell merchandise or provide a service similar to that specified in the tenant's lease. (Because state laws on this sensitive issue vary, advice of legal counsel should be sought before using this type of clause.) See also *exclusive.*

exculpate   To free from blame. Hold-harmless clauses are exculpatory.

execution   The signing and delivery of an instrument; also, a legal order directing an official to enforce a judgment against the property of a debtor.

executive property manager   Another name for *property supervisor.* Also sometimes used in referring to the chief executive officer of a (usually small) real estate management firm.

executive search firm   Employment agency that specializes in recruiting managerial and professional personnel; also called *headhunter.*

exemplary damages   See *damages.*

exemption   Release from some (usually) legal liability or requirement to which others are subjected. In regard to income taxes, a deduction allowed because of a taxpayer's status or circumstances. In regard to property taxes, a deduction based on homeowner or senior citizen status.

exhibit   An attachment to a lease document that elaborates on points agreed to in the lease.

expense   Any business-specific cost incurred in operating a business (or investment real estate). For income tax purposes, costs that are currently deductible from income, as those for goods or services.

expense allowance   An allowance to provide for reimbursable expenses.

expense cap   See *expense stop*.

expense stop   In an office lease, a clause obligating the property owner to pay operating costs up to a certain amount per square foot per year; tenants pay their pro rata share of any costs in excess of that amount. When used in a retail lease, a clause obligating the tenants to pay a pro rata share of operating expenses up to a certain amount per year *(expense cap);* the owner pays any costs in excess of that amount.

experience   Knowledge or skill acquired by direct observation of or participation in an activity or profession over time.

experience exchange   A compilation of operating data on comparable properties generated through annual or other regular surveys of property managers. The Institute of Real Estate Management (IREM) publishes *Income/ Expense Analysis®: Conventional Apartments, Income/Expense Analysis®: Federally Assisted Apartments, Income/Expense Analysis®: Office Buildings, Income/Expense Analysis®: Shopping Centers,* and *Expense Analysis®: Condominiums, Cooperatives, and Planned Unit Developments* annually. The Building Owners and Managers Association (BOMA) International publishes an annual *Experience Exchange Report* on office buildings. The National Association of Industrial and Office Properties (NAIOP) publishes *Industrial Income and Expense Report* every other year. *Dollars and Cents of Shopping Centers* is published every other year by ULI—The Urban Land Institute. Shopping center operating data are also published periodically by the International Council of Shopping Centers (ICSC).

experience rate factors   Derived from the number of workers' compensation insurance claims filed against an individual company and from the number of claims filed within the state for specific job classifications. In many states, the basis for the rates a company must pay for workers' compensation insurance for its employees.

expert   One who has acquired special skill or knowledge from specific training, wide experience, or long practice.

extended coverage (EC) endorsement   An addition or rider to a fire insurance policy that adds coverage against financial loss from certain other specified hazards beyond those of fire and lightning. Examples typically include damage from windstorms, civil commotions, smoke, hail, aircraft, vehicles, explosions, and riots. However, coverage for water damage from most causes, including broken pipes and fire hoses, may have to be obtained as a separate endorsement.

extended coverage insurance   A policy that extends a basic fire policy to cover property loss caused by additional perils, usually windstorm, hail, explosion, riot and civil commotion, aircraft, vehicles, and smoke. May also be written as an *endorsement.*

external audit   Analysis by an outside firm (generally a firm of Certified Public Accountants) of the acceptability of the financial records of a business. See also *audit; internal audit.*

external recruitment   Seeking candidates for employment from sources outside of the existing staff.

F

facility manager A type of real estate manager who, when employed directly by a corporation that owns real estate incidental to its primary business, may be responsible for acquisition and disposition in addition to physical upkeep of the property, record keeping, and reporting on its management, although acquisition and disposition are likely to be handled separately by a corporate asset manager. More broadly, the responsibilities involve coordinating the physical workplace with the people and purpose of the organization.

failure Default; dereliction of duty. To not perform as expected, as a venture that was unsuccessful financially. The inability of a bank or other financial institution to honor the withdrawals of its depositors. Also used in referring to the wearing out of machine parts.

Fair Credit Reporting Act (FCRA) A federal law that gives people the right to see and correct their credit records at credit reporting bureaus. It also requires real estate managers to inform rental applicants if a credit bureau is contracted to investigate their credit (and obtain the applicant's written authorization to do so), advise them in writing if a lease is denied because of a poor credit report, and identify the source of credit information that resulted in their being denied a lease.

Fair Debt Collection Practices Act (FDCPA) A federal law that created a series of guidelines for debt collectors to follow. Designed to prevent collection agencies from harassing debtors, the law was later expanded to include any organization that collects consumer debt (including real estate managers). The law is governed and regulated by the Federal Trade Commission (FTC).

Fair Housing Act Alternate name for section VIII of the Civil Rights Act of 1968, which prohibits housing discrimination on the basis of race, color, religion and/or national origin in both rental and sales practices. The Act makes several types of activities illegal, including refusal to rent, discriminatory language or images in advertising, and denying the availability of units. The law is enforced by the U.S. Department of Housing and Urban Development (HUD).

Fair Housing Amendments Act of 1988 See *fair housing laws*.

fair housing laws   Laws promulgated at all levels that prohibit discrimination in the sale and rental of housing.· There are federal, state, and local fair housing laws. Specifically, Title VIII of the U.S. *Civil Rights Act of 1968* prohibits discrimination in the sale or rental of housing based on race, color, religion, or national origin. The Act was amended in 1974 to include sex as a protected class. The *Fair Housing Amendments Act of 1988* further prohibits discrimination on the basis of familial status (children) or mental or physical disability.

Fair Labor Standards Act (FLSA)   The federal law that regulates the minimum wage per hour and the number of hours employees can work per day and per week in positions that are paid an hourly wage and requires overtime compensation (one and one-half times their regular hourly wage) for time worked in excess of 40 hours per week; also called *Federal Wage and Hour Law*. Employees whose role is primarily management of operations or supervision of employees or administrative office support that is compensated by a minimum weekly salary regardless of hours worked are exempt from the overtime compensation requirement. State laws may establish additional or different requirements; employers must comply with the most stringent law in place locally.

fair market value   The price paid, or one that might be anticipated as necessarily payable, by a willing and informed buyer to a willing and informed seller (neither of whom is under any compulsion to act), if the object sold has been reasonably exposed to the market. In real estate, the price at which a property is sold to a willing buyer by a willing seller.

fair market wage   A fair wage in comparison with wages being offered for the same position within the area.

familial status   Defined as a protected class under the Fair Housing Amendments Act of 1988, the presence in a household of children under age 18 living with parents or guardians, pregnant women, or people seeking custody of children under age 18.

family   Most commonly used in referring to a group of persons consisting of parents (father and mother) and their children. A group of blood relatives (extended family). As defined by HUD, this is a group of persons or individuals considered a family and consisting of either a single person, an elderly family, a displaced family, or the remaining member of a resident family. Compare *household*.

Family and Medical Leave Act (FMLA)   Passed in 1993, a federal law that requires employers to grant eligible employees up to 12 weeks of unpaid job-protected leave in the event of a serious health condition or to care for a family member. This is more likely to affect a management firm than a single property (a firm must have at least 50 employees within 75 miles of its main office).

Fannie Mae   A common nickname for *Federal National Mortgage Association (FNMA)*.

Farmer's Home Administration (FmHA)   A program authorized by the Housing Act of 1949 to provide a full range of technical services, loans, and grants for the improvement of farm housing. The program was later expanded to serve other rural housing. Unlike the majority of other housing assistance programs, which are administered by HUD, Farmer's Home Administration programs fall under the jurisdiction of the Secretary of Agriculture. In 1995, the Farmer's Home Administration was replaced by an agency called *Rural Development*. Rural Development is further subdivided into a variety of rural agencies designed to provide housing assistance, sewer and water programs, and rural business programs.

feasibility study   Analysis done to discover the practicality, possibility, and reasonableness of a proposed undertaking (e.g., real estate development), especially regarding proposed costs and revenues.

Federal Deposit Insurance Corporation (FDIC)   An agency established by the U.S. government to insure deposits in Federal Reserve member banks and qualified state banks. Accounts of an individual depositor are insured up to a defined limit (currently $100,000).

federal discount rate   The interest rate that banks pay to borrow funds from their regional federal reserve bank.

Federal Environmental Pesticide Control Act (FEPCA)   See *Federal Insecticide, Fungicide, and Rodenticide Act (FIFRA)*.

federal funds rate   The interest rate charged on short-term loans made between financial institutions (e.g., between mortgage bankers and commercial banks).

Federal Home Loan Mortgage Corporation (FHLMC)   Often referred to as *Freddie Mac*, a private corporation authorized by the U.S. Congress that buys qualifying residential mortgages from lenders then packages them as new securities and resells the securities on the open market.

Federal Housing Administration (FHA)   A division of the U.S. Department of Housing and Urban Development (HUD) whose main activity is insuring residential mortgage loans from private lenders. The FHA does not lend money; nor does it plan or construct housing, but it does set standards for construction and loan underwriting.

Federal Insecticide, Fungicide, and Rodenticide Act (FIFRA)   Enacted in 1947, this law originally called for all pesticides to be registered with the U.S. Department of Agriculture (USDA) and established labeling requirements. FIFRA was amended by the Federal Environmental Pesticide Control Act (FEPCA) of 1972 as well as FIFRA amendments in 1975, 1978, 1980, and 1988 to further regulate the use and distribution of pesticides under the U.S. Environmental Protection Agency (EPA).

Federal Insurance Contributions Act (FICA)   The law under which employer and employee are required to contribute equally to the Social Security fund and Medicare. Employee contributions are deducted as payroll withholdings along with income taxes.

Federal National Mortgage Association (FNMA)   Often referred to as *Fannie Mae*, a U.S. government-sponsored private corporation that buys mortgages from banks and other lending institutions and sells them to investors to create a fund for mortgage lending.

Federal Reserve Bank   One of twelve district banks established to act as agents for maintaining money reserves, issuing bank notes, lending money to banks at a discount, and supervising banks.

Federal Reserve System   The central banking system of the United States whose functions include setting monetary policy, influencing the cost and availability of credit, supervising bank regulation and bank holding companies, and overseeing international banking operations. The "Fed" was established to provide currency flexibility and facilities for discounting commercial paper and to improve the supervision of banking. The system comprises a network of twelve central (district) banks whose members include participating national and state-chartered banks.

Federal Trade Commission (FTC)   A U.S. government agency charged with protecting the system of free enterprise and competition in the marketplace to maintain a strong economy.

Federal Unemployment Tax Act (FUTA)   The law which established the federally mandated unemployment insurance program. Individual states establish specific eligibility requirements and payout amounts and timing. Employers are required to contribute funds to compensate employees who are laid off or terminated. Contributions are based on total payroll and claims made. While payment is made to the federal government, specific unemployment compensation programs are usually administered at the state level.

Federal Wage and Hour Law   Another name for *Fair Labor Standards Act (FLSA)*.

Federal Water Pollution Control Act (FWPCA)   See *Clean Water Act (CWA)*.

fee   A payment for a service. Services of a managing agent are compensated by a *management fee*.

feedback   In communication, signals from the recipient of a message which indicate that he/she has understood the message.

fee simple   The most complete type of private ownership of real estate which gives the titleholder the right to possess, control, use, and dispose of the property without time limitation, including the unlimited right to divide the property among one's heirs. Sometimes called *fee* or *fee simple absolute*.

felony   A crime punishable by death or imprisonment in a state prison for more than one year. Assault with a deadly weapon is an example of a felony. Compare *misdemeanor*.

festival center   A type of specialty shopping center, usually located in an historic section of a city, which creates a unique shopping environment using imaginative architecture and nearby natural resources. Customers are drawn mostly from the tourist trade, and merchandising is concentrated in restaurants and souvenir-type goods. This type of center may be anchorless.

FHA   See *Federal Housing Administration (FHA)*.

fiat money   Currency not backed by gold or silver (e.g., U.S. currency in the form of federal reserve notes).

fidelity bond   A contract issued by a third party (usually an insurance company) that protects one individual against financial loss that might result from dishonest acts of another specific individual. A bond obtained by an employer to protect against the loss of money or property sustained because of the dishonesty of an employee. A suretyship agreement. See also *suretyship*.

fiduciary   One charged with a relationship of trust and confidence, as between a principal and agent, trustee and beneficiary, or attorney and client, when one party is legally empowered to act on behalf of another.

fiduciary relationship   An agreement based on trust in which one person or group of persons handles financial transactions for another person or group.

financial accounting   A system of classifying financial transactions that documents a company's financial position in the form of a balance sheet and an income (profit and loss) statement and is auditable. See also *managerial accounting.*

financial analysis   Projection of income and expense, financing considerations, tax implementations, and value charged; used in a management survey. A complete evaluation of real estate as an investment including valuation, depreciation, tax benefits, and cash flow calculations.

financial management rate of return (FMRR)   A method that relies on investor-selected rates of return in calculating positive cash flow as a basis for decision-making. FMRR varies from *internal rate of return (IRR)* with regard to reinvestment rates and tends to project a more market-driven return.

financing   The availability, amount, and terms under which money may be borrowed to assist in the purchase of real property, using the property itself as the security (collateral) for such borrowing. See also *collateral; mortgage loan.*

finish allowance   An amount allowed by the landlord for constructing tenant improvements to leased commercial space.

finish schedule   In office building leasing, a list of items such as floor and wall coverings and paint colors that are made available by the property owner to finish off a suite design. See also *workletter.*

fire and extended coverage (EC) insurance   Insurance for property that covers not only loss by fire but also from such causes as windstorm, hail, explosion, riot, civil commotion, aircraft, vehicles, and smoke (as specified in the policy).

fire insurance   The most basic type of property casualty insurance. Insurance against all direct loss or damage by fire. See also *extended coverage (EC) endorsement.*

fire warden   A member of a building *emergency response team* who serves as the team leader for a floor or a specific area of the building and supervises the *evacuation* process.

first-class   Something considered to be of the best quality or of the highest excellence. Often used in office leases in reference to building condition (e.g., building will be maintained in first-class condition) to imply the very best or the highest level.

first mortgage   A mortgage that has priority as a lien over all other mortgages.

fiscal year   Any twelve-month accounting period ending with a date other than December 31.

fixed assets   Properties, goods, or other things of value that cannot be readily sold or otherwise converted on short notice at their true and fair value. Things possessed mainly of value in their use as is, and of little value if removed, such as trade fixtures and machinery. Tangible assets of a long-term nature such as land, buildings, machinery, and equipment that are not intended for resale within the regular operation of a business.

fixed-bid basis   The method of cost estimating that requires the contractor to state that a project will cost a certain amount based on the plans and specifications provided.

fixed expense   A cost that does not change. A regular expenditure that does not vary according to sales volume.

fixed-minimum rent   See *minimum rent.*

fixed-rate mortgage   A loan for real property in which the interest rate is constant over the term of the loan.

fixed rate option   The tenant's guaranteed right to renew at the end of a lease term at a previously determined rental rate.

fixture   An article of personal property installed in or attached permanently to a building or to land and legally considered part of the real estate because it cannot be removed without causing irreparable damage. In retailing, personal property in the form of cabinets, shelving, and other devices used for displaying merchandise that usually are not permanently installed are called *trade fixtures.*

flat fee   A uniform rate charged for service. Condominium management services are typically compensated by a flat fee.

flex space   A single-story commercial structure that can be configured to accommodate a single tenant or multiple tenants or with varying proportions of office and warehouse or manufacturing space according to individual tenants' needs.

float   In banking, the time that lapses after a deposit or withdrawal is made and before the transaction is credited or deducted. When used in reference to currency, having no fixed rate or value. Specifically, the value of the U.S. dollar is allowed to float against other currencies (e.g., the Japanese yen, the British pound Sterling, the Deutsche mark, and more recently the Eurodollar or euro).

floor area   Used in regard to shopping centers, another name for *gross leasable area.*

floor-ceiling loan   A type of mortgage loan that is paid out in two separate amounts. A combination loan that is tied to reaching predetermined occupancy rates and rent levels, usually used in new buildings or conversions. The *floor* loan obligates the lender to furnish a minimum amount (less than the full loan value) when construction has been completed in conformance with the terms of the loan commitment. The remainder (the *ceiling*) is paid out when predetermined occupancy and/or cash-flow requirements of the loan commitment are met. Also called *floor-to-ceiling loan.*

floor load   The weight that a floor in a building is capable of supporting if such weight is distributed evenly, calculated in pounds per square foot; also called *floor-load capacity.* The *live load* of a floor.

floor loan   See *floor-ceiling loan.*

floor plan   Architectural drawings showing the floor layout of a building and including precise room sizes and their interrelationships. The arrangement of the rooms on a single floor of a building, including walls, windows, and doors.

focus group   A market research tool that consists of a number of people brought together in a group interview setting to focus on a specific product, organization, or service. The intent is to obtain personal viewpoints, so the group is usually small (rarely more than twelve people). Panel members are carefully chosen so the group will represent the same general demographic characteristics as the target market (age, economic status, occupations, etc.) and therefore be representative of their attitudes or opinions. In short, a focus group consists of people with similar demographic characteristics gathered together for the purpose of exploring psychographic factors.

food court   An area in a shopping center, usually in an enclosed mall, where different kinds of food are available from individual vendors selling from separate stalls. Typically there is a shared (common) seating area for customers.

footcandle   A unit of illumination measured on a surface that is one foot away from the light source.

force majeure   An event or effect that cannot reasonably be anticipated or controlled. A clause commonly included in construction and other contracts to protect the parties in the event that part of the contract cannot be performed due to events or causes beyond the parties' control (e.g., weather, natural disaster, war, strikes, or riot).

forcible detainer   Statutory proceeding to regain possession of property by a person entitled to possess it. Forcible detainer exists when someone originally entitled to possession of real estate (as a tenant under a lease) refuses to surrender possession upon termination of that right (i.e., expiration/termination of the lease). It may take place after peaceable entry as well as after forcible entry; more commonly called *forcible entry and detainer.*

foreclosure   A court action initiated by the mortgagee, or a lienor, for the purpose of having the court order the debtor's real estate sold to pay the mortgage or lien (e.g., a mechanic's lien or court judgment).

form   Established method of expression or practice. A printed or typed document having blank spaces for insertion of specific information. Also, such a printed document attached to an insurance policy as an endorsement that provides for specific additional coverages or modifies provisions of the basic policy.

franchise   An exclusive right to sell a product or perform a service. In retailing, an individual (franchisee) will purchase this right from a chain store or other type of parent corporation and operate the store according to the rules and regulations of the franchisor.

fraud   A generic term that encompasses all means resorted to by one person to take advantage of another, whether via making false statements or suppressing the truth or otherwise attempting to cheat the other person. See *actual fraud* and *constructive fraud* for specific distinctions.

Freddie Mac   A common nickname for *Federal Home Loan Mortgage Corporation (FHLMC).*

free-and-clear return   A comparison of the net operating income (NOI) and total property cost designed to measure the potential return of a property that is free of debt. The result is expressed as a percentage.

free enterprise   Business conducted primarily according to the laws of supply and demand and without direct government intervention.

free on board (FOB)   Used in transportation of goods to mean that the invoice price includes delivery to a specified point (and no further) at the seller's expense. *FOB destination* means the seller pays freight to the destination (the buyer); *FOB origin* means the buyer pays all freight from the point of shipment or other designated place.

freestanding retail space   A store that is not an integral part of a shopping center, enclosed mall, or mixed-use development; also called *pad space*. Many downtown department stores are freestanding. See also *outlot.*

Freon   Trademark for refrigerants used in air-conditioning systems. See also *chlorofluorocarbons (CFCs); Montreal Protocol.*

frequency   In advertising, the number of times an ad will appear in a particular medium. In print media, each placement is called an *insertion.*

friable   Easily crumbled or pulverized (i.e., reduced to powder), as when rubbed between the fingers.

fringe benefits   Extra compensation paid by an employer that accrues to an employee's benefit but does not affect the employee's basic wage or salary. Examples include pension plans, insurance programs (medical, dental, life), paid vacation and sick time, and the like.

frontage   Linear measure of a piece of land that lies along a street, highway, river, or lake. Such property is often priced on a per-front-foot basis. In regard to retail property, the section of a store that faces the street or the pedestrian walkway in a mall; also used in referring to window display area and entrance.

full agency management   A plan for handling all or designated aspects of the affairs of a condominium association whereby a managing agent is contracted to perform a full range of administrative, maintenance, and operational tasks for an association.

fully amortized loan   A loan characterized by periodic payments that include a portion applied to interest and a portion applied to retiring the loan principal. Compare *balloon loan.*

functional obsolescence   A condition of obsolete design or use of a property. Defects in a building or structure that detract from its value or marketability. Such defects may be curable or incurable. See also *curable obsolescence; incurable obsolescence; obsolescence.*

funding   Providing money to finance a project. Money set aside for a specific activity or objective.

funds from operations   Commonly abbreviated *FFO* and used by a *real estate investment trust (REIT)* in referring to operationally derived funds (as opposed to investment capital). Also used in referring to property income collected before payment of any expenses or debt service has been made.

future value (FV)   A concept derived from the time value of money that describes how much an investment will be worth after a specified time span at a given rate of interest.

G

GAFO A way of categorizing merchandise. The acronym stands for General merchandise, Apparel, Furniture, and Other.

gap financing A short-term second loan used by a developer to make up the difference between a minimum (floor) loan amount and the maximum (ceiling) amount committed for permanent financing; also called *gap loan*. See also *floor-ceiling loan*.

garagekeepers' legal liability insurance Protection against loss arising out of the insured party's legal responsibility and as a result of damage to vehicles left in the care, custody, and control of the insured. A common type of insurance carried by condominium associations.

garden apartment building A low-rise building, usually a two- or three-story walk-up that may have its first floor at or slightly below grade, designed for multifamily living, usually located in a suburban area. Also called *garden-style apartments* and *terrace apartments*.

garden condominium A multifamily dwelling under condominium ownership that usually is no more than three stories tall, has units arranged horizontally and vertically, and may be built around a courtyard or a pond; also called *low-rise condominium*.

garden office building An office building one to three stories tall, usually located in a suburban area.

garnishment A legal proceeding whereby a portion of a debtor's wages, property, or assets are withheld to satisfy a creditor.

general advertisement An ad used for a group of products or services or for a company's entire line of products and services. For rental single-family homes, a general ad would list the range of rental rates and various features of available homes along with how to contact the leasing agent or management company. Compare *laundry-list advertisement*.

general and administrative (G&A) costs See *indirect costs*.

general contractor An individual or company that undertakes the construction or renovation of a property and agrees to perform (provide) or procure all of the various construction disciplines necessary to complete the building of the structure and install the necessary mechanical and other equipment and systems. A construction specialist who enters into a formal agreement or contract with the owner of real property to construct a building or complete a remodeling project.

general damages   A type of *compensatory damages*. See also *damages*.

general journal   An original-entry record of miscellaneous entries that do not apply to other accounting journals; see also *cash disbursements journal; cash receipts journal*. When other, specialized journals are not used, the general journal is a daily record of all receipts, disbursements, and non-cash bookkeeping entries.

general ledger   A formal record of all the financial transactions of a business. Accounts are transferred as final entries from the various journals to the general ledger, where they are posted as debits and credits and thus show the accumulated effects of transactions.

general maintenance   Upkeep of a property that can be anticipated and performed on a regular basis or that is minor in nature.

general partner   A co-owner of a partnership who is able to enter into contracts on behalf of the partnership and is fully liable for debts of the partnership. In a limited partnership, the individual who manages the limited partnership and is its fiduciary.

general partnership   The business activity of two or more persons who agree to pool capital, talents, and other assets according to some agreed-to formula, and similarly to divide profits and losses, and to commit the partnership to certain obligations. General partners assume unlimited liability. Compare *limited partnership*.

general warranty deed   A deed that contains several warranties from the grantor to the grantee. For example, it protects the grantee against any other claim to the title of the property.

gentrification   Inmigration of middle and upper income people into a deteriorating or recently renewed area so they gradually displace lower income residents. A form of urban neighborhood renewal.

geographics   Those variables pertaining to the region, climate, and size of a city and county. Also used in reference to the locational characteristics of a potential customer or tenant, as being in an urban, suburban, or rural area.

Ginnie Mae   A common nickname for *Government National Mortgage Association (GNMA)*.

giveaway   Another name for *promotional aid*.

go dark   A provision sometimes included in shopping center leases that allows a tenant to cease operations at the property if a predefined event occurs (e.g., sales at the location are below an agreed-upon dollar amount in two or more consecutive years or a specific anchor tenant vacates its premises in the center). The tenant may be required to continue to pay the minimum guaranteed rent for the remainder of the lease term. Also used in referring to the vacating of a retail space by a tenant whose lease has a *continuous operation* provision.

gold standard   A guarantee that for each currency unit issued a certain weight of gold could be redeemed on demand.

goodwill An intangible business asset arising from a firm's reputation, good relations with customers and suppliers, favorable location, etc., beyond the mere value of the goods it sells or the service it provides. When a business is sold, an addition to the purchase price above and beyond the value of its tangible assets.

governing documents The set of legal papers, filed by a developer with the appropriate local government office, that submit land to condominium use and create and govern a condominium association.

government-assisted housing Residential rental property in which the lessor (landlord) receives part of the rent payment from a governmental body, either directly from the government on behalf of a resident or indirectly from a grant to a public housing authority, or from the residents in the form of a voucher. Compare *public housing*; *subsidized housing*.

Government National Mortgage Association (GNMA) Often referred to as *Ginnie Mae,* a U.S. government-owned corporation created to invest in mortgages not suitable for the private Federal National Mortgage Association (FNMA), as those for government-subsidized housing.

grace period A period allowed after a due date for payment of a mortgage, rent, insurance premiums, etc. In financing, a specified period before a late fee is imposed. In real estate management, use of a grace period for rent payment varies by property type. In insurance, the 30-day period after the date a premium is due; coverage continues during the period even though the premium has not yet been paid.

graduated rent Rent that has two or more levels in the same lease term.

Graduate, REALTOR® Institute (GRI) A designation awarded by the National Association of REALTORS® (NAR) to members involved in residential real estate who complete a prescribed educational course.

graffiti Inscriptions or other markings scratched on walls or other artifacts made of stone, plaster, or clay. Also used in referring to the use of markers and spray paint to deface public and private property. A type of *vandalism.*

grandfather clause A provision in a new law or regulation that exempts those already established in the system or activity that is being regulated. In a new zoning ordinance, an exemption for a previously existing building that would otherwise be in violation of the new ordinance or "non-conforming." Such an exemption may no longer apply if the ownership or user of a building changes.

graphics Artwork and/or design, as for advertising or a business symbol *(logo).*

gray shell Used in referring to the condition of the interior of a retail shell space that has been partially improved by the landlord (i.e., stubbed plumbing has been installed and concrete floors have been poured, but there is no finish on *demising walls.* Compare *vanilla shell.*

Great Depression The 1929–1939 economic slump during which private capital investment came to a virtual standstill, unemployment was very high, and consumer expenditures declined by nearly one half.

grievance A wrong, injury, or injustice that provides cause for complaint.

gross area   All of the floor area inside a building.

gross building area   Area equal to length times width of the building(s) times the number of living floors, expressed in square feet.

gross domestic product (GDP)   The market value of all finished goods and services produced by an economy within the country in one year's time. Since 1991, U.S. economic activity has been measured as GDP to facilitate comparison with other economies that use the same measure. Compare *gross national product (GNP)*.

gross domestic product (GDP) deflator   A price index tracked by the federal Council of Economic Advisors. The deflator adjusts prices so that growth in GDP can be related to a base year and thus give corrected growth figures that are not skewed by inflation and other factors.

gross income   Total monthly or annual revenue from all sources, such as rents and other receipts, before any deductions, allowances, or charges.

gross leasable area (GLA)   The size of an individual retail tenant's area of exclusive use in a shopping center, usually expressed in square feet. The total square feet of floor space in all store areas of a shopping center, excluding common area space; also called *floor area*.

gross lease   A lease under which the tenant (lessee) pays a fixed rent. The landlord (lessor) is responsible for paying all property expenses (e.g., taxes, insurance, utilities, repairs, etc.), and these costs are factored into the rent paid by the tenant. Compare *net lease*.

gross national product (GNP)   The market value of all finished goods and services produced by an economy in one year's time. It measures output attributable to a country's residents regardless of their geographic location. Thus, productivity of U.S. residents and businesses owned by U.S. companies outside the United States is included in the calculation of GNP for the United States. See also *gross domestic product (GDP)*.

gross possible income   The total monthly or annual possible income before uncollected income is deducted.

gross potential income (GPI)   The maximum amount of rent a property can produce. The sum of the rental rates of all spaces available to be rented in a property at 100 percent occupancy. In assisted housing, GPI includes payments from governmental agencies as well as tenant payments.

gross potential rental income   The sum of the rental rates of all spaces available to be rented in a property, regardless of occupancy. The maximum amount of rent a property can produce. Also called *gross possible rental income*.

gross profit   The retailer's sales income minus the cost of the goods sold. Sometimes the cost of returns is also subtracted from the total.

gross receipts   The total cash income from all sources during a specific period of time (e.g., a month or a year).

gross rent   The rent before deduction of concessions. In assisted housing, the sum of the contract rent and utility allowance. If there is no utility allowance, contract rent equals gross rent.

gross rent multiplier (GRM)   A figure that, when used as a multiplier of the gross income of a property, produces an estimated value of that property.

gross sales   The total sales that the retailer makes during a financial period, usually a calendar or fiscal year.

gross square feet   The total number of square feet in a building or on a floor of a building, without regard for whether the space is usable by a tenant or not. A unit of space measurement particularly useful in measuring and evaluating building energy consumption.

gross up   In commercial leasing, adjustment of variable operating expenses that are passed through to tenants in a new building or one that is not fully occupied to more closely reflect those expenses under full occupancy (usually around 90 percent; in shopping centers, between 80 and 90 percent).

ground lease   A lease for land only, it gives the tenant the right to use and occupy the land under a property. Under a *subordinated ground lease,* the owner offers the land as collateral for the mortgage commitment on the property. If the ground lease is *unsubordinated,* the land will not become collateral for the mortgage, and the lender will be in a second lien position.

ground rent   Rent that is paid for the right to use and occupy the land under a building. (The building is called a *leasehold improvement.*)

groundskeeper   One who cares for the grounds of a large property such as an estate or a rental development (apartment complex, suburban office park).

group insurance   A plan subscribed to by an employer to provide various kinds of insurance to employees (e.g., health care). Professional organizations sometimes sponsor such plans to provide specific insurance that their members may not be able to obtain as individuals at reasonable cost or at all.

group relamping   Systematic replacement of all lamps in a building or lighting system after a specific time period, based on when the lamps were installed and the rated life for the type of lamp, as opposed to replacing individual lamps as they burn out.

guarantee   An expressed or implied assurance of quality or use life, as of goods sold. When in writing, a *warranty.* One who provides such assurance is a *guarantor.*

guaranteed rent   See *base rent; minimum rent.*

guarantor   One who acts as a surety or gives security, as for payment of a debt. In real estate management, one who agrees to assume responsibility for a financial obligation of another in the event the other person cannot perform (e.g., payment of rent under a lease)

guaranty   In real estate management, a pledge by a third (outside) party who agrees to assume responsibility for a tenant's obligations under a lease in the event of tenant default, including payment of rent and performance of all other terms, covenants, and conditions of the lease. The arrangement is specific to a particular tenant and the lease for specified premises. The individual or organization making such a pledge is called a *guarantor.*

guest   In apartments, condominiums, and mobile/manufactured home parks, a nonresident who stays in a resident's private dwelling (with that resident's consent) for one or more nights. See also *visitor*.

H

habitability A state of being fit for occupancy (e.g., sanitary, safe, in compliance with applicable codes). Under landlord-tenant law, the landlord is bound by an *implied warranty of habitability,* by which he/she warrants the condition of the leased premises at the time the tenant takes possession and during the period of tenancy.

half-bath A term used in real estate to describe a bathroom with a basin and toilet but no bathing facilities such as a tub or shower.

handbook A book of rules or guidelines designed to provide information on policies, procedures, and requirements of a property or governmental agency.

handicap As defined in the *Fair Housing Amendments Act of 1988,* a physical or mental impairment which substantially limits one or more major life activities, a record of having such impairment, or being regarded as having such impairment. See also *disability.*

handicap aide A member of a building *emergency response team* who is responsible for moving handicapped individuals to safe areas in stairwells where they can be rescued by firefighters. The role is more common at commercial properties and the title may vary.

handout Another name for *promotional aid.*

hardware See *computer hardware.*

hazard A dangerous condition. In insurance, a condition that increases the frequency, severity, or likelihood of a loss. See also *peril.*

hazardous materials Any of a variety of gaseous, liquid, or solid materials that can pose a potential hazard (e.g., flammability, combustibility, toxicity, corrosivity) to persons who are exposed to them or damage property in the event of a spill. Some types of materials have been declared as specific hazards by federal, state, or local laws. Commercial leases often include a provision that identifies specific hazardous materials that may be allowed (or prohibited) for use on the property and provides remedies for the parties in the event of a spill or other incident.

headhunter   Another name for an *executive search firm.*

head rent   Rent charged to a person or persons occupying the same premises independently of each other. A frequent practice in the rental of privately owned student housing.

health insurance   Coverage for medical and other expenses arising out of sickness, accidental injury, or disability.

heating degree-day   See *degree-day.*

heating, ventilating, and air-conditioning (HVAC) system   The combination of equipment and ductwork for producing, regulating, and distributing heat, refrigeration, and fresh air throughout a building.

herbicide   A pesticide used to kill undesirable plants (weeds) or prevent their emergence and growth.

hidden defects   Another name for *latent defects.*

highest and best use   That use of real property which will produce the highest property value and develop a site to its fullest economic potential. In appraisal, the reasonably probable and legal use of vacant land or an improved property that is physically possible, appropriately supported, financially feasible, and results in the highest value. The four criteria for highest and best use are: physical possibility, legal permissibility, financial feasibility, and maximum profitability.

high-rise   A multistory building with elevators. Though sometimes defined as a building with ten or more stories, the definition may vary depending on locale and property type. When used in regard to office buildings in an urban setting, a building containing forty or more stories.

high-rise apartment building   A multiple-unit dwelling that is ten or more stories in height. Such buildings often average 25 stories and 100 units and are usually located in a major metropolitan area where space is at a premium.

high season   The busiest season at a resort area, when rental rates are highest.

hold harmless   A declaration that one is not liable for things beyond his/her control. A clause in contracts (e.g., management agreements) through which one party assumes liability inherent in a situation and thereby eliminates the liability of the other party. See also *indemnification.*

holding over   A tenant retaining possession of the leased premises after the lease term has expired.

holdover tenancy   A situation in which a tenant retains possession of leased premises after the lease has expired, and the landlord, by continuing to accept rent from the tenant, thereby agrees to the tenant's continued occupancy as defined by state law. Some leases stipulate that such holding over may revert to a month-to-month tenancy, often at a higher rent. See also *month-to-month tenancy.*

home-officing   A work strategy in which employees use computers, fax machines, telephones, and the Internet (e-mail) to connect with the central office from their homes. Compare *telecommuting.*

homeowners' association (HOA)   An organization of homeowners in a condominium, cooperative, or housing subdivision whose major purpose is to maintain and provide for the rights of owners to have easement in the use of common areas. Homeownership is a requirement for membership. An HOA may, in some instances, be organized by the builder or developer of a condominium, cooperative, or planned unit development (PUD).

home visit   A means for management to check the condition of a rental applicant's current residence and to develop a one-on-one relationship with a prospective resident.

horizontal property   Another name for a *condominium*. The term is more appropriately applied to townhouse condominiums where units are built side by side.

horizontal property laws   Laws originally enacted to regulate individually owned dwellings with shared common walls (townhouses, rowhouses). Also used in referring to statutes that deal with condominium and cooperative ownership of real estate. In the latter instance, the laws state that property owners own only the confines of the dwelling unit (apartment, townhouse) within a condominium or cooperative building or complex and thus do not allow the individual property owner to own the land on which his/her dwelling unit is located. (This is an exception. Most property law regards ownership as vertical ownership, including mineral rights below and air rights above the owned land.)

host liquor liability insurance   Protection against loss arising out of the insured party's legal responsibility as a result of an accident attributed to the use of liquor dispensed (but not sold) on the premises at functions incidental to the insured party's business. Recommended coverage for condominium associations and other properties where liquor may be served in the common areas of the premises. Usually purchased to cover specific events.

household   All persons, related or not, who occupy a housing unit. Compare *family*.

housekeeping   The regular duties involved in keeping a property clean and in good order, sometimes called *custodial maintenance*. Also used in referring to the level of care given to a leased space by the occupant.

house rules and regulations   In a condominium, guidelines regarding day-to-day conduct in common areas and relationships between unit owners. See also *rules and regulations*.

housing act   Any of several laws passed by the U.S. Congress creating programs and procedures for obtaining federal assistance in the creation and improvement of housing in the United States.

Housing and Community Development Act   Passed in 1974, this Act included a provision adding sex as a protected class under the *Fair Housing Act*.

Housing Assistance Payment (HAP) contract   A contract that indicates the specifics of the subsidy payments to be made to an owner of a public housing or an assisted housing property. When a public housing agency (PHA) is involved, the HAP contract is made between the PHA and HUD. If there is no PHA involved, the HAP contract is made directly between the property owner and HUD.

housing for the elderly   See *elderly housing.*

Housing Quality Standards (HQS)   Standards established by the federal government to ensure that the apartments of residents who receive assistance under any of the several categories of the Section 8 program meet minimum standards of habitability.

housing unit   Any residential arrangement that constitutes separate living quarters.

HUD   See *Department of Housing and Urban Development.*

HUD code   See *Manufactured Home Construction and Safety Standards Act of 1974.*

hundred-percent location   The site, usually in a central business district (CBD), where a retail business would achieve maximum sales volume compared to other locations in the same market area; also *one-hundred-percent location.* The site in a downtown business district that commands the highest land value and rental rate and reflects highest desired traffic count.

HVAC   See *heating, ventilating, and air-conditioning system.*

hypermarket   A very large individual store, sometimes occupying in excess of 150,000 square feet of gross leasable area (GLA), that offers groceries, apparel, appliances, furniture, and other types of merchandise at discount prices.

I

illiquid Not readily converted to cash; often used in referring to real estate as an asset because it cannot be converted to cash (i.e., sold) quickly.

Immigration Reform and Control Act (IRCA) Federal law requiring employers to verify an employee's identity and eligibility to work in the United States at the time of employment. Employees must complete Immigration and Naturalization Service (INS) form I-9.

implied warranty of habitability See *habitability*.

improvement Any addition to raw land (e.g., buildings, infrastructure) that adds value. A major replacement that becomes a permanent part of a property that reduces or stops deterioration and/or appreciably prolongs the useful life of a property and adds to its value. The investment in an improvement must be capitalized rather than expensed.

impulse tenants Used in referring to ancillary or shop tenants in a shopping center or mall because the merchandise they offer is usually not specifically sought out by consumers (e.g., candy, hosiery, magazines) but more likely to be bought on the spur of the moment by passersby traveling between stores. Compare *destination tenants*.

incentive Payment that is tied directly to standards of productivity and represents a financial inducement to perform. Often used in referring to a rental *concession*.

incentive fee In real estate, a type of management fee tied to the level of management performance. This may be structured such that management is compensated on a cost-plus basis, with specific incentives for achieving prescribed results, such as increased occupancy or gross collections, paid as a percentage of the excess over an agreed-to minimum level.

income Money or value received. A periodic benefit derived from labor or capital or both and usually measured in money.

income approach The process of estimating the value of an income-producing property by capitalization of the annual net income expected to be produced by the property during its remaining useful life.

income capitalization approach   A method of property valuation based on the net operating income (NOI) of the property. See also *appraisal; capitalization; capitalization rate.*

income/expense analysis   Evaluation of the relationship between gross income and operating expenses. See also *experience exchange.*

income/expense projection   An estimation of income and expenses for a future specified time period; a *budget.*

income participation loan   See *participation.*

income property   Real estate that produces income in the form of rents.

income tax   A levy on the earned incomes of individuals and businesses after certain deductions and exemptions have been taken into account.

incorporation   The process of forming a corporation via state charter. See also *articles of incorporation.*

incurable obsolescence   Irreversible loss of value of a building because of changes in style or market preference. This type of loss may be physically impossible or financially unfeasible to improve; *economic obsolescence.*

indemnification   Legal exemption from responsibility for a loss that may occur in the future or for a loss or damage already suffered. The condition of being indemnified. The action of indemnifying.

indemnify   To exempt from incurred liabilities or penalties. To secure against harm or damage or loss. Contracts and insurance policies usually include an *indemnification clause;* see also *hold harmless.*

independence of clauses   In a lease, a clause stating that if any one clause of the lease is in violation of the law, that clause becomes void but the balance of the lease remains in full force and effect.

independent adjuster   An independent contractor, not associated with a particular insurer, who adjusts claims for different insurance companies and may negotiate with the insurer on behalf of the victim of a casualty loss. Often used by insurers whose claims volume and/or financial resources do not warrant direct employment of in-house adjusters. Also employed by an insured party to assist in negotiating the settlement of a claim. Independent adjusters may also serve as a neutral third party to avert a conflict of interest. See also *adjuster.*

independent contractor   A person who contracts to do work for others by using his/her own methods and without being under the control of the other person(s) regarding how and when the work should be done. Unlike an employee, an independent contractor pays for all expenses including income and Social Security taxes, receives no employee benefits, and is not covered by workers' compensation.

independent living   The ability of senior citizens (retirement age and beyond) to maintain their persons and their lifestyle by remaining in their current owned or rented housing.

independent retailer   A local, nonchain store owned by a single individual or family.

index escalation clause   A provision in a commercial (office, retail, industrial) lease whereby the rental rate is adjusted according to a specified cost-of-living index.

indirect costs   In construction estimating, the costs for workers' compensation insurance, payroll taxes, and liability and other insurance carried by the contractor plus a factor for overhead and profit; sometimes called *general and administrative (G&A) costs*.

indirect loss   Economic loss, as of income and profits, that is consequential to the direct loss from an insured peril (e.g., property damage by fire). See also *direct loss*.

indoor air quality (IAQ)   An environmental concern related more specifically to the work environment (e.g., office buildings). In particular, certain symptoms in employees have been related to poor IAQ. See *sick-building syndrome*. The four major contributors to IAQ, as defined by the U.S. Environmental Protection Agency, are outside air sources, HVAC systems, activities of building occupants, and construction materials. The American Society of Heating, Refrigerating, and Air-Conditioning Engineers (ASHRAE) has established an IAQ standard specific to ventilation rates in relation to occupancy levels. Other IAQ issues continue to be considered for establishment of specific standards.

industrial park   A controlled park-like development designed to accommodate specific types of industry (e.g., manufacturing) and usually located at a distance from the center of a city. Often such properties are also specially zoned for heavy manufacturing or for light manufacturing and warehouse operations.

industrial relations   All relations between management and individual employees concerning terms and conditions of employment, including wages, benefits, and safety issues.

industrial shopping center   A type of specialty center based around stores and services having to do with plumbing fixtures, hardware items, or the care of automobiles.

inflation   An economic condition occurring when the money supply increases in relation to the amount of goods available, resulting in substantial and continuing increases in prices. Inflation is associated with increasing wages and costs and decreasing purchasing power. Compare *deflation*.

infrastructure   In land development, the permanent installations that provide for water supply, sewerage, and other utilities at a site and for access to it (roads, transportation systems).

inherent physical deterioration   Loss of value due to normal wear and tear and/or deferred maintenance; *physical obsolescence*.

in-house agents   Leasing representatives who work for a particular developer, owner, or retailer (e.g., a national chain). Typically they are paid a salary rather than a commission, but they may receive incentive bonuses as additional compensation.

in-house management   Management originating from within an organization or company (i.e., by the staff of the corporation owning the property) rather than being contracted with an independent third party (i.e., professional management services).

initial investment base   The difference between the loan amount and the purchase price of a property (i.e., the owner's initial equity).

initial markup   In retailing, the first price set for a new item after purchasing it wholesale. The difference between the merchandise cost (including freight) and the original retail price placed on the goods expressed as a percentage of the retail value; also called *initial mark-on.*

innovation   Something that differs from established forms or practices and is (usually) an improvement on them; introduction of something new, as a product or procedure.

insecticide   A pesticide used to kill or repel insects or prevent their reproduction.

insertion   In advertising, the placement of an ad in print media.

inspection checklist   A printed form used when property managers or other staff members inspect a building and its leased spaces. Usually set up in a grid format with the items to be inspected being listed at the left and separate columns to note the condition of the item and identify repair work to be done. Some forms include columns that facilitate scheduling of the work and estimating repair costs.

Institute of Real Estate Management (IREM®)   A professional association of men and women who meet established standards of experience, education, and ethics with the objective of continually improving their respective managerial skills by mutual education and exchange of ideas and experience. The Institute is an affiliate of the National Association of REALTORS® (NAR). See also *ACCREDITED MANAGEMENT ORGANIZATION® (AMO®); ACCREDITED RESIDENTIAL MANAGER® (ARM®); CERTIFIED PROPERTY MANAGER® (CPM®).*

institutional advertising   A technique designed to increase the prestige of the advertiser (e.g., building or management firm) through the use of specific promotional media.

instrument   A written document that formally expresses a legal arrangement, as a contract, deed, or lease.

insufficient funds   Another name for *nonsufficient funds (NSF).*

insurable value   The value of property for insurance purposes. Insurance may be based on the *replacement cost* of a building and other improvements to land or on the *actual cash value (ACV)* of the property (i.e., the cost to replace the building or structure less certain depreciation factors).

insurance   An agreement by one party (the insurer, carrier, insurance company) to assume part or all of a financial loss in the event of a specified contingency or peril (e.g., liability, property damage) in consideration of a premium payment by a second party (the insured). A means of reducing economic risk in which funds are accumulated from a group of insured parties and used to pay the losses of an individual member of the group. As a form of risk management, insurance substitutes regular payment of insurance premiums for the unpredictable cost of an economic loss, based on the probability of a particular type of loss occurring.

insurance adjuster   See *adjuster; independent adjuster; public adjuster.*

insurance agent   A representative of a specific insurance company, either an employee or an independent businessperson under contract, who represents that company exclusively. In most states, an application, an insurance policy, or endorsements to it must be countersigned by a licensed agent.

insurance broker   An independent operator who represents the client and not the insurance company. These individuals seek the best coverage for their clients, bargain with selected insurers, and place the order at the best terms and lowest possible premium. In most states, business written by a broker must be countersigned by a licensed agent of the insurance company that issues the policy.

insurance claim   Money demanded for a loss in accordance with the terms of an insurance policy.

insurance clause   A provision in commercial leases that requires the tenant to obtain specified types and amounts of insurance, including a certain amount of liability insurance, and to include the building owner as an additional named insured party on the policy.

insurance producer   Any of several entities who can sell insurance policies, including an *insurance agent* who represents a specific insurance company, an *insurance broker* who represents the client in obtaining insurance, and an *independent agent* who contracts with selected insurance companies. Usually insurance written by a broker must be countersigned by an agent of the insurer.

insurance trustee   A person or entity who administers recovery funds collected from an insurance company.

insured   The person or other entity for whom insurance is provided. The person whose property, life, or physical well-being is covered by insurance. A property policy covers the interest of the insured in the property rather than the property itself. A liability policy covers a particular activity of the insured.

insurer   A person or entity that contracts to indemnify another through insurance. An insurance company or *underwriter.*

intangible asset   A right or resource that has no physical form. Licenses, permits, patents, trademarks, copyrights, and goodwill of a business are intangible assets. In real estate management, leases and management agreements would be included in this category. Compare *tangible asset.*

intelligent office building   See *smart building.*

intentional tort   A purposeful act, such as assault, battery, false imprisonment, or defamation. See also *personal injury.*

intercept survey   A market research method often used at shopping centers in which customers patronizing the center are stopped at random and asked questions concerning their shopping habits (e.g., visits to competing centers) and their likes, dislikes, and preferences regarding their shopping experience. To ensure uniform collection and evaluation of information, the interviewer completes a preprinted standard questionnaire. See also *market research.*

interest   The cost of borrowing money, expressed as a percentage of the amount borrowed to be paid in one year. The yield required by lenders on their investment. Also, right, title, or legal share in something, as a share in owner-ship of a property.

interest-only loan A type of financing that requires payment of interest only during the term of the loan, and the principal is paid in full at the end of the term.

interest rate The percentage of an amount of money charged for its use, as of a loan. Also, the rate of return on an investment, as of capital.

interim financing Short-term, high-interest financing for new and existing projects. Financing during the period from commencement of a project to clos-ing of a permanent loan, usually in the form of a construction or development loan; an *interim loan*. See also *permanent loan*.

interim period In a condominium, the time during which owners are living in their units but the developer controls the association.

internal audit Review of a company's accounting records conducted by an employee, generally performed to ensure that company accounting policies are being followed. See also *audit; external audit*.

internal rate of return (IRR) The rate of return at which the discounted value of all benefits received during ownership is equal to the value of the owner's equity in the investment. The true annual earnings of an investment expressed as a percentage. A method used by investors to determine cash re-turns in relation to cash invested. (The calculation assumes that the annual *proceeds* can be invested at the same rate as the IRR.) In financial analysis, the specific discount rate for which the net present value (NPV) is zero, which gives a percentage that indicates the viability of a project or the profitability of an in-vestment. See also *financial management rate of return (FMRR); modified in-ternal rate of return (MIRR)*.

internal recruitment Seeking candidates for employment from among a company's existing staff.

Internal Revenue Code Laws that govern the filing of income tax returns with the United States Treasury.

Internal Revenue Service (IRS) The federal agency that administers and enforces most U.S. tax laws.

International Code Council (ICC) A nonprofit organization established by the three organizations—*Building Officials and Code Administrators (BOCA) International, International Conference of Building Officials (ICBO),* and *Southern Building Code Congress International (SBCCI)*—whose model build-ing codes are used in the United States and Canada to develop a single set of coordinated building codes. The three code groups became a single entity in 2003. See also *building code*.

International Conference of Building Officials (ICBO) See *Interna-tional Code Council (ICC)*.

International Council of Shopping Centers (ICSC) Membership organi-zation of retailers and owners, developers, and managers of shopping centers as well as other professionals and businesses that provide services to those in the shopping center industry.

International Facility Management Association (IFMA)   Membership organization of professional managers and others involved in facility management; formerly the National Facility Management Association

Internet   An open information network of computer links that allows users to access and search databases, advertise services, and deliver messages around the world via *e-mail*.

inventory   Materials owned and held by a business; a detailed list of such items showing the value of each. Also used in referring to residential units under construction; see *upcoming inventory*.

investment   Expenditure of money to purchase something of intrinsic value or to generate income or profits. Purchase of property that will be held for a relatively long period, during which it is expected to increase in value.

investment bank   A specialized bank that underwrites public offerings of securities sold in the stock market, including securities for real estate investment. Wall Street stock brokerage firms sometimes provide investment banking services.

investment value   The worth of a property to a particular investor based on predetermined criteria. The price that an investor bound by special circumstances and restraints will agree to pay. Investment value relates to equity ownership and is an individualized or personal value as compared to market value, which is impersonal and detached. See also *market value*.

invoice   An itemized bill presented to a buyer by a seller that specifies the price of goods sold or services delivered and the terms of the sale.

involuntary ownership   Ownership of a property that has been acquired involuntarily, as by inheritance.

IRV formula   A basic equation in real estate that relates three variables—income, rate, value—to calculate a property's value. As a formula, its basic form is Income ÷ Rate = Value. The investor's equation—the income-to-value ratio—is the same terms, rearranged (income ÷ value = rate of return).

J

janitorial maintenance   Day-to-day upkeep and cleaning of the interior and exterior of a building; sometimes also called *custodial maintenance.*

job analysis   Determination of the characteristics of a job based on observation of the sequence of tasks, needed tools and equipment, working conditions, and the skills and other qualifications required of a worker who would perform it.

job description   A listing of regular and ongoing tasks to be performed by the person occupying a given position and assignment of parameters of responsibility and authority. Usually derived from a job analysis, such descriptions are used in job evaluation and classification and employee selection and placement.

job specification   A list of the skills, experience, educational background, and working knowledge needed to fill a particular job within an organization. Also, an in-depth analysis of the characteristics, both required and desirable, to be sought in an applicant for a particular position and used to develop a specific job description.

joint and several liability   A situation in which all the participants in a legal agreement are individually responsible for performing the obligations of the agreement and one or more or all of them can be sued for a breach of the agreement. In real estate management, when a lease is signed by nonrelated adults who agree that they are all individually, and as a group, responsible for rent payments and other duties of the tenant.

jointly and severally   As a group and individually.

joint tenants   Two or more owners of real or personal property who have been specifically named in one conveyance as joint tenants. Upon the death of a joint tenant, his/her interest passes to the surviving joint tenant or tenants by the *right of survivorship,* which is the important element of joint tenancy.

joint venture   An association of two or more persons or businesses to carry out a single business enterprise for profit, for which purpose they combine their assets and agree to share the risks. In real estate, a combination of owners and money partners may be involved in a joint venture.

journal   In accounting, a record of current transactions maintained on a daily or other regular basis. A financial record book in which certain business transactions are recorded chronologically and for the first time. See also *cash disbursements journal; cash receipts journal; general journal.*

judgment   A court decree of one person's or entity's indebtedness to another; also, the amount of such indebtedness.

judgment clause   A provision in notes, leases, and contracts by which the debtor, tenant, and others authorize any attorney to go into court and confess a judgment against them for a default in payment; sometimes called a *cognovit.* Use of this clause is prohibited in many jurisdictions.

judgment lien   An encumbrance against real property that arises by law as a result of a judgment to recover money owed by the property owner.

junior mortgage   Any mortgage or financing instrument involving real estate that is subordinate to the first mortgage; a *junior lien.* Junior mortgages are often given numbers: second mortgage, third mortgage, and so forth. See also *second mortgage.*

jurisdiction   The district over which the power of the court extends. The geographic area of authority for a specific government entity.

K

k The symbol used for the *loan constant*.

keystone markup In retailing, a standard apparel markup that sets a selling price for merchandise at double its cost. See also *markup*.

kilowatt-hour (kwh) A unit of energy equal to 1,000 watts expended for a period of one hour.

kiosk A booth or stall set up in a shopping center, sometimes on a temporary basis, to sell goods such as tobacco, newspapers, magazines, seasonal merchandise, candy, keys, and other small impulse-purchase items.

L

labor The human effort expended to produce goods or provide services and thereby generate income.

labor and material payment bond Another name for *payment bond.*

labor cost The total compensation (salaries or wages and benefits) paid to workers employed by a business.

labor relations Relations between labor and management and, in particular, collective bargaining and maintenance of the (union) contract.

labor turnover See *employee turnover.*

labor union An organization created to advance the interests of its members, especially as regards wages and working conditions, through collective bargaining.

laissez-faire An economic philosophy which states that government should not interfere with commerce and economic affairs.

land lease A lease under which a tenant pays rent to use the land, usually for a period of years that will allow for construction on the land (and use) of a custom building. Typically, ownership of the improvements to the land reverts to the land owner at the expiration of the lease term. Compare *build-to-suit; ground lease.*

landlord One who owns real property that is leased to a tenant; see also *lessor.*

landlord-tenant law Laws enacted by various jurisdictions (at the state or local level) that regulate the relationship between landlord and tenant. As applied to mobile home parks, landlord-tenant laws usually set forth specific guidelines and include requirements for providing tenants with other documents in addition to the lease.

landscaping The improvements made to and maintenance done on a specific parcel of land. Landscaping may involve contouring the land; planting grass, flowers, trees, and shrubs; and installing items to enhance the appearance or utility of the land (e.g, a fountain, a pathway). Regular upkeep (cutting grass, trimming hedges, weeding, picking up litter, etc.) is also considered landscaping.

larceny   Unlawful taking and carrying away of the property of another with the intent to deprive the rightful owner permanently of its use; theft.

late fee   A fee charged for late payment of rent.

late notice   Notification that payment of rent is past due. While sometimes handled informally, such notification may be provided for specifically in a lease. When that is the case, the usual requirement is that notice be sent in writing to a specified address and include a statement of what additional charges (i.e., late fee) apply if the delinquency is not cured immediately (or within a specified time period).

latent defects   Physical deficiencies or construction defects not readily detected from a reasonable inspection of the property, such as a defective septic tank or underground sewage system or improper plumbing or electrical wiring; also called *hidden defects.*

lateral turnover   A type of turnover that occurs when tenants move from one rented apartment to a similar rented apartment in the same general market. See also *economic turnover; turnover.*

laundry-list advertisement   An ad in which each individual product is listed and described briefly. In single-family home management, such an ad would describe each individual rental home. Compare *general advertisement.*

laws of supply and demand   In relation to pricing, when demand exceeds supply, prices rise. If supply exceeds demand, prices drop. Prices are stable when supply equals demand. In regard to rental real estate, when demand exceeds supply, absorption of space is favorable (vacancy decreases); when supply exceeds demand, absorption is unfavorable. *Stabilization* occurs when landlords are able to increase rents in parallel with inflation rates.

lawsuit   A legal action between two parties. See also *defendant; plaintiff; tort.*

lawyer   An attorney at law. See *attorney.*

leaking underground storage tank (LUST)   See *underground storage tank (UST).*

lease   A contract, written or oral, for the possession of part or all of a landlord's property for a stipulated period of time in consideration of the payment of rent or other compensation by the tenant. Leases for more than one year generally must be in writing to be enforceable. A residential lease is sometimes called *occupancy agreement* or *rental agreement.*

lease abstract   A summary of the pertinent facts agreed to in a particular lease document; also called *lease brief.*

lease amendment   See *amendment.*

lease commencement   The date specified in a lease when the obligations of the parties legally begin.

lease conditions   The provisions or covenants setting forth the agreed privileges, obligations, and restrictions under which a lease is made; also called *lease terms.*

lease deposit   Another name for *security deposit.*

lease extension agreement   A covenant or other written and executed instrument extending or agreeing to extend the lease term beyond the expiration date as provided in the body of the original lease.

leasehold   Land held under a lease.

leasehold improvement   Improvement to leased property made by a tenant; such improvements remain in place and revert to the property owner when the lease expires. Also, improvements (a building) constructed under a *ground lease.*

leasehold interest   The position of a tenant in a leased property, including the right of use and possession for a specified period of time in return for payment of rent.

lease log   A form or document maintained by an appropriate member of the leasing staff and used to record every movement of a lease document from draft through authorizations and signatures.

lease proposal   A written presentation made to a prospective tenant setting forth the general terms and conditions of a proposed lease for commercial (office, retail, industrial) space. Also referred to as a *letter of intent.*

lease renewal   A goal of marketing in which qualified tenants are encouraged to renew their leases. The benefits of lease renewal include reduction or elimination of marketing costs, lower turnover costs, and assured income from the leased space. See also *renewal.*

lease terms   Another name for *lease conditions.*

lease-up   Another name for *rent-up period.*

lease-up budget   Projection of income and expenses for a newly developed property; also called *rent-up budget.* Having such a separate budget allows the developer or property manager to account for the wide variances in income and expenses that occur before there is sufficient occupancy to stabilize its financial picture.

lease-up costs   Expenses involved in obtaining tenants for a new building, including advertising and promotional programs and materials, leasing commissions, and space studies (office buildings).

lease-up period   Another name for *rent-up period.*

lease-up program   The advertising, public relations, brochures, printings, and mailings necessary to lease space in a newly developed building; also called *rent-up program.*

lease year   In retail leasing, the twelve-month period (either calendar or fiscal year) specified in the lease for which the tenant is to report retail sales information.

leasing   The process of marketing and renting a building's space.

leasing agent   The individual in a real estate brokerage firm (or management organization or development company) who is directly responsible for renting space in assigned properties. In some states, leasing agents must have a real estate broker's license unless they are employed directly by the property owner. Residential leasing agents may be called *leasing consultants.*

leasing fee   In single-family home management, a fee charged to the owner when a home is leased. This may be a fixed dollar amount or a percentage of the rental rate. It should be distinguished from the monthly management fee and described specifically in the management contract. The term also applies to fees paid to firms that assist in leasing apartments or commercial (office, retail, industrial) space when that activity is outsourced. Commercial leasing fees may be a percentage of the total rent amount, an agreed-to fixed amount, or a rate per square foot. See also *commission.*

leasing plan   For a given retail site, the statement of rental rates and suitable tenants for specific spaces, usually presented to the owner or developer in the early stages of prospecting.

ledger   A permanent accounting record. A book of accounts to which debits and credits that result from business transactions are posted from books of original entry, such as a *journal.*

legal counsel   Legal advice. Also, an attorney giving such advice and/or pleading a case in court.

legal description   The description of real property by metes and bounds, lot and block numbers of a recorded plat, or government survey, including any easement or reservation, used to locate and identify a particular parcel of land in legal instruments (e.g., leases, sale/purchase contracts, management agreements).

legal notice   A notice which the law requires to be given for a specific purpose or action.

lender's loss payable   An endorsement to a policy of hazard insurance providing that any compensation for losses sustained shall be made to the order of a lender to whom the property has been pledged as security for a loan.

lessee   The tenant in a lease.

lessor   The landlord in a lease.

let   To lease. To grant the use of a thing for compensation.

letter of intent   A letter or document stating the intention of the parties to take (or not take) a particular action, sometimes contingent on certain other action(s) being taken. In commercial leasing, a preliminary step to finalizing specific lease terms.

level-payment loan   Another name for *direct-reduction loan.*

leverage   The use of borrowed funds to increase one's purchasing power. In real estate, use of borrowed funds to purchase investment property with the expectation of realizing a return that exceeds the cost of the borrowed funds. Also used to describe how effectively an investor is using debt. Positive leverage means that debt increases return on equity. Negative leverage decreases such return.

liability   An obligation to do or to refrain from doing something. In legal terms, a duty or responsibility owed to another from which a claim may arise against an individual or a business. In accounting, a debt owed by an individual or a business. In a balance sheet, cash inflows and outflows are classified as assets and liabilities; see also *current liabilities; long-term liabilities.* In insurance, legal responsibility for bodily injury or damage to another person's property caused by negligence.

liability insurance   Insurance protection against claims arising out of injury or death of people or physical or financial damage to other people's property that is a consequence of an incident occurring on an owner's property. A form of coverage in which the insured (property owner) is the first party, the insurer (insurance company) is the second party, and the claimant (person who experienced the loss) is the third party; also called *third-party insurance.*

libel   Defamation that maliciously or damagingly misrepresents by written or printed words; see also *slander.*

license   Permission granted by a government or other authority to engage in a business, profession, or other activity that is regulated by law. Freedom to act or express oneself. Also, the revocable permission for a temporary use (a personal right that cannot be sold).

lien   A claim against property by a creditor under which the property becomes security for the debt owed to the creditor. The legal right of a creditor to have his/her debt paid out of the property of the debtor. Mortgages, mechanic's liens, and tax liens are monetary liens against a property for the satisfaction of debt. See also *mechanic's lien.*

lien release   A document executed by a provider of contract services (labor and materials) under which the contractor relinquishes the claim imposed against the property where its services are being performed.

lien theory   In some states, a lending practice in which title to the mortgaged property remains with the borrower and a lien on the property is given to the lender by means of the mortgage.

lien waiver   A voluntary relinquishing of a subcontractors' right to make a claim *(mechanic's lien)* against a property for payment of labor or materials already provided. Such waivers are required for release of construction loan funds from the lender. Also, an agreement between management, contractor, and subcontractor that no liens will be placed against the property for failure to meet the contract terms.

lifecare facilities   Often used in reference to a retirement village or high-rise building or complex that includes a health care center or nursing home. Entry into such a facility may require transfer of assets under a contract in return for care, or there may be a simple monthly rental arrangement. Lifecare typically assures the resident of lifelong shelter and care regardless of the number of years and the resident's financial resources.

life insurance   Insurance that pays a stipulated amount to the designated beneficiaries of the insured. A form of financial protection that provides for payment of benefits to a deceased person's survivors or involves enforced savings to build a reserve of funds, especially for old age. *Whole life insurance* builds cash reserves. *Term life insurance* pays benefits only if the insured dies within the term (number of years) the policy is in effect. An *endowment policy* pays face value if the insured dies within a stated period; otherwise, if the insured is living at the end of the stated period, the value of the policy is distributed as a lump sum or in installments.

lifestyle center   A type of strip shopping center composed entirely of *destination tenants*. Such centers may or may not include anchor tenants.

life-support systems   The safety and security devices and procedures adopted by a property's management.

limited common areas   In a condominium, property that physically is part of the common areas but is reserved for the exclusive use of a particular unit owner or group of unit owners (e.g., entry doors, balconies, windows, roofs). Also called *limited common elements*.

limited liability   Responsibility for the debts of a business (e.g., real estate investment) that is restricted to the size of one's investment in it. Corporations, their stockholders (usually), and limited partners have this benefit.

limited liability company (LLC)   Created by state statute, a business ownership form that functions like a corporation (its members are protected from liability) but for income tax purposes is classified as a partnership. Income and expenses flow through to the individual members. The arrangement offers considerable flexibility in its organization and structure.

limited liability general partnership (LLGP)   A form of general partnership that limits the liability of the general partners.

limited liability limited partnership (LLLP)   A form of limited partnership that limits the liability of the general partners.

limited liability partnership (LLP)   Terminology used in some states for either a *limited liability general partnership (LLGP)* or a *limited liability limited partnership (LLLP)*.

limited partner   A partner in a business venture who by agreement shares in the profits of the business but is not liable for any portion of the net losses or other obligations of the business beyond the value of his/her original investment.

limited partnership (LP)   A partnership arrangement in which the liability of certain partners is limited to the amount of their investment. Limited partnerships are managed and operated by one or more general partners whose liability is not limited; limited partners have no voice in management. Compare *general partnership*.

limited power of attorney   A legal authorization to act on behalf of another for a specified purpose.

line-item budget   A budget format that lists expenses by type.

liquid asset   A holding in the form of cash or one that is easily converted to cash—e.g., savings accounts (including money market accounts and certificates of deposit), stocks, bonds, mutual funds, and precious metals. Real estate is an *illiquid* asset because it is not easily converted to cash.

liquidity   The ability to convert assets into cash. The ease with which a person or business can meet its obligations without selling fixed assets.

list broker   An organization that compiles and rents mailing lists.

listing fee   Payment to a referral service for listing in their file or database. Such a fee may apply to real estate for sale, space for lease, or jobs to be filled.

litigation   A lawsuit or other legal action. See also *lawsuit*.

live load   The load (weight or force) on a structure that may be removed or replaced, including the weight of people, furniture, and equipment but not accounting for movement resulting from the force of wind against the exterior.

load-bearing wall   A supporting wall that sustains its own weight as well as other weight. A wall that supports a portion of a building above it, usually a floor or roof; also called *bearing wall*.

load factor   The percentage of space in a (usually commercial) building that is added to its usable area to account for lobbies, corridors, and other common areas; sometimes also called *add-on factor*. In utility consumption, the ratio of the average load carried by a power station for a given period to the maximum load carried during the same period (kilowatt-hours ÷ kilowatts of demand consumed). The ratio between the capacity of an elevator (weight of passengers or freight) and its actual utilization, stated as a percentage.

loan   A sum of money borrowed at interest for a specific period of time with the promise of repayment.

loan agreement   The document agreed to between the lender and the borrower setting forth certain nonmonetary conditions the borrower must meet during the term of the loan, otherwise the loan may be considered in default.

loan amortization schedule   See *amortization schedule*.

loan commitment   An agreement by a lender, usually in writing, to loan a specified amount of money at a future date provided certain conditions are met. More specifically, an agreement by a lender to provide a shorter term loan at a higher interest rate to finance construction until permanent financing for the project can be arranged. Sometimes used in referring to a *takeout commitment*.

loan constant   The percentage of the loan amount needed to pay annual debt service (principal and interest), usually represented mathematically as k and sometimes referred to simply as *constant*. The formula is: annual debt service ÷ loan amount = loan constant (k). The loan constant represents the amount to be paid for each dollar borrowed. Because the constant includes both principal and interest, it is higher than the interest rate of the loan. As the original loan amount is amortized, the constant will increase. (The term refers to a constant method of calculation rather than a constant value.)

loan cost   The cost in money for securing a loan, as in loan fees, legal charges, appraisal fees, title or abstract costs, recording charges or notary fees, etc. The total charges for effecting a loan, customarily paid by the borrower.

loan origination fee   The fee charged by a lender to a borrower for administrative costs of preparing the mortgage loan, usually as a percentage of the loan amount.

loan package   A proposal submitted by a potential borrower to a lender with extensive documentation of the purposes and terms of the potential loan, the benefits to the lender of making the loan, and a complete background and financial history of the borrower.

loan payment   The payment of an installment on the principal balance plus accrued interest on the entire unpaid balance that accrued since the immediately preceding interest payment.

loan payment cost   The cost paid by the borrower for securing a loan (e.g., origination fee, points).

loan-to-value (LTV) ratio   A measure of the lender's risk of loss in making a loan. The relationship between the amount of the principal of a loan and the market value of the real estate securing it; usually expressed as a percentage using the formula: loan amount ÷ property value. The value may be the price being paid for the property or the appraised value. An LTV above 85 percent would be considered high risk.

location   A site or position that is occupied or available for occupancy. An area or tract of land. Commonly used in real estate to refer to the comparative advantages of one site over another in consideration of such factors as transportation, convenience, social benefits, specific use, and anticipated pattern of change.

locational analysis   A comprehensive evaluation of the external factors that affect the value of real property, including local business climate, governmental policy (tax structure, zoning), demographic data, employment and household income, transportation, markets, and geographic features.

lockbox   An electronic device that allows a real estate salesperson to use an access code to enter a home without having to obtain a key elsewhere. Such lockboxes log time and date of entry, and sales personnel are required to use a *personal identification number (PIN)* so that entries can be tracked. Older style lockboxes simply stored keys to the house that were available to those who had a key (or combination) to the lockbox.

lock-in provision   A loan clause that prohibits the borrower from paying off a loan for a specified term; *lock-in period.* Also called *closed period.*

loft building   A structure of two or more stories designed for industrial use. In urban areas, many such buildings that are no longer used for their original purpose may be candidates for *change of use* to offices, condominium dwellings, or rental apartments.

log   A record of performance, as of maintenance services.

logo   A graphic symbol or other device (a company name or trademark) used in identifying a product or business.

London Inter-Bank Offering Rate (LIBOR)   An average of the rates at which five major banks would be willing to deposit U.S. currency for a set period, comparable to the U.S. rate on one-year treasury bills (T-bills). A benchmark interest rate. See also *risk-free rate of return.*

long-range budget   A budget covering a longer period of time than an annual budget, usually three to five years.

long-range plan   A formal written plan that details beforehand the means of accomplishing an objective; a *strategic plan.*

long-term assets   See *capital assets.*

long-term liabilities   In accounting, obligations whose maturity dates are more than a year from the date on the balance sheet. In finance, debts whose due dates are more than ten years in the future; *long-term debt.*

long-term loan Permanent financing required to purchase an existing structure or to replace a construction loan, usually for a term of ten to thirty years.

loss In accounting, any excess of costs over income. In insurance, the basis of a valid claim for damages or indemnity under the terms of a given policy.

loss adjustment See *adjustment.*

loss assessment insurance Condominium unit owner protection that covers special assessments the owner may be obligated to pay because a loss incurred by the association was not otherwise adequately insured.

loss leader In retailing, an item sold at a lesser markup than would normally be obtained on that item in order to attract customers in the hope that they will buy more-profitable items as well.

loss-of-income insurance A policy that protects against loss of earnings as a result of a direct loss from an insured peril.

low-income household A household whose annual income is 80 percent or less of median income for the jurisdiction as defined by HUD and adjusted for household size by HUD.

low-income housing Housing units that, by reason of rental levels or amount of other charges, are available to households or individuals whose incomes do not exceed the maximum income limits established for continued occupancy in federally assisted low-rent public housing.

low-rise A building containing five or fewer stories. The definition may vary depending on locale and property type. When used in regard to office buildings in an urban setting, a building containing up to twenty stories.

low-rise apartment building Multiple-unit residential dwelling of three or fewer stories. See also *garden apartment building.*

low-rise condominium Another name for *garden condominium.*

low season In a resort area, the months just before and after *high season.* An intermediate period differentiated from *off season* when demand is lowest.

lump sum A total or an amount paid at one time.

M

macroeconomics The study of large-scale economic and financial structures, practices, and trends. Study of the economic system as a whole, its general level of income and output, and the interrelationships among various sectors of the economy. Compare *microeconomics*.

maintained markup In retailing, the average markup of an item sustained over a period of time, allowing for future markdowns and other reductions in selling price. The difference between the cost of goods sold and net sales; also called *maintained mark-on*. See also *markup*.

maintenance The effort expended to keep a property in good physical and operating condition and appearance. In real estate management, several types of maintenance are differentiated. *Corrective maintenance* is the ordinary repairs made on a day-to-day basis; when this work is not done, such *deferred maintenance* negatively affects the use, occupancy, and value of the property. *Routine maintenance* (also called *janitorial maintenance*) is the day-to-day upkeep—mopping and waxing floors, washing windows, polishing fixtures, and generally keeping the interior and exterior of the building clean—that is essential to preserving the value of a property. While *preventive maintenance* is a program of regular inspection and care designed to detect and resolve potential problems before major repairs are needed, *emergency maintenance* refers to unscheduled repairs that must be done immediately to prevent further damage or minimize danger to life or property. *Cosmetic maintenance* does not affect function; rather, it makes the property more appealing in appearance.

maintenance program A schedule of all tasks (e.g., inspection, cleaning, lubrication, repair) necessary to keep something in proper working order.

maintenance schedule A listing of specific maintenance tasks, how often they are to be performed, and when the work is to be done.

maintenance yield A lender requirement under many loan placements, which requires a borrower, in the event of prepayment of the loan balance, to supply securities in an equivalent yield to prevent a loss of return to the lender through maturity of the loan (i.e., to guarantee that the lender will receive the full amount of profit from the loan as if it had run its full term). Also called *yield maintenance.*

majority   The age set by state law at which individuals have the legal right to manage their own affairs and are responsible for their own actions. The age of majority varies from state to state. See also *minor.*

malicious mischief   Intentional destruction of another's property based on ill will or resentment toward the property's owner. See also *vandalism.*

malpractice   Failure of a professional to provide proper services as a result of ignorance, negligence, or criminal intent. In real estate management, misconduct or unreasonable lack of skill or fidelity in the discharge of one's professional or fiduciary duties.

management   The job of planning, organizing, and controlling a business enterprise. The persons in an organization who are engaged in management.

management agreement   A contractual arrangement between the owner(s) of a property and the designated managing agent, describing the duties and establishing the authority of the agent and detailing the responsibilities, rights, and obligations of both agent and owner(s).

management company   A real estate organization that specializes in the professional management of real properties for others as a gainful occupation; a *management firm.*

management fee   The monetary consideration paid monthly or otherwise for the performance of management duties, usually defined in the management agreement as a percentage of the gross receipts (effective gross income) of the property and/or as a minimum monthly amount.

management firm   Another name for *management company.*

management plan   The fundamental document for the short-term operation of a property that represents a statement of facts, objectives, and policies and details how the property is to be operated during the coming year. Such a plan usually includes the annual budget.

management records   Historical and accounting documents designed for the interpretation and understanding of the physical and financial welfare of a managed property.

management review   In regard to housing that receives government funds, a multifaceted examination performed by the governmental agency monitoring the property. The process used to determine whether a property meets all specified management requirements, including record keeping, occupancy practices, property inspections, maintenance operations, financial administration, and subsidy contract administration.

managerial accounting   Use of financial information and records to make business planning decisions. A system designed to facilitate decision-making, planning, and control. Because managerial accounting forecasts are not actual transactions, they are not auditable. See also *financial accounting.*

managing agent   An agent duly appointed to direct and control all matters pertaining to a property that is owned or controlled by another. One who supervises the operation of a property on behalf of the owner and in consideration of a management fee.

man-hour   A unit of one-hour's work by one person used as a measure to estimate labor costs and productivity.

Manufactured Home Construction and Safety Standards Act of 1974 (the HUD code)   The construction of every manufactured home in the United States must comply with this federal building code. The HUD code was adopted on June 15, 1976. The legal differentiation between the terms "mobile home" and "manufactured home" is based on the passing of the HUD code.

manufactured housing   A dwelling that is built in a factory, transported to and anchored on a site, and used as a year-round residential unit. All manufactured homes must be in compliance with the federal Manufactured Home Construction and Safety Standards Act of 1974 (the HUD code) which became effective in 1976. (Usage note: The term *"mobile home"* is commonly used to identify all manufactured housing even though the legal nomenclature is manufactured homes for units built after the enactment of the HUD code.)

margin   The amount of profit a retailer makes from a certain item. It is always expressed as a percentage of the sales price. Compare *markup.*

margin of safety   A measure of a company's financial position. In financing, the extent to which the fair market value of the property held as collateral exceeds the outstanding loan amount. In real estate and its management, used in referring to the difference between net operating income (NOI) and annual debt service. Additional funds available for payment of annual debt service; a lender's margin of safety.

markdown   In retailing, a reduction in the original or previous retail price of an item stated as a percentage of net sales. A retail price reduction taken for a hard-to-sell item.

market   Broadly, any interaction between buyers and sellers. In real estate management, the geographic area within which a rental property competes for tenants.

market analysis   An evaluation of supply and demand conditions in a particular area for a particular type of goods or services. A determination of the characteristics, purchasing power, and habits of a given segment of the population. See also *demographics; psychographics.* In real estate development, a study of the supply of and demand for a specific type of property in a specific area. In real estate management, the process of identifying the specific group of prospective tenants for a particular property and then evaluating the property by that market's standards for rental space. A market analysis is usually a component of a management plan.

market approach   A method of valuation based on a comparison of data from recent sales of similar properties in the market. See also *appraisal.*

market area   The geographic region from which a product or service can expect its greatest demand. See also *trade area.*

market cap rate   A capitalization rate used to compare the values of properties, found by using net operating income (NOI) divided by property value to give a decimal number that is converted to a percentage.

market data approach   Also called *comparable sales approach.* See *market approach.*

marketing The process of moving goods from producers to consumers by finding out what consumers want or need and then determining whether a product that meets those needs can be made and sold at a profit. All business activity a producer uses to expose potential consumers to available goods and services, from product development and determination of cost through generating demand via advertising to packaging and selling. In real estate leasing, methods used to rent space and to retain current tenants.

marketing fund In a shopping center, an account controlled by the landlord that is specifically for funding shopping center promotions and advertising. Merchants in the center contribute to this fund based on a predetermined amount stated in their leases. Compare *merchants' association*.

marketing plan A short-term business tool to generate profits by increasing business. In real estate management, a comprehensive marketing program for a rental property for a defined period of time, including how the program will be coordinated, who will be responsible for marketing and/or leasing tasks, and the allocation of budgeted funds. In the absence of a budget or as a prelude to preparing a budget, a marketing plan may outline specific marketing strategies, project their estimated costs as a basis for comparison, and make specific recommendations as to which alternatives would be most efficient or cost-effective or both. In shopping centers, typically an annual plan outlining how *marketing fund* income will be spent (types of media and frequency of ad placement, specific promotional activities, etc.) to increase customer traffic and sales volume at the center. A marketing plan incorporates *marketing strategy*.

marketing research A methodology for determining the general characteristics of the marketplace (population size, age, income distribution, etc.) and assessing the competition. In residential property management, a tool used to establish the location and extent of the market for a particular apartment property. Compare *market research*.

marketing strategy A plan of action for meeting marketing objectives. Advertising and other techniques used to promote and lease space in a building.

market penetration The percentage of a specific type of retail market that a retailer has captured.

market price The price for a good or service at which supply and demand for it are equal. The price a property can actually be sold for at a given time as agreed to by a willing buyer and a willing seller; the amount actually paid in a real estate transaction. Often, but not always, synonymous with *market value*.

market rate of interest The interest rate determined by the supply of money available for lending and the demand by those wishing to borrow it for capital investment.

market rent Rent that a property is capable of yielding if leased under prevailing market conditions; *economic rent*. Also, the amount that comparable space would command in a competitive market. Often used interchangeably with *street rent* and *contract rent*. (By definition, the latter is the rent stated in a specific lease.) For apartments, the basis is unit type and size. For office buildings, the basis would be dollars per rentable square foot; for retail space, it would be dollars per square foot of gross leasable area (GLA). In government-assisted housing, the rent HUD authorizes the owner to collect from families who are ineligible for assistance; also called *maximum rent*.

market research   Collecting information about consumer wants, needs, and preferences by surveying consumers directly. A methodology used to explore product design, packaging, size (quantity), and other marketing-related issues, including price. In residential property management, a tool for identifying what apartment renters in a particular market want in terms of unit size, features and amenities, and rental price. In shopping center management, the gathering of information about a trade area and a particular retail site pertaining to population, economy, local industries, per capita expenditures, competing retail sites, and sales potential. Specific information about shoppers is often gathered via *focus groups,* telephone interviews, and *intercept surveys.* Compare *marketing research.*

market segmentation   Division of a market into identifiable submarkets as a way to focus on specific users whose requirements can be met by the subject building. Marketers of office space often segment the local market based on location (the neighborhood of the building), user size (users of large versus small spaces), and/or user type (government versus corporate versus service providers). For marketers of retail space, the process of reducing the number of available tenant prospects by classifying retailers into categories on the basis of type of goods sold, form of ownership, size of store, and other criteria.

market share   That portion of consumer dollars spent on a particular merchandise category which a given retailer can capture.

market survey   A detailed and comprehensive evaluation of a given market that provides market research data. Collection and analysis of up-to-date information on other products distributed in a given area. See also *market research.* In real estate management, the process of gathering information about specific comparable properties for comparison to data about the subject property in order to weigh the advantages and disadvantages of each property and establish a market rent for the subject. In the office building market, a survey is made of comparable buildings located in the subject property's neighborhood and includes such information as number of stories, net rentable area, building features and amenities, rental rates, and load factors. For shopping centers, a market survey of competing centers would include location specifics, gross leasable area (GLA), anchor and ancillary tenants, rental rates, and sales volumes. Amount and availability of parking are important considerations in market surveys for all types of properties.

market value   The price at which a seller would willingly sell an item and a buyer would willingly buy it in an open market if neither were acting under unusual pressure. The price that a piece of property might be expected to bring if offered for sale in an open market comprised of willing buyers and sellers where the property has been available for sale for a reasonable period of time. Compare *market price.*

markup   In retailing, the difference between the selling price of an item and its cost; also called *mark-on.* Compare *margin.*

markup percentage   In retailing, the difference between cost and retail price expressed as a percentage of the retail price (or, less commonly, as a percentage of cost).

mart building   A multistory interior-finished property that is a cross between a retail arcade and a loft building and is used by wholesalers and jobbers to display sample merchandise.

master association   An organization of unit owners created by a developer when a property will comprise two or more incorporated condominiums and the separate condominiums will share certain amenities; also called *common association* or *umbrella association.* The master association is responsible for maintaining, operating, managing, and financing the shared recreational facilities and other amenities.

master deed   A legal document filed by a condominium developer or converter to record all of the individual condominium units owned within a condominium development. It may also include restrictions and covenants. See also *declaration.*

master key   A key that opens many or all of a property's locks.

master meter   A single meter, owned and operated by the utility company, which measures the total amount of energy from one source that is required to operate an entire building. When a master meter is in place, individual tenants' spaces may be submetered to measure their discrete energy use. See also *submeter.*

master policy   In insurance, another name for *blanket policy.*

material safety data sheet (MSDS)   A compilation of information regarding the hazardous properties of chemicals. Usual information includes composition, physical and chemical properties, and known hazards (e.g., toxicity, flammability, explosion potential); recommended cautions for handling (e.g., protective clothing and devices), storage, and disposal; clean-up procedures, and first aid treatment in the event of exposure. An MSDS is provided when chemicals (e.g., solvents, cleaning compounds) are shipped in bulk in pails or drums and when the information cannot be fitted on the labels of small containers. These documents must be retained for reference by maintenance and other on-site personnel.

maximum rent   See *ceiling rent; market rent.*

mean   A statistical term, also called arithmetic mean or *average,* which is calculated by adding together a set of related values (in real estate management, the rental rates for all of the competing or comparable properties) and dividing the sum by the number of values in the set. See also *arithmetic mean; weighted mean.*

mechanical maintenance   Inspection, cleaning, lubrication, and repair of machines and tools to keep them in proper working order.

mechanic's lien   A lien created by statute that exists in favor of contractors, laborers, or material suppliers who have performed work or furnished materials in the erection or repair of a building. A claim against a property to collect payment for materials or labor provided, it restricts clear title to the property until the amount owed is paid in full.

media   Various forms of communication, such as publications and broadcasting, which carry advertising.

median   A statistical term meaning the middle value among a series in which there are an equal number of items above and below it. In a data set with an even number of data points, the two middle figures are averaged to find the median.

mediation   Private, informal process of dispute resolution in which a neutral third party (mediator) helps disputing parties reach an agreement. However, the mediator has no power to impose a decision on the parties. Compare *arbitration.*

medical payments insurance   A type of liability insurance policy that covers medical, hospital, and/or funeral expenses that are incurred when members of the public are injured on the premises, regardless of any actual liability.

megamall   An enclosed mall three or four times the size of an ordinary regional shopping center (usually in excess of two million square feet of gross leasable area) and including retail space, hotels, restaurants, entertainment facilities, and amusement park-type amenities.

Member of the Appraisal Institute (MAI)   Professional designation conferred by the Appraisal Institute.

merchandising   An aspect of marketing that involves advertising, promoting, and organizing the sale of a particular product or service. A comprehensive approach to sales promotion that encompasses market research, product development, coordinated manufacturing and marketing, and effective advertising and selling.

merchants' association   An organization formed in shopping centers and controlled by the tenants to plan promotions and advertisements for the good of the center as a whole and usually established as a not-for-profit corporation. All tenants are required to participate, and both tenants and landlord pay dues. Compare *marketing fund.*

merger   In business, the combination of two companies by purchase, sale, or an exchange of stock.

metered fee   A charge for legal services based on the attorney's time, experience, and expertise.

metes and bounds   Boundaries of a tract of land established by referring to natural features or man-made constructs (e.g., a river, a road) as the point of origin. This is differentiated from boundaries established by measuring from a fixed starting point and stating specific distances in reference to compass directions. See also *survey.*

metropolitan area (MA)   A designation by the U.S. Bureau of the Census applied to metropolitan areas with a central city or core area having a large population nucleus and including adjacent communities that are interdependent with the core area economically and socially. *Metropolitan statistical areas (MSAs), consolidated metropolitan statistical areas (CMSAs)* and *primary metropolitan statistical areas (PMSAs)* are defined by the Office of Management and Budget as a standard for federal agencies in preparing statistics relating to MAs.

metropolitan statistical area (MSA)   See *metropolitan area.*

microeconomics   The study of the economic behavior of individual decision-makers (e.g., consumers, farmers). Compare *macroeconomics.*

mid-month convention   An Internal Revenue Service rule for calculating cost recovery that allows only half of a month's depreciation to be claimed in the months that a property is bought and sold.

mid-rise Definition varies by property type and geographic location. When used in regard to office buildings in an urban setting, a building containing twenty to forty stories.

mid-rise apartment building A multiple-unit dwelling ranging from four to nine stories tall.

mid-rise condominium A multifamily dwelling under condominium ownership that usually is four to ten stories high and has a single front entrance and lobby and common corridors.

midstream analysis The part of the cash flow analysis that is prepared after a property is bought, thus allowing new figures to be added and a revised, more accurate investment base to be calculated.

millage rate A property tax rate under which the assessment basis is one dollar for every one thousand dollars of assessed property value (1 mill = $1/$1000). Thus, the owner of a property with assessed valuation of $100,000 and property taxes assessed at a millage rate of 20 mills would pay $2,000 in property tax.

minimum fee The lowest fee for which service can be provided while maintaining a margin of profit.

minimum rate In insurance, a rate that is applied uniformly to all risks within a given class regardless of possible differences in hazards. In property insurance, a rate that applies to a whole group of buildings of similar construction and hazard.

minimum rent In retail leasing, the rent which will always be due each month in a tenant's lease term, regardless of sales volume and exclusive of any additional charges. Often used in conjunction with a percentage rent arrangement; sometimes called *fixed-minimum rent*. See also *base rent*.

minimum wage The lowest hourly wage rate permitted either by state or federal law or a labor contract. See *Fair Labor Standards Act (FLSA)*.

miniperm loan An interest-only mortgage on income property put in place because a longer-term permanent loan cannot yet be supported by the property's cash flow, usually made in conjunction with a construction loan and for a term of three to five years. Also called *minipermanent loan*.

miniwarehouse A facility that provides self-storage units to private individuals and businesses on a rental basis; also called *ministorage* and *self storage*. See also *self-service storage facility*.

minor One who has not reached the age set by state law to be legally recognized as an adult and, therefore, is not legally responsible for contracting debts or signing contracts. See also *majority*.

minority Any group that can be distinguished in a particular situation from some other group on any disallowed basis (color, race, national origin, religion, sex, familial status or handicap/disability). See also *protected class*.

minutes The official record of proceedings of a meeting, as of a condominium or homeowners' association.

miscellaneous income Income a property produces from sources other than rent, such as parking fees, rental of storage space or common area facilities, coin-operated laundry equipment, vending machines, late fees from delinquent rents, and forfeited application and security deposits. Also called *ancillary income* or *unscheduled income*.

misdemeanor A crime punishable by fine, penalty, or imprisonment in a county facility for less than one year. According to federal law and most state laws, any offense other than a felony is classified as a misdemeanor. Compare *felony*.

mixed-use development (MXD) A large-scale real estate project having three or more significant revenue-producing uses (e.g., retail, office, residential, hotel, recreation or entertainment), incorporating significant physical and functional integration of project components (thus an intensive use of land), and conforming to a coherent plan. MXDs are often found in central business districts (CBDs) in large urban areas.

mobile home A transportable, factory-built dwelling that is designed to be used as a year-round residence. Although it is more appropriately applied to mobile housing built prior to the HUD code, the term "mobile home" is commonly used to identify all forms of manufactured housing even though the U.S. Congress changed the legal name of all HUD-code dwellings from "mobile home" to "manufactured home" in 1980. (Prior to 1974, a mobile home was defined as a movable dwelling constructed to be towed on its chassis, connected to utilities, and remain *without* permanent foundation for year-round living.) Prior to the HUD code, mobile homes were built to voluntary industry standards established by the American National Standards Institute (ANSI). See also *manufactured housing*.

mobile home park A community designed to receive manufactured, mobile, and/or modular housing. The resident typically owns the dwelling unit and leases the lot on which the home is placed. The lot includes the pad plus utility connection, lawn, parking space, etc. Other arrangements also exist; the resident may purchase his/her lot, for example. Parks are frequently categorized on the basis of the ownership of the property (e.g., land lease, subdivision, condominium), services provided (e.g., with or without pool and playground), or types of residents who live in the park (e.g., retirement community, family park). The term "mobile home park" reflects the common use of the term "mobile home" to describe all kinds of mobile, manufactured, and modular housing.

mobile home site A parcel of rentable land, with sewer and utility connections, designed to accommodate a mobile home. Also called a *pad*.

mode A statistical term meaning the most frequently occurring value or amount. Unlike the mean and the median, which can be found for all sets of data, a mode does not exist in every data set. See also *mean; median*.

model apartment A furnished apartment that serves as a display for prospective residents.

model office A fully equipped office to be shown to prospects, usually used as an aid in leasing space in a new building. Often a model office is built out with the building standard finishes (e.g., paint surfaces, window treatments, carpeting or other floor covering) to show prospects how their office interiors would look.

modernization Adaptation to modern (current) needs, taste, or usage. Change that is related to market perception of what is currently acceptable.

The removal or upgrading of original or existing features of a property, primarily to reflect technological improvements such as energy-saving equipment.

Modified Accelerated Cost Recovery System (MACRS) The schedule put in place by Internal Revenue Service tax codes for depreciating property and equipment.

modified accrual accounting A method of accounting in which items that repeat at regular intervals are accounted on a cash basis while those requiring accumulation of funds toward a large dollar payout are accounted on an accrual basis; sometimes also called *modified cash-accrual system*.

modified gross lease A lease under which the tenant and landlord each pay part of the operating expenses of the property in addition to the tenant paying a fixed (base) rent. Compare *gross lease; net lease*.

modified internal rate of return (MIRR) In financial analysis, an indicator that uses investor-selected rates of return in calculating positive cash flow as a basis for decision-making.

modular home A factory-built year-round dwelling unit that is built to the specifications of the local or state building code applicable to modular housing. Unlike a "mobile home," a modular home is permanently secured to a foundation. Some modular homes are delivered to a home site on a removable chassis; others are shipped in pieces (components) and erected on site.

money A universally valued commodity used as a medium of exchange.

money supply The total volume of currency in circulation plus the total amount of demand deposits (checking and savings accounts) in all of the nation's banks, sometimes differentiated as *M1* and *M2*.

monthly financial statement A statement that summarizes one month's income and expenses.

month-to-month tenancy An agreement to rent or lease for consecutive and continuing monthly periods until terminated by proper prior notice by either the landlord or the tenant. Notice of termination must precede the commencement date of the final month of occupancy. State law usually establishes the time period of prior notice.

Montreal Protocol An international agreement (made in 1987) that establishes a comprehensive schedule for the phase-out of ozone-depleting chemicals, specifically *chlorofluorocarbons (CFCs),* which were to be eliminated by January 1, 2000.

mortgage An interest in land or real property conveyed by a written instrument as security for the payment of a debt. Often used in referring to the loan itself, the debt instrument usually creates a *lien* against the property until the debt has been paid in full. A conditional transfer or pledge of real property as security for the payment of a debt; see also *collateral*. The document used to create a mortgage loan.

mortgage bonds Securities issued by a local government to accumulate tax-exempt financing for real-estate ventures and housing.

mortgagee The lender in a mortgage loan transaction.

mortgage-equity analysis A method of determining value by dividing net operating income into debt and equity components and using these components to find cap rates and the rates of return for lender and investor.

Mortgage Guarantee Insurance Company (MGIC) A private company that insures lenders against borrowers' defaults and foreclosures.

mortgage insurance A form of decreasing term (life) insurance that is intended to make the periodic payments on a mortgage as they come due in the event of disability or death of the insured (the mortgagor). With this type of insurance, the principal (loan amount) covered by the policy declines as the mortgage is amortized. The term is also used in referring to the practice of the government insuring privately borrowed loans. If the borrower defaults, the government guarantees to pay off the balance or purchase the property. Compare *private mortgage insurance.*

mortgage interest differential Compensation provided to a transferred employee to cover some or all of the difference between the employee's mortgage in his/her original location and a higher mortgage payment in the location of the transfer.

mortgage lien The claim on real estate granted to the mortgagee when a mortgage or trust deed is executed by the mortgagor (property owner) to secure a loan.

mortgage life insurance A type of life insurance on the mortgagor that is intended to pay the balance due on a mortgage in the event of the death of the insured. It prevents loss to the mortgagee if, in the event of default, the mortgaged property cannot satisfy the balance due plus the cost of foreclosure.

mortgage loan A loan secured by a mortgage (lien) on real property.

mortgage loan insurance A government program for insuring mortgages and loans made by private lending institutions for the purchase, construction, rehabilitation, repair, and improvement of single-family homes and multifamily housing.

mortgage market The demand for and supply of mortgages. Borrowers seeking loans and lenders willing to invest in mortgages. Interest rates and terms offered to potential borrowers by competing lenders.

mortgagor The borrower in a mortgage loan transaction. The owner of the real estate who conveys his/her interest in the property as security for a loan.

motion A formal proposal put before an assembly (e.g., a condominium association, a merchants' association, or committee meeting) on which action must be taken.

motor vehicle insurance Another name for *automobile insurance.*

move-in The process of moving a resident into an apartment or a commercial tenant into its leased space.

move-in checklist An inspection checklist used to document the condition of an apartment at the time a new resident moves in. Usual practice is for a member of the management staff to conduct this inspection in the presence of the resident and for both management and resident to sign the completed form acknowledging its accuracy. This will be compared to a *move-out checklist* to determine if there has been any excessive damage (beyond normal wear and tear) that the resident is responsible for repairing (or for the cost of repairs made by management). In commercial leasing, a punch list serves a similar purpose in documenting completion of tenant improvement construction and identifying work that remains to be done. See also *punch list*.

move-out   The process of moving a resident out of an apartment or a commercial tenant out of its leased space.

move-out checklist   An inspection checklist used to document the condition of an apartment at the time a resident moves out. This is compared to a previously used *move-in checklist* to identify repairs to be made and responsibility for the cost of such repairs. Often combined with the former as a *move-in/move-out checklist* that facilitates comparison of the before and after condition. Here again, usual practice is to have the management person and the resident sign the completed form and acknowledge responsibility for repair costs to be deducted from the resident's security deposit.

mulch   Protective covering, usually organic material, placed around plants to protect against weed growth and help soil retain moisture.

multitenant floor   A floor of an office building that is divided into office suites for several businesses; also called *multiple-tenancy floor*.

multi-use development   A term applied to multiple uses of a single site and encompassing densely configured developments that achieve physical and functional integration but include only two uses, mixed-use developments as such, and developments with two or more uses but lacking physical and functional integration (usually because of large scale, low density, or lack of a coherent plan). Compare *mixed-use development (MXD)*.

mutual savings bank   A kind of thrift institution that exists in a limited number of states. Mutual savings banks are owned and operated by their depositors and managed by a board of trustees. Unless required by state law, they need not be incorporated or supervised under state banking regulations.

N

named insured The entity or entities specifically identified in an insurance contract as the insured parties. One of several parties provided coverage, which may include others in addition to the purchaser of the policy.

National Apartment Association (NAA) Organization comprised of state and local associations of professionals and others involved in the multifamily housing industry.

National Association of Home Builders (NAHB) Trade association serving the single-family home industry. Serves the multifamily housing industry through education and professional certifications, including the Registered in Apartment Management (RAM) program.

National Association of Industrial and Office Properties (NAIOP) Membership organization of owners and developers of industrial, office, and related properties and others involved in the commercial real estate industry. Formerly the National Association of Industrial and Office Parks and, subsequently, NAIOP—The Association for Commercial Real Estate.

National Association of Real Estate Investment Trusts (NAREIT) The national trade association for real estate investment trusts (REITs) and other real estate companies.

National Association of REALTORS® (NAR) National nonprofit professional organization of licensed real estate practitioners who are members of subscribing local real estate boards throughout the United States and its possessions.

National Center for Housing Management (NCHM) See *Certified Occupancy Specialist (COS)*.

National Environmental Policy Act (NEPA) A federal law, passed in 1969, that sets forth U.S. national environmental policy and goals. In particular, it requires federal agencies to file environmental impact statements on all legislative recommendations or programs that affect the quality of the environment.

National Housing Act The first significant housing legislation in the United States, this 1934 act created the *Federal Housing Administration (FHA)*.

National Register of Historic Places   Federal agency established to record and preserve buildings of architectural and historic significance. Such registration places restrictions on rehabilitation or restoration of buildings designated as historic places.

natural breakpoint   Another name for *breakpoint.*

negative cash flow   A deficit or loss. When operating expenses and debt service exceed revenues collected (effective gross income).

negative rent   See *tenant rent.*

negligence   Failure to use the level of care a reasonable and prudent person would use under the same circumstances, characterized by inattention, inadvertence, and thoughtlessness that results in harm. Failure to exercise reasonable care which, though not accompanied by harmful intent, directly results in an injury to an innocent party. A person (e.g., a property manager) or a business entity (e.g., a property management company) can be held liable for negligent acts.

negligent hiring   Hiring someone about whom it is known or should have been known that the person could reasonably be expected to cause injury to another person. A cause of action against an employer if an employee's actions cause harm to co-workers or others and if a background check that would have revealed the potential for such harmful action (e.g., prior conviction for assault, which is a felony) had not been done prior to the individual's employment.

negligent retention   Failure to terminate an employee whose behavior on the job has been problematic. A cause of action against an employer if an employee who exhibits dangerous behavior on the job (e.g., showing a weapon, making threats) is allowed to repeat the behavior and someone is hurt.

negligent supervision   Failure to supervise an employee adequately that results in foreseeable injury to another person. A cause of action against an employer if an incident results in injury to another person because training and oversight of an employee have been inadequate.

negligent tort   A breach of the legal duty to act reasonably (e.g., negligent operation of a vehicle, negligent hiring, negligent security).

negotiation   The process of bargaining on price, quantity, quality, payment, or other terms of a business transaction that precedes an agreement. In commercial leasing, the bargaining to reach a mutual agreement on rental rates, term of the lease, options, and other points.

neighborhood   An area within which there are common characteristics of population and land use. A district or locality, often defined by referring to its character or inhabitants. An area limited as to size and used for residential, commercial, or other purposes or a combination of such uses integrated into an accepted pattern. In real estate market analysis, a section of a larger region or market area, within which buildings generally compete with one another for tenants. The area surrounding and adjacent to a property, especially as it is characterized by similarity of demographic, economic, and other parameters.

neighborhood analysis   A study of a neighborhood and comparison with the broader economic and geographic area of which it is a part to determine why individuals and businesses are attracted to the area. A usual component of a management plan.

neighborhood center   A shopping center typically anchored by a supermarket or drugstore and having 30,000–100,000 square feet of gross leasable area (GLA).

net charges   Another name for *pass-through charges.*

net cost   Cost after all incidental charges are added and all allowable credits are deducted.

net lease   A lease under which the tenant pays a prorated share of some or all operating expenses in addition to base or minimum rent. The terms net-net (or *double-net*) and net-net-net (or *triple-net*) are also used, depending on the extent of the costs that are passed through to the tenant. Used most often for commercial tenants, the definitions of the terms vary with location and type of property (e.g., office, retail, industrial). In retail leasing, the tenant pays a prorated share of property taxes under a net lease, prorated shares of both property taxes and insurance under a net-net (or double-net) lease, and prorated shares of all operating expenses (including common area maintenance) under a net-net-net (or triple-net) lease. Compare *gross lease.*

net operating income (NOI)   Total collections (gross receipts) *less* operating expenses; may be calculated on an annual or a monthly basis. More broadly, cash available after all operating expenses have been deducted from collected rental income and before debt service and capital expenses have been deducted.

net present value (NPV)   The difference between the cost of a real estate or other investment and the discounted present value of all anticipated future fiscal benefits of that investment. In financial analysis, a method that discounts expected future cash flows to their present value using a predetermined desired rate of return. NPV is calculated by subtracting the present value of the capital outlay from the present value of the expected returns.

net prior to debt service (NPDS)   The cash available from collected rental income after all operating expenses have been deducted and before capital expenses and debt service have been deducted; *net operating income (NOI).*

net proceeds   The amount, usually in the form of cash (or cash equivalents), received from the sale of property or distribution of stock dividends. Also, the amount received from a loan or from the sale or issuance of securities after all costs incurred in the transaction have been deducted. See also *proceeds.*

net profit   See *after-tax cash flow.*

net rentable area   See *rentable area.*

net rentable square foot   The unit of measurement used to determine the area that is occupied and used exclusively by tenants on a multitenant floor in an office building.

net sales   A retailer's sales income after exchanges, refunds, and allowances have been deducted from the total.

net terms   In retailing, requiring payment for the billed amount of the invoice (no cash discount is allowed).

networking   Making use of business and professional contacts.

net worth   The excess of assets over liabilities. In real estate and its management, this represents the owner's equity.

newsletter   A printed periodical report devoted to news of and for a special-interest group, such as a condominium association. Newsletters are used by managers of all types of properties to communicate with tenants as part of a tenant-retention program. Management companies also publish newsletters directed to their clients.

news release   Another name for *press release.*

nominal damages   See *damages.*

noncompetitive space   Commonly used in referring to office space that is occupied by building owners or long-term tenants (i.e., with leases for ten or more years into the future) and therefore not available to satisfy immediate demand; also called *noncompetitive office space.* The term can also apply to retail, industrial, and flex space. Compare *competitive space.*

nonconforming loan   A construction loan that is made without a pre-arranged permanent loan commitment and carrying a higher interest rate.

noncontrollable expenses   Operating expense items over which property management has no control (e.g., real estate taxes, insurance premiums, labor-union wages).

nonexclusive authorization to lease   A document stating that the leasing agent will only receive a commission if his/her efforts actually result in an executed lease with a prospect within a certain time frame.

nonperforming assets   Properties whose as-is value is below that which would be acceptable to a lending institution's board or whose upside potential is marginal or achievable only in the distant future. Such properties are potential candidates for *rehabilitation* or *change of use.*

nonperforming loan   A loan that is not in conformity with its terms. A loan on which no payments (principal or interest) are being made. A financial asset of a lending institution regulated by the Federal Deposit Insurance Corporation (FDIC) that has been declared by the FDIC as nonperforming.

nonrecourse   Having no personal liability. In the case of a loan that is non-recourse, the lender must rely solely on the property pledged as collateral for payment in the event of default by the borrower; other assets of the borrower cannot be taken.

nonstandard specification   See *specification.*

nonsufficient funds (NSF)   Usually used as the acronym in referring to a check drawn on a bank account that does not contain enough cash to cover the draft; an NSF check. Also sometimes called *insufficient funds.*

nonyield space   Space that is essential to the operation of a building but does not produce direct revenue. See also *efficiency factor.*

North American Industry Classification System (NAICS)   A numerical classification system developed jointly by the United States, Canada, and Mexico to provide easier comparability of business activity statistics, in particular across the three countries. The NAICS superseded the *Standard Industrial Classification (SIC) System* in 1997.

notary public   An individual licensed by the state to certify documents to make them authentic and to take affidavits.

notes payable   The amount owed by a business to lenders in the form of short-term loans (promissory notes).

notes receivable   The amount owed to a business on promissory notes from customers and other debtors.

notice clause   In a lease, the clause that establishes the proper method and time frame each party must use to inform the other of matters that require notification as provided in the lease.

notices   Documents used to communicate with tenants, in particular residents in government-assisted housing.

notice to vacate   Legal notification requiring a tenant to remove him/herself and all removable possessions from the premises, within a stated period of time or upon a specified day and date, and to deliver the premises to the owner or agent or to a designated successor.

nuisance rent increase   The amount of additional rent a tenant will pay to avoid the expense, discomfort, and inconvenience of moving.

O

observed depreciation   In appraisal, the loss in utility of a property compared to its value new, based on inspection and analysis of observable conditions that affect the property and its desirability.

obsolescence   Generally speaking, a loss of value brought about by a change in design, technology, taste, or demand. *Physical obsolescence* (deterioration) is a result of aging (wear and tear) or deferred maintenance. *Functional obsolescence* is an internal condition of a property related to its design or use. *Economic obsolescence* is an inability to generate enough income to offset operating expenses, usually due to conditions external to the property (changes in populations and/or land uses, legislation, etc.). Also used in referring to the process by which property loses its economic usefulness to the owner/taxpayer due to causes other than physical deterioration (e.g., technological advancements, changes in public taste); an element of *depreciation*. See also *curable obsolescence; incurable obsolescence.*

occupancy agreement   A lease agreement that spells out the conditions of occupancy of a property for a specified length of time for a specified amount of rent; a *lease.*

occupancy cost   The tenant's total cost for the leased space. For commercial tenants, this includes base rent plus a pro-rata share of property operating expenses (e.g., insurance, real estate taxes, utilities, common area maintenance, and management fees) and may include reimbursement of a tenant improvement allowance. In addition, retail tenants may pay percentage rent (usually as overage) and contribute to a marketing fund or merchants' association.

occupancy date   Used in reference to the date an occupant (owner or tenant) takes possession of the premises or to a move-in date or a date that move-in is authorized, separate from a construction completion date, although the term may be used as another name for *completion date.* Also, occupancy date may (or may not) be the commencement date of a lease or the closing date of a sale.

occupancy level   The relation of space already rented to the total amount of leasable space in a property, expressed as a percentage; also called *occupancy rate.* In office buildings, the measure is rentable square feet; in shopping centers, it is gross leasable area (GLA). In apartments, the number of leased units is compared to the total number of units in the building or property. See also *vacancy rate*.

occupancy rate   The number of residential units or rentable square feet of commercial space that is occupied by tenants, expressed as a percentage of the total number of units or square feet. When subtracted from the total, the difference is the *vacancy rate*.

occupancy report   A statement of the number of occupied units in a building and, consequently, the vacancy factor. A usual component of the periodic management report to ownership.

occupancy restrictions   Limitations on who may and may not buy and/or live in condominium units.

occupancy standards   Guidelines that state the number of bedrooms or square footage required for specific numbers of people living in a unit. Standards should be designed to avoid overcrowding or underutilization of units at the property. Governmental agencies may have specific requirements as to the number of bedrooms or square footage required per person.

occupant   One who occupies a particular space. In the case of leased premises, a resident or tenant.

occupational hazard   Any danger of accident or disease directly associated with performing a particular type of work.

Occupational Safety and Health Act (OSHA)   A law passed in 1970 requiring employers to comply with job safety and health standards issued by the U.S. Department of Labor. The law regulates safety conditions in the workplace and mandates use of protective clothing and devices for certain types of tasks.

Occupational Safety and Health Administration (OSHA)   An agency of the federal government that oversees compliance with the *Occupational Safety and Health Act*.

office building   A single- or multistory structure designed for the conduct of business, generally divided into individual offices and offering space for rent or lease.

office building classification   The categorization of office buildings according to their age, condition, amenities, and location for comparison purposes. Definitions vary from market to market, but the following generally hold true. Class A buildings are the most attractive in their markets and command the highest rents. Class B buildings offer fair to good facilities and services at average rents. Class C buildings provide very basic facilities and services for lower-than-average rents.

office park   A controlled park-like development composed of office buildings that includes access roads and a unique identification. Often these developments are located outside the central business district (CBD) of major urban centers and buildings are single-story or low-rise structures; also called *suburban office park*.

off-price center   A type of specialty shopping center comprised of tenants offering name-brand merchandise at large discounts (20%–60%) off normal retail prices because special bulk purchases allow cost savings to be passed on to the customer. Compare *outlet center*.

off season   The least busy season at a resort area, when rental rates are lowest.

off-site management   Management of a property by persons not residing or keeping office hours at the subject property.

on call   The status of an employee or other person who is available and may be called upon outside of normal business hours.

one-hundred-percent location   Another name for *hundred-percent location*.

on-site management   A plan for managing a condominium association whereby a person is hired and works exclusively for the association and handles all or specifically designated aspects of the association's affairs.

on-site manager   The direct representative of management and ownership on the property site; a *site manager*. See also *resident manager*.

open space plan   An office design that eliminates the use of fixed partitions and permits tenants to rearrange workstations as their operational needs require.

operating budget   A listing of all anticipated income from and expenses of operating a property, usually projected on an annual basis. While funds for accumulation of capital reserves would be deducted from net operating income (NOI) in an operating budget (and the accumulated funds would be recorded as a capital or asset item), actual expenditures of such reserve funds would be anticipated in a *capital budget*.

operating covenant   See *continuous operation*.

operating expense escalation clause   A lease provision under which increases in building operating expenses are passed on to tenants on a pro rata basis.

operating expense ratio   A measure of management risk that relates operating expenses to gross potential income. The result is written as a percentage. The lower the percentage, the more efficiently a property is run. Differentiated from *operating ratio,* which is the relationship between operating expenses and effective gross income (i.e., gross potential income minus vacancy and collection loss).

operating expenses   The normal costs of running a business. In real estate, the expenditures for real estate taxes, salaries, insurance, maintenance, utilities, and similar items paid in connection with the operation of a rental property that are properly charged against income. More broadly, all expenditures made in connection with operating a property with the exception of debt service, capital reserves (and/or capital expenditures), and income taxes. At commercial properties, increases in operating expenses are often used as a basis for rent increases. Items included for this purpose can vary by property type and geographic location.

operating reserves   Funds set aside for the payment of an annual expense.

operating statement   The primary record of money received and paid out relative to a property produced by the accounting function. It details expenditures and the percentage of income that can be expressed as profit. In real estate management, this is a regular component of the management report submitted to the owner by the managing agent (property manager or management firm).

operations manual   An authoritative collection of information that describes the organization and its goals, explains policies that guide its operations, outlines specific procedures for implementing those policies on a day-to-day basis, assigns responsibility for performing various functions, and contains the various documents (forms) for performing the work; also called *standard operating procedures manual.* In real estate management, an operations manual is usually also developed to guide the management and business operations of a specific property.

opportunity cost   The cost of not selling and reinvesting the proceeds of an investment, calculated by an investor at a certain time as a measure of performance. The return that could have been earned if the money were available for investment immediately. The monetary or other advantage that is foregone today in order to obtain something that will have value in the future. Investors use the *discounted cash flow (DCF) method* to determine whether an investment in real estate will have a comparable or better yield than other investments. The discount rate is based on the rate of return on financial assets whose risk is equivalent to the risk of investing in the particular property under consideration. See also *internal rate of return* and *time value of money.*

optimum rent   Another name for *street rent.*

option   The right to purchase or lease something at a future date for a specified price and terms. The right may or may not be exercised at the option holder's (optionee's) discretion. Options may be received, negotiated, or purchased. In a lease, the right to obtain a specific condition within a specified time (e.g., to renew at the same or a pre-agreed rate when the lease term expires; to expand into adjacent space at a pre-agreed time when that space is expected to be available; to cancel the lease). Options are often incorporated in the lease as an *addendum.*

organization chart   A graphic representation of the levels of employee responsibility and authority. The chain of command within a business.

original basis   An income tax term. See *basis.*

origination fee   A charge made by a lender for placing a loan.

outdoor advertising   Advertising used outside (e.g., billboards, electric spectaculars, painted displays, and ads on buses, commuter trains, and transit cars and platforms).

outlet center   A type of specialty shopping center comprised of at least 50 percent factory outlet stores offering name-brand goods at discounted or wholesale prices. Usually the manufacturer will operate the store, eliminating the retail markup. Merchandise is usually manufacturers' surplus (e.g., seconds, irregulars, factory overruns). Compare *off-price center.*

outlot   In a shopping center, a site that is not attached to the main center; also called *out parcel* or *pad space.* The term is often applied to freestanding space in the parking lot. Outlot tenants usually include restaurants, gas stations, and drive-up banking services.

outside broker   Another name for *cooperating broker.*

outsourcing   The practice of having discrete business activities performed by entities other than direct employees of the business, often under a contractual arrangement, in order to operate the business more efficiently and reduce overhead expenses. Outsourcing is sometimes used as a means of handling short-term or one-time assignments rather than hiring staff to do the work.

overage   In retail leases, rent payments in excess of a guaranteed minimum, usually a percentage of the tenant's sales; also called *rent overage.* See also *breakpoint; percentage rent.*

overall capitalization rate (OAR)   The rate used to capitalize net operating income by relating it to value is called either the *overall rate of return* or the overall capitalization rate. The overall capitalization rate is the most common capitalization rate used. Higher cap rates result in lower values, and lower cap rates give higher values. See also *capitalization rate.*

overbuilding   A component of the *real estate cycle.* A period when real estate activity is high as a consequence of prosperity. Money is readily available from lenders for development of housing and office, store, and warehouse space to meet pent-up demand. Demand that cannot be sustained or is miscalculated leads to declining real estate values.

over-building standards   Improvements to leased office space that are installed at the tenant's expense (e.g., because they differ materially and/or cost-wise from the building standard allowance).

overdraft   The amount by which a check exceeds the funds on deposit in the account on which it is drawn.

overhead   The cost of doing business (i.e., wages, salaries, rent, insurance, taxes, utilities, etc.) that cannot be charged to a particular part of the operation. A general accounting item for all business costs that are neither direct labor nor material; *indirect costs.* In retailing, usually all expenses exclusive of the cost of goods sold or inventory.

owner   The individual or entity with the legal right of possession of a property; can also be the developer. See also *landlord.*

owner by choice   An entity who actively invests in real estate. Examples include individual investors, corporations, and partnerships.

owner by circumstance   Ownership acquired other than by choice. Examples include individuals who inherit property from relatives or others and REO (real estate owned) departments of financial institutions that hold property acquired through foreclosure.

owner's equity   An individual owner's or investor-participant's share of a business enterprise or an investment property measured as the value of the business less all financial obligations of the business and the result multiplied by the investor's percent of ownership.

owner's goals and objectives   A statement given orally or in writing by an owner of income property as to what benefits he/she wishes to receive from the income property; an important consideration in developing a management plan.

ownership   Legal right of possession. The owner or owners of a rental (apartment, office, retail, or industrial) building who contract for professional property management and/or employ a leasing agent(s).

ownership interest   The legal share (undivided interest) each unit owner of a condominium has in the common areas of the property, expressed as a percentage.

owners', landlords', and tenants' (OLT) liability insurance   Insurance that covers liability for bodily injury or damage to others' property arising out of the ownership, maintenance, or use of premises owned or occupied by the insured for which the insured may be liable. This insurance covers claims against a property owner, a landlord, or a tenant arising from bodily injury to a person or persons in or about a subject property and including the improvements on the land and any other contiguous areas for which the insured is legally responsible, such as sidewalks. This coverage is commonly included in "all risk" policies.

owner's requirements   Demands made on a budget by the owner's objectives for the property.

P

package policy An insurance plan that combines many forms of coverage.

pad See *mobile home site; outlot.*

Parcel Identification Number (PIN) Another name for *Property Identification Number* or *Property Index Number.*

parity Equivalence in value.

parking area ratio The relationship between the size of the parking area and the size of the building it is intended to serve.

parking index For a retail property, the number of parking spaces per 1,000 square feet of gross leasable area (GLA).

parking ratio At residential properties, the number of parking spaces provided for each dwelling unit constructed. At office buildings, the number of spaces per 1,000 rentable square feet.

parliamentary procedure Established rules of parliamentary law and unwritten rules of courtesy used to facilitate the transaction of business in deliberative assemblies, such as condominium or homeowners' association board meetings.

participation An agreement by a lender to join in an investment. In *income participation,* the lender receives a certain percentage of the cash flow each year. In *equity participation,* the lender receives a payment based on the appreciation or market value of the property; also called *additional interest provision (AIP).*

partition Legal action brought by a condominium unit owner to separate the owner's share of the property's common areas or common funds, based on *ownership interest.* More generally, division among several individuals of real or personal property that belongs to them as co-owners (joint tenants, tenants in common). Instead of physically partitioning the property, the court may order it sold and the proceeds divided among the owners.

partnership A form of business organization in which two or more individuals enter into business as co-owners to share in profits and losses as spelled out in a written *partnership agreement.* A form of ownership that binds the participants in shared responsibility for its debts. In a general partnership, all partners are equally and fully liable for its debts. In a limited partnership, there are one or more general partners who actively manage the business plus one or more passive partners whose liability is limited to the amount of their investment. See also *general partnership; limited partnership.*

partnership agreement   The document that spells out the roles and financial obligations of participants in a partnership.

party   An individual, partnership, corporation, or other entity engaged in a lawsuit, transaction, or agreement.

passive activities   In income tax terminology, business or trade activities in which a person does not materially participate during the year and real estate rental activities, even if the person does materially participate in them, unless the individual is a real estate professional.

passive activity income   In income tax terminology, income derived from *passive activities* and gains from disposition of an interest in a passive activity or a property used in a passive activity. Specifically excluded from this classification are portfolio income, personal service income, and a variety of other specific sources of income. See also *Tax Reform Act of 1986.*

passive activity loss(es)   In income tax terminology, losses incurred as a result of participation in *passive activities.* Under the Tax Reform Act of 1986, passive activity losses can only be deducted from passive activity income. If there is no passive income as such, passive losses can be deducted from capital gains at sale.

passive income   For tax purposes, income from investments that a taxpayer does not participate in substantially, income from activities in which the taxpayer has a limited business interest, and income from rent.

passive infrared (PIR) motion detector   A device designed to detect movement based on rapid temperature changes, as from body heat.

passive loss rules   Clauses in the tax law that allow losses from passive business activities to be used only to offset income from other passive business activities. See also *Tax Reform Act of 1986.*

pass-through charges   In commercial leasing, operating expenses of a property that are paid by the tenants, usually on a pro rata basis in addition to base rent, including real estate taxes, insurance on the property, and common area maintenance (CAM) costs. Also sometimes called *tenant charges, net charges,* or *billback items.* See also *net lease.*

pass-through clause   The terms of a lease document that specify and define which (if any) costs of operating the building are to be paid by the tenant. Such costs are often called *pass-throughs.*

pass-through escalation clause   In a retail lease, the article that passes increases in operating expenses to the tenant.

payback period   The amount of time required to recover the cost of a capital investment.

payment bond   A guarantee or assurance by a third party (surety) that a contractor will pay for all labor, material, equipment, supplies, and subcontractors used on a project, thereby protecting the property owner against claims and liens brought after the project has been completed and final payment to the contractor has been made; a type of *contract bond*. Sometimes called *labor and material payment bond*.

payroll   The total amount owed by a business to its employees for work performed during a given period. Also, the list of monies so owed and the monies to be distributed.

payroll expenses   The cost to a business of wages, vacation and sick pay, holiday pay, group medical benefits, and other employee benefits.

payroll journal   An original-entry record in which all salary and related transactions are recorded chronologically.

peaceful enjoyment   The use of real property without illegal or unreasonable interference or annoyance within the control of the party granting the use. See also *quiet enjoyment*.

pedestrian flow   The direction and patterns in which people move through a shopping center, which can be influenced by architecture and design.

pedestrian mall   In downtown shopping areas, a blocked-off set of streets containing stores where people can shop without interference from automobile traffic.

penalty   Loss or forfeiture imposed for failure to fulfill an obligation to another. Specifically, a provision in contracts often employed as an incentive to on-time performance of the contracted obligation.

pension fund   A fund into which a regular payment is made by an employer and/or the employee to provide the funds to make payments to the employee upon retirement. Also, a type of institutional investor in real estate.

per capita expenditure   A way of measuring how much each individual consumer spends in a particular retail category over the course of a year.

percentage fee   Used in referring to compensation paid monthly for management of real property based on a percentage of the gross receipts (e.g., collected rents and related revenues). The basis of the fee is negotiated individually and stated specifically in the management agreement.

percentage lease   In its most restricted use, a lease agreement used at retail properties in which the rent is a percentage of the tenant's gross sales (or net income) made on the premises. Such a percentage lease may also stipulate a minimum or a maximum rental amount. See also *percentage rent*.

percentage-of-gross fee   A property manager's regular compensation based on an agreed-to percentage of monthly gross collections.

percentage-of-loss deductible   An insurance plan under which the deductible increases as the size of the loss increases, usually up to a specified maximum amount.

percentage-of-sales clause   Used exclusively in retail leases, this clause requires the tenant to pay a specified percentage of gross sales revenue in addition to the base rent. Often the percentage rent is only required after an agreed-upon breakpoint is reached by the tenant. See also *breakpoint; overage*.

percentage rent   In retail leasing, rent that is based on a percentage of a tenant's gross sales (or sometimes net income or profits), often compared to the guaranteed minimum or base rent under the lease and paid as *overage* (i.e., the amount of percentage rent in excess of the minimum or base rent due). See also *breakpoint.* A percentage rent provision may also be written such that the tenant in a shopping center is required to pay a percentage of gross sales in lieu of minimum rent under certain circumstances (e.g., loss of an anchor tenant).

perception   Awareness developed through the senses. The term is synonymous with recognition and discernment and implies knowing and understanding. The perception of a property by potential tenants and other users affects its desirability. See also *curb appeal.*

per diem   Allowance, payment, charge, or rent established on a daily basis.

performance   Fulfillment of terms of a contract or lease.

performance appraisal   A formal evaluation of an employee's fulfillment of the duties and responsibilities of the job. The periodic and realistic assessment of an employee's progress on the job; also called *performance evaluation* or *performance review.*

performance bond   A guarantee or assurance by a third party (surety) that a contractor will perform and complete the contract as per agreement; a type of *contract bond.*

performance evaluation   Another name for *performance appraisal.*

performance review   Another name for *performance appraisal.*

performing assets   Properties that are currently profitable but which could be more profitable.

peril   In insurance, a condition that can cause loss (e.g., fire).

perimeter security   Security measures that protect the exterior of a building, extended to include the boundaries of the property when there is land area surrounding the building.

period of transfer   The time during which the developer transfers control of a condominium association to the unit owners, and the owners must learn to accept responsibilities for running the association.

permanent loan   Financing for a period of ten or more years; a *permanent mortgage.* A long-term loan that finances the purchase of an existing building or replaces a construction loan for a new development. A permanent mortgage loan commitment is often necessary before a construction loan can be arranged. See also *mortgage.*

personal identification number (PIN)   A numeric code (a type of password) used to access electronically controlled security devices (e.g., locks, lockboxes). Also required for electronic access to an individual's protected financial information and accounts when using an automated teller machine (ATM) or the Internet. See also *lockbox.*

personal income tax   See *tax.*

personal injury   In insurance, injury or damage to one's reputation, as by libel, slander, false arrest, defamation, or invasion of privacy, differentiated from *bodily injury* (physical pain, illness, impairment) to one's person and *property damage.* Liability insurance coverage is sought to protect against claims for money damages by an injured party.

personal injury liability insurance   A policy that covers alleged injury due to a social injustice such as libel or slander (defamation of character), invasion of privacy (wrongful entry or eviction), or false arrest (detention or imprisonment and malicious prosecution).

personal property   Movable property belonging to an individual, family, or other entity that is not permanently affixed to real property, such as clothing, fixtures, and furnishings; distinguished from real property; also called *personalty* or *chattel*. In real estate, the furniture, blinds and drapes, office equipment, appliances, and other items that belong to the property owner apart from the land and the improvements to it. Also, the items owned outright by the tenant in leased premises. In states in which mobile homes are considered personal property, no property taxes are levied on individual mobile homes (only the land they stand on).

personalty   Another name for *personal property.*

pesticide   A substance used to inhibit, destroy, or repel a pest.

pet agreement   A lease addendum that authorizes a tenant to keep a specific pet on the premises as long as certain conditions are met. A pet agreement is actually a separate document that constitutes a license granted by the landlord to the tenant. As such, it can be revoked or canceled without affecting the lease itself.

phantom space   Another name for *shadow space.*

physical life   The length of time for which a building is a sound structure, which depends on the quality of maintenance. In appraisal, the estimated period of time that a building will remain functional and habitable. See also *useful life.*

physical maintenance   Inspection, cleaning, and repair of a physical plant to keep it in proper working condition.

physical obsolescence   A condition of aging (deterioration) or deferred maintenance of a property.

physical security   A system of tangible countermeasures designed to control or limit access to a building or a property, including barriers designed in concentric layers surrounding the property, with security growing progressively tighter the closer you get to the center or objective.

physical vacancy   The number of vacant units in a building or development that are available for rent, usually expressed as a percentage of the total number of units. See also *economic vacancy.*

physical vacancies   Commonly used in rental housing to mean units that are unoccupied but actually available for rent.

pilot circles   Another name for *quality circles.*

plaintiff   The person (injured party) who files a lawsuit or complaint.

planned unit development (PUD)   A type of development that usually includes a mixture of open space, single-family homes, townhouses, condominiums or cooperatives, rental units, and recreational and commercial facilities within a defined area under a specific zoning arrangement. Generally, PUDs are large in scale and built in several phases over a number of years. Typically, all infrastructure for the site is constructed before the improvements are built. Also, a *zoning* classification that allows flexibility in the design of a subdivision, usually setting an overall density limit which allows clustering of units to provide for common open space.

plat   A survey plan or map and descriptions of a tract of land showing property lines, easements, and other appropriate features.

plumbing chase   A duct space or enclosure inside partition walls to house plumbing lines and vent stacks.

points   An upfront percentage fee paid for a loan that increases the overall yield to the lender. One point equals one percent of the original amount of the loan; also called *discount points*. Lenders may charge one or more points at closing of a real estate purchase as a service fee to secure the loan or as additional interest (lender's profit).

police   The department of local government charged with maintaining public order and enforcement of the law. Also, the act of patrolling an area to maintain a clean and orderly appearance.

police power   The right of a governmental agency to enact and enforce regulations regarding the health, safety, and general welfare of the population within its jurisdiction.

policy   A statement of general intent that tells what is permitted or expected. A previously established guiding principle, rule of action, or method of action. When written policies exist, management responds to a variety of events more consistently and effectively because decisions have been given careful consideration before an incident occurs or an issue arises. In mobile home park management, applicable landlord-tenant law may require presentation of written statements of policy to prospects and residents. In insurance, the written contract made between an insurance company and a person or business entity (the insured) to provide specific insurance coverage.

policyholder   The person or business entity for whom an insurance policy is written.

polychlorinated biphenyls (PCBs)   Organic compounds produced by replacing hydrogen atoms on a biphenyl with chlorine (Cl) atoms. PCBs are used in various industrial applications, including heat transfer agents in electrical transformers. Because of their toxicity, new use was banned by law in 1979.

population   The total number of individuals occupying a defined geographic area.

population shift   Movement of a large number of people from one place to another over a period of time.

portable presentation   Drawings, models, slide programs, films, and other transportable means used to promote a product or to lease rental space.

portfolio   A selection of assets held by an investor.

portfolio income   For tax purposes, income derived from investments, interest, and dividends.

portfolio theory   In financial analysis, a concept used in portfolio management that involves assessing risks and making decisions about what level of risk is acceptable for certain kinds of investments.

possession   Occupancy or control of property. The right to use and enjoy leased premises.

power center   A large strip shopping center anchored by several large promotional, warehouse, or specialty stores that dominate their merchandising categories and having very few small shops; originally called *promotional center*.

power of attorney   A written instrument authorizing another to act in one's behalf as his/her agent or attorney.

preamble   An introduction to a contract that identifies its purpose and establishes its legality.

preferred stock   See *stock*.

preleasing   The leasing of space in a project under construction in order to achieve a high occupancy level upon completion. Usually a certain percentage of space is required to be preleased to obtain construction financing.

premium   An amount paid in addition to the nominal value of an item, as an amount paid to obtain a loan apart from or in addition to interest. The amount paid periodically by an insured party to obtain and retain insurance coverage.

prepaid expense   An expense incurred for future benefit or paid before it is currently due.

prepayment clause   A provision in a mortgage or other loan instrument that gives the borrower the right to pay off the indebtedness before it becomes due. See also *prepayment penalty*.

prepayment penalty   An extra stipulated charge for paying off all or part of a loan on real property in advance. A cash penalty for paying off a mortgage loan before its date of maturity.

prepayment provision   A loan document clause that imposes a penalty if the borrower pays off the loan before the due date.

presentation book   A visual aid used by leasing agents to stimulate the interest of a prospective tenant in specific office space.

present value (PV)   The current dollar value of a sum of money to be received in the future which has been discounted by a given percentage rate. The amount one would have to invest today at a given rate for the period to yield the future sum.

press release   A straightforward, newsworthy story for release to the print and broadcast media, usually prepared following a standard format and including information about the entity distributing it; also called *news release*.

prestige   One's standing or estimation in the eyes of other people; esteem. In real estate, the status that individuals or businesses acquire from a property's desirable location and tenancy.

pre-tax cash flow   See *cash flow*.

prevailing rental rate   The rental rate a current resident pays for an apartment. Also, the typical rate being charged in an area for similar size apartments.

preventive maintenance   A program of regularly scheduled inspection and care that allows potential problems to be prevented or at least detected and solved before major repairs are needed. See also *corrective maintenance; deferred maintenance.*

price   The exchange value of a good or service at a particular time as expressed in terms of money.

price fixing   Collusion between members of a group (e.g., owners and managers) to set prices (or rental rates).

price index   A database that traces the changes in prices of a selection of representative commodities over specified time spans.

pricing   The method of setting a price (in money) for a good or service.

primary financing   The first loan that is recorded on a property, which has a lien priority ahead of any other loan filed or recorded after it.

primary metropolitan statistical area (PMSA)   See *metropolitan area.*

prime rate   The lowest interest rate available from commercial banks for short-term loans to their most creditworthy customers (i.e., those whose credit standing is so high that little lender risk is involved), such loans being repayable on demand by the lender.

prime tenant   A tenant that occupies more space than any other tenant in a commercial property. A major tenant in a shopping center or office building.

principal   In real estate, one who owns property. In real estate management, the property owner who contracts for the services of an agent. In finance, the amount of money that is borrowed in a loan as distinct from the interest on such loan; the original amount or remaining balance of a loan. Also, the original amount of capital invested. In law, the individual being represented in a business transaction by an agent authorized to do so.

principle of substitution   The premise that when several similar or commensurate commodities, goods, or services are available, the one with the lowest price attracts the greatest demand and widest distribution.

print media   Any and all printed advertising vehicles, including newspapers, magazines, and trade journals.

private limited partnership   A type of *limited partnership* having thirty-five or fewer investors and not usually required to register with the Securities and Exchange Commission (SEC) although a certificate may have to be filed with state authorities.

private mortgage insurance (PMI)   Insurance that protects lenders making risky loans in financing real estate purchases, including single-family housing, multi-family housing, and commercial and industrial properties, often required when the buyer's downpayment is minimal. Compare *mortgage insurance.*

probationary status   A step in the process of *progressive discipline.* The status upon which an employee is placed for a specified period of time, during which the employee must rectify the unacceptable behavior or action.

procedure   The specific series of related chronological steps that are adopted as the accepted way of performing a given activity or function.

proceeds   Money received by the seller of an asset after debt payment, costs of sale, and commissions are deducted. Funds given to a borrower after all interest costs and fees have been deducted from the loan amount. The income (cash flow) from an investment property. See also *net proceeds.*

Producer Price Index (PPI)   A price index tracked by the federal Bureau of Labor Statistics based on goods, services, labor, and raw materials used by American manufacturers. It measures cost pressures on manufacturers.

professional association   A group of professionals organized for education, social interaction, lobbying, and such other activities as will benefit individual members. Compare *trade association.*

Professional Community Association Manager (PCAM)   A designation conferred by the Community Associations Institute (CAI) on individuals who have met certain minimum requirements as to experience, education, and participation in the profession of association management.

professional liability insurance   Insurance against a monetary loss caused by failure to meet a professional standard or resulting from negligent actions (e.g., malpractice). In real estate management, insurance to protect against liabilities resulting from honest mistakes and oversights (no protection is provided in cases of gross negligence); also called *errors and omissions (E&O) insurance.* Policies that protect directors and officers of corporations are also available. See *directors' and officers' liability insurance.*

profit   Any excess of revenues over the costs incurred to obtain those revenues. The surplus earned in a business when the price received for a good or service exceeds the cost of producing it.

profit and loss statement   A summary of the revenues and expenses of a business (or an investment property) for a particular period of time, generally one year; also called *operating statement.*

profit margin   The percentage of profit realized by a business for each dollar of sales. The difference between gross sales dollars and net sales dollars—what remains after all costs are accounted for—expressed as a percentage of net sales.

profit sharing   The practice of distributing a portion of a firm's profits to some or all of its employees, usually as a bonus in addition to regular wages and salaries.

pro forma   According to prescribed form. In reference to preparing financial statements or budgets, use of hypothetical numbers for illustrative purposes. In real estate development, a financial projection for a proposed project based on certain specified assumptions and reflecting construction costs, financing, leasing rates and velocity, and operating costs. An unofficial financial statement that projects gross income, operating expenses, and net operating income (NOI) for existing rental real estate based on specific assumptions; a *pro forma statement.* Also, a projection of gross income and net operating income of a stabilized property; a *budget.*

pro forma statement   A projection of future earnings and expenses based on specific assumptions.

program budget   A budget format in which expense items are listed according to the program or activity for which they will be disbursed (e.g., all anticipated maintenance expenditures, possibly including related contract and payroll costs, would be consolidated in a single maintenance line item).

progressive discipline   A step-wise process for dealing with problem employees that may start with an oral reprimand(s) and progress through one or more written reprimands and, if the situation or behavior is not corrected, lead to termination. See also *probationary status.*

projected completion date   The date the contractor expects to have a building completed and ready for occupancy. A term used in renting up a residential property when a unit is more than 60 days away from completion. See also *scheduled completion date.*

promissory note   A written promise to pay a specified sum of money to a specific person or firm under specified terms (a stated interest rate, a schedule of payments, and a due date).

promotion   The overall activity intended to further or advance a business, particularly by increasing sales of its products and services. In staffing, appointment to a position of higher rank. In real estate management, the entire spectrum of marketing activities related to leasing.

promotional aid   A gift, usually marked with the name of the giver, used as part of a promotional campaign for a product or service; also called *handout* or *giveaway* and sometimes referred to as a *promotional item.* Used in real estate management to interest prospective tenants in leasing space at a particular property.

promotional center   The original name for *power center.*

promotional fund   Another name for *marketing fund.*

proof of loss   A formal written statement of a claim for payment of a loss, with supporting data. A requirement for insurance claims.

property analysis   In-depth investigation of the various characteristics of a property. Usually undertaken as a complete study of a piece of real estate, including its architectural design, buildings and improvements, physical condition, location, services provided, and tenant profile. Also, a study of a property referring to such items as deferred maintenance, functional and economic obsolescence, land location and zoning, exterior construction and condition, plant and equipment, unit mix, facilities, and expected income and expenses with the intent of developing a management plan.

property-based assistance   Housing assistance that is tied to a particular property instead of to residents. In one program, government buys down a portion of the owner's mortgage and reduces the rate of interest on a loan. The owner must offer reduced rents to eligible tenants to comply with the mortgage terms. In another program, a local housing authority provides mixed-income housing by leasing a portion of a rental complex from the property owner for low-income residents or pays a certain percentage of eligible tenants' rents at designated properties. Compare *resident-based assistance.*

property damage insurance   Insurance protecting against liability for damage to or destruction of others' property that may result from occurrences in or about a specified property, or because of the insured party's negligent action or inaction, and for which the insured is legally liable. Also called *property damage liability insurance.*

property grading system   See *office building classification.*

Property Identification Number (PIN)   A numeric code assigned by local jurisdictions to identify specific parcels of real estate for property tax purposes; also called *Property Index Number* and *Parcel Identification Number.*

property inspection   A systematic process of examining a property to determine which items require physical maintenance.

property insurance   A policy that protects the insured against direct or indirect loss arising out of damage, destruction, or other loss of real or personal property.

property management   A professional activity in which someone other than the owner supervises the operation of a property according to the owner's objectives; also referred to as *real estate management.* The operation of income-producing real estate as a business, including leasing, rent collection, maintenance of the property, and general administration. Usually, this is performed by someone who acts as the owner's agent (i.e., a professional property manager).

property management fee   See *management fee.*

property manager   A knowledgeable professional who has the experience and skills to operate real estate and understands the fundamentals of business management. The person who supervises the day-to-day operation of a property, making sure it is properly leased, well maintained, competitive with other sites, and otherwise managed according to the owner's objectives. The chief operating officer or administrator of a particular property or group of properties.

property supervisor   Service- and detail-oriented professional who oversees operations of a property or group of properties and is responsible for the performance of personnel and maintenance of properties under his/her supervision in accordance with company policies and procedures; sometimes also called *regional property manager* or *executive property manager.* The term is applied to those in a higher-level position. A property supervisor would have more experience and greater expertise than a property manager.

property tax   A tax levied on various kinds of real and personal property by state and local governments based on the nature of improvements to the land, fair market value, and assessed valuation.

proposed completion date   A term used when construction of a residential unit is within 60 days of completion but more than 30 days away. See also *projected completion date.*

proprietary lease   A document that gives a shareholder in a cooperative the right to occupy a specified unit subject to certain conditions. See also *cooperative.*

pro rata   Proportionately. In real estate ownership and leasing, based on the size of individually owned or leased spaces in relation to the whole. Condominium owners and commercial tenants commonly pay proportionate shares of operating expenses and other costs. See also *pass-through charges.*

pro rata share   A retail tenant's share of operating expenses—e.g., HVAC charges, common area maintenance (CAM) fees, taxes, insurance, etc.—computed as a percentage by dividing the gross leasable area (GLA) of the tenant's space by the GLA of the shopping center.

prorate   To divide, distribute, or assess in proportionate shares.

prorated   Divided proportionately, as rent for a period of less than a month.

prospect   A potential customer. In real estate and its management, a potential client (property owner) or potential residential or commercial tenant.

prospect card   A (usually standardized) card form on which information about a potential tenant is recorded for purposes of future contact. May also be used to document all follow-up with a prospect until a decision is made whether or not to sign a lease.

prospecting   The systematic search for potential tenants through personal interaction, which includes referrals, canvassing, and cooperation with business colleagues (e.g., leasing brokers). See also *canvassing; cold calling.*

prosperity   Part of the *business cycle,* a period of economic growth characterized by business expansion, increased consumer spending, and low levels of unemployment.

protected class   A group, usually a *minority* in the population, specifically protected against discrimination under the U.S. Civil Rights Act of 1964 and later amendments to that law. Protected classes include race, religion, color, national origin, and sex; in regard to housing, familial status and disability are also protected classes. Other protected classes may be created under state and local laws. See also *fair housing laws.* Color, race, national origin, sex, and disability are also protected classes in regard to employment; specific protections are delineated in the *Civil Rights Acts of 1964/1968* and the *Americans with Disabilities Act (ADA).*

psychographic profile   An analysis of a retail trade area that goes beyond numbers and dollars to examine values, attitudes, and similar phenomena. See also *demographic profile; trade area.*

psychographics   A qualitative methodology for compiling information about people's individual personalities and lifestyles, it goes beyond demographics to uncover personal preferences and attitudes that numbers alone do not reveal; a tool of market research. In leasing, used to determine what factors about a property are likely to appeal to particular prospective tenants (more specifically applicable to individual consumers in regard to apartment leasing). See also *market research.*

public accommodation   Under the *Americans with Disabilities Act (ADA),* a facility operated by a private entity whose operations affect commerce, including places of lodging, establishments serving food or drink, places of exhibition or entertainment, places of public gathering, sales or rental establishments, service establishments, stations used for public transportation, places of public display or collection, places of recreation, places of education, social service centers, and places of exercise or recreation. In order to comply with ADA accessibility requirements, public accommodations must (1) modify discriminatory practices, policies, and procedures; (2) provide auxiliary aids and services to facilitate communication with disabled people; and (3) remove structural and communications barriers where removal is "readily achievable." (The law defines an array of twenty-one alterations that are considered readily achievable.)

public adjuster   The name commonly used to refer to the individual or company that represents the insured party in an insurance claim. See also *adjuster; independent adjuster.*

public area   Space in a property for general public use that is not restricted for use by any lease or other agreements, as a lobby, corridor, or court.

public housing   Housing owned by and/or managed for a local or state governmental agency. The principal form of low-income housing available in the

United States. A form of *property-based* housing *assistance.* Compare *subsidized housing; government-assisted housing.*

public housing agency (PHA) The state, county, municipal, or other local governmental agency or public body established to administer funds and manage the operation of housing for low-income persons.

public image The image (perception) of a firm created in the public's mind by public relations.

publicity The technique of drawing attention to a person or a company by telling a story. Real estate management firms use publicity techniques to establish and enhance their position in the local market and the industry at large, to build name recognition, and to enhance their image.

public limited partnership A type of *limited partnership* with an unlimited number of participants that is required to register with the Securities and Exchange Commission (SEC) when the number of partners and the value of their assets reach certain levels.

public relations A business activity whose purpose is to secure publicity, contacts, and market exposure by means other than paid advertising. Activities undertaken to improve the public image of a firm in order to meet its marketing objectives. The promotion of goodwill between one entity and other entities by distribution of information and assessment of public reaction. Public relations is aimed at developing a good rapport between the public, a business, and the business's clients. Also an important component of emergency procedures planning and implementation *(crisis public relations).*

Pullman kitchen A small non-walk-in kitchen, often in a closet-sized space, with appliances and equipment aligned in a row.

punch list A list of office space improvements, both building standard and tenant paid, that should be finished or accounted for before move-in. Used for reference by management to guide final inspection of built-out premises before delivery. A marked punch list documents that the items punched were completed by the contractor in a good, workmanlike manner in respect to the contract documents and makes clear the items yet to be completed.

punitive damages Monetary damages in larger amounts, above what will compensate for the loss itself, awarded to compensate the complainant for aggravating circumstances (e.g., mental anguish). They are also intended to punish and make an example of the wrongdoer.

purchase option A chance to buy a property if specific conditions are fulfilled.

purchase order (P.O.) Written authorization to an outside vendor to provide certain goods or services in a given amount, at a given price, to be delivered at a certain time and place. Purchase orders are usually preprinted, sequentially numbered forms with multiple copies to ensure that appropriate departments of the company have a record of all such transactions. Once accepted by the supplier, the purchase order becomes a legally binding contract.

Q

qualification   In real estate management, the process of judging prospective tenants' financial status or creditworthiness to determine their ability to fulfill the terms of the lease, especially the payment of rent and other charges. In commercial property management, determination that a potential tenant will be acceptable to the building and that the building will meet the tenant's needs. Retail tenants are also evaluated on their ability as merchants and their compatibility with the array of tenants in the shopping center. Also used in referring to degree of expertise, including licensing or certification, as of real estate managers and other professionals.

quality circles   A marketing program for shopping centers whereby retail tenants are divided into groups, also called *pilot circles,* with each group responsible for planning and supervising at least two promotional programs or marketing "flights" in a year's total program. The quality circle is a compromise between the *merchants' association* and the *marketing fund.*

quiet enjoyment   The use of real property by a tenant without illegal or unreasonable interference or annoyance by the landlord or others. A right granted under landlord-tenant law—the right to privacy, peace and quiet, and use of the leased space, common areas, and facilities. A clause included in most leases stating that the tenant has a right of possession of the leased premises without undue disturbance by others (the owner, other tenants). See also *peaceful enjoyment.*

quitclaim deed   A deed that does not convey warranties of ownership; only the rights and interests of the grantor are transferred to the grantee. A quitclaim (or release) deed is often used to clear some kind of title problem. See also *general warranty deed.*

quotation   Also called *quote.* Another name for *bid.*

R

radon A naturally occurring radioactive gas, chemical symbol Rn, formed by the disintegration (radioactive decay) of radium. Radon migrates through soil and enters buildings through porous foundation materials and along water and gas lines. It is considered a potential hazard to human health, most particularly in residential buildings, especially those that have been tightly sealed to prevent heat loss because they are usually less well ventilated than commercial buildings.

radius clause A provision in a retail lease that prevents a retailer from opening and operating a similar—and therefore competitive—business within a certain radius (distance in all directions) from the shopping center, normally expressed in miles.

range A statistical term used when expressing the lowest and highest prices or rental rates.

rape Unlawful sexual intercourse against a person's will or under threat of bodily injury. Rape is classified as a *felony*. Assault with the intent to commit rape is likewise a felony. Failure to report a rape, which is a violent crime, is a *misdemeanor*. In addition to filing a police report, instances of rape are often documented in order to monitor the effectiveness of security at a managed property. Documenting crime is a critical component of *risk management*. All instances of rape should be documented and, in the event of any liability exposure, such documentation would be used to report a potential claim to the insurance company.

rate holder A type of advertising *contract rate*.

rate of return (ROR) The percentage of income derived from an investment over a specific time span, often for a single year.

reach In advertising terms, the specific audience a medium touches—the paid subscriptions to a periodical, the listening or viewing audience of broadcast media.

real estate Land; also, freehold estates in land. A portion of the earth's surface extending downward to the center of the earth and upward into space including all things permanently attached to the land by nature or by mankind.

real estate broker   Any person, partnership, association, or corporation who, for compensation or valuable consideration, sells or offers for sale, buys or offers to buy, or negotiates the purchase, sale, or exchange of real estate, or who leases or offers to rent any real estate or the improvements on it for others. Unless employed directly by the owner to offer the owner's property, such a broker must have a state license.

real estate cycle   Recurring periods of high and low activity in real estate markets, sequentially identified as *overbuilding, adjustment, stabilization,* and *development,* which generally follow their counterparts in the business cycle.

real estate investment trust (REIT)   An entity that sells shares of beneficial interest to investors and uses the funds to invest in real estate or real estate mortgages. Real estate investment trusts must meet certain requirements such as a minimum number of investors and widely dispersed ownership. No corporate taxes need to be paid as long as a series of complex Internal Revenue Service qualifications are met. See also *shares of beneficial interest.*

real estate management   A profession in which someone other than the owner (a real estate manager) supervises the operation of a property according to the owner's objectives; also referred to as *property management.*

real estate mortgage investment conduit (REMIC)   For income tax purposes, a separate legal entity, created by the Tax Reform Act of 1986, into which mortgage issuers (e.g., lenders) can "sell" mortgage assets which then become the basis for issuance of mortgage-backed securities.

real estate owned (REO) property   A property whose ownership has reverted to the lender due to foreclosure.

real estate portfolio   All real estate investments owned by an investor (e.g., an individual, a corporation).

real estate tax   See *property tax; tax.*

real property   The rights, interests, and benefits inherent in the ownership of real estate. Also used as a synonym for the terms real estate and realty, which refer to the land itself and everything attached to it.

Real Property Administrator (RPA)   A professional designation granted by BOMI Institute.

REALTOR®   A registered trademark reserved for the sole use of active members of local boards of REALTORS® affiliated with the National Association of REALTORS® (NAR).

realty   Another name for *real estate.*

reasonable accommodations   Changes to policies and procedures that may be required to allow a disabled person to use and enjoy the property, specifically housing.

reasonable modifications   Physical changes to a property that allow a disabled person full use of the premises. Modifications may be made to a unit interior or to any common area not open to the public (e.g., laundry rooms or storage areas). Modifications may be made at any time during a tenancy, and the disabled person is responsible for the cost of such modifications and for restoring the unit to original condition, as may be appropriate, when tenancy terminates. Accessibility of public accommodations (at residential properties, lobbies, rental offices, and other areas open to the public) are covered under the *Americans with Disabilities Act (ADA)*.

rebate   Return of part of a payment representing a deduction from the full amount previously charged and paid.

recapitulation statement   An annual balanced cash statement customarily prepared by real estate managers showing all receipts, disbursements, and reserves accumulated for an established twelve-month period; also called *recap statement*.

recapture   An income tax term describing money taken back or forfeited; a kind of tax penalty. For example, if a tax deduction was taken but does not meet all conditions, the deduction will be disallowed and the taxpayer will be required to pay tax on the income that had been offset by the deduction. This money is said to be recaptured by the taxing body.

receiver   An individual appointed by a court to manage a property that is the subject of a pending *bankruptcy* or *foreclosure*. A receiver's role is to preserve property that has been abandoned or for which there have been allegations of fraud or mismanagement by the owner. In some states, property is assigned to a receiver during the statutory redemption period after a foreclosure sale.

receivership   Court-ordered turnover of a property to an impartial third party *(receiver)* so that it may be preserved for the benefit of the affected parties. A special trust set up to hold and administer property under litigation.

recertification of income   In assisted housing, verification of tenant income and status to ensure that a tenant is still eligible for the housing program. Occurs annually for all public housing or assisted/subsidized tenants. However, if tenant status or income changes, interim recertification is required.

recession   Part of the *business cycle,* a period of reduced general economic activity characterized by tightened credit, reduced consumer and business spending, and declining employment, profits, production, and sales that is not as severe or protracted as a depression.

reciprocal easement agreement (REA)   In shopping centers, an agreement between anchor tenant(s) and landlord regarding rights of use of each other's property, specifically the use of each other's parking area for customer parking.

reconciliation   In accounting, the bringing into agreement of two or more financial records by accounting for all outstanding items. At commercial properties, comparison of actual operating expenses to estimated expense amounts used to collect *pass-through charges,* usually done at the end of the calendar year or the fiscal year established for the owner or the property.

reconciliation billing   Billing to tenants to reconcile the difference between estimated pass-through charges paid by the tenant and actual operating expenses of the property owed by the tenant. The difference is billed or credited (or refunded) to the tenant as appropriate.

record keeping   The overall process of accurately accounting for income and expenses, as of a managed property, in order to facilitate budgeting for future operations and preparation of regular financial statements for the owner.

records retention   Usually used in reference to the archiving and storage of business records and documents. Many types of accounting and personnel records are required to be retained for specific periods of time prescribed by law.

recourse   The right to demand payment, as of a loan.

recourse covenant   A loan provision that allows the lender to require the borrower to pay the debt out of his/her own personal assets. In the event of default, the lender can claim other assets of the borrower in addition to the property pledged as collateral for the loan.

recovery   Part of the *business cycle,* a period of economic upturn following a depression characterized by increasing demand for goods and services and rising prices. Also, obtaining something by a court judgment.

recreational lease   A long-term agreement under which a developer retains ownership of a condominium's recreational facilities and allows unit owners to use them for a specified time in exchange for compensation in the form of rent.

recreational vehicle (RV)   A dwelling unit not intended for year-round use (although some are so used). Generally perceived as movable vacation homes, recreational vehicles are often motorized and can be driven or towed from site to site. Specific definitions of recreational vehicles exist for state licensing purposes; these definitions may differ from state to state.

recurring expenses   Operating expenses that recur monthly or periodically, such as those for utilities, supplies, salaries, waste disposal services, insurance, and taxes.

recyclables   Materials that can be recovered and reused rather than disposed of as waste. Used specifically in regard to products manufactured from metals, glass, and various types of plastics that can be re-used as raw materials to create new products.

recycle   To reuse materials, usually reclaiming raw materials for use in another form. In real estate, to change the use of a building, as to convert office or warehouse space into rental apartments; *adaptive use.*

recycling   Minimizing the generation of waste by recovering usable materials that might otherwise be disposed. Also, the reprocessing of various materials (e.g., paper, glass, aluminum, and various types of plastic) into usable new products.

redemption period   A period established by state laws during which the property owner has the right to redeem his/her real estate from a foreclosure or a tax sale by paying the sale price, interest, and costs. (Many states do not have mortgage redemption laws.)

referral fee   A fee paid to a referral service by management or by a prospective apartment resident when a referral results in a signed lease. A fee paid by one real estate broker to another for the referral of a prospective tenant or client.

referral program   In apartment leasing, a marketing vehicle that offers residents incentives to refer others to a property. If a prospect is accepted for tenancy, the referring resident receives some material benefit such as an improvement to his/her apartment. (In some states, real estate law prohibits this practice, defining such payment as a *commission.*)

referrals   Potential occupants (residents, tenants) suggested by satisfied current occupants, business associates, persons in influential positions, and friends.

referral service   A business that specializes in locating apartments for prospective residents or locating residents for vacant apartments.

refinancing   Obtaining a new loan to pay off an existing loan, using the same property as collateral.

refurbishing   Superficial change, the minimum that one might do to a property. To freshen up or clean is to *refurbish*.

region   The market area in which changes in economic conditions (e.g., employment, population, income) are likely to affect the fiscal performance of a particular property and thereby determine its value. For purposes of market analysis in real estate management, the *metropolitan statistical area (MSA)* in which a property is located.

regional analysis   An examination of the general economic and demographic conditions and physical aspects of an area surrounding a property and the trends that affect it. A detailed study of a region, usually the area surrounding and including one or more neighboring cities, to determine the force of various factors affecting the economic welfare of a section of the region, such as population growth and movement, employment, industrial and business activity, transportation facilities, tax structures, topography, improvements, and trends. A usual component of a management plan.

regional center   A large shopping center anchored by two or three major retailers, at least one of which is a full-line department store, and usually developed as an enclosed mall having 250,000–900,000 square feet of gross leasable area (GLA). See also *super regional center.*

regional property manager   Another name for *property supervisor.*

Registered in Apartment Management (RAM)   A professional certification granted by the National Association of Home Builders (NAHB).

regulatory agreement   In assisted housing, the contract between a property owner and a particular governmental agency that establishes, among other things, the conditions that must be met to obtain financial assistance.

rehabilitation   The process of restoring something damaged or deteriorated to a prior good condition. The restoration of improvements to real property to a satisfactory condition without changing their plan or style.

re-lease   To rent again, usually involving a cancellation of the previous lease; to *re-let.*

release deed   Another name for *quitclaim deed.*

reminder notice   A notice sent to tenants when rent is past due. See also *late notice.*

remodeling   Physical changes to a building or property short of changing its use (i.e., reconstruction).

rendering   A perspective drawing finished with ink or color to bring out the effect of a design (e.g., an architect's drawing of a proposed building or development).

renewal   The granting or obtaining of an extension, as of a lease, for an additional period upon expiration of the original term. In residential rentals, a new lease may be presented to the current tenant, or the tenant may be sent a *renewal notice* that states the new term and any required adjustment of the rental rate. As with a lease, the renewal notice (document) must be signed by both parties to be valid. Once signed, it becomes part of the lease (i.e., a *lease amendment*).

renewal clause   A lease provision giving a tenant the right to renew the lease for an additional period upon the expiration of the original lease term; also called *renewal option*. The clause will provide for notification to landlord of the tenant's intention to renew. Adjustment of rent may also be addressed.

renewal rate   The rental rate a current tenant will pay when the lease is renewed.

renovation   The process of restoring to a former state of soundness or newness. A general term covering the modernization, rehabilitation, or remodeling of existing real estate.

rent   Payment for the use of space or personal property owned by another. In real estate, a fixed periodic payment by a tenant to an owner for the exclusive possession and use of leased property.

rentable area   In a residential property, the combined rentable area of all dwelling units. The rentable area of a unit is calculated by multiplying length times width of the apartment, with no discounts for interior partitions, plumbing chases, and other small niches. Balconies, patios, and unheated porches are not included in these measurements. Sometimes called *net rentable area*. In an office building, the area on which rent is based and which generally includes the space available for tenants' exclusive use plus identified common areas less any major vertical penetrations (air shafts, stairways, elevators) in the building. The term is applied to the building as a whole, to individual floors, and to portions of floors. Compare *usable area*.

rental agent   A staff member responsible for leasing apartments.

rental agreement   A *lease*.

rental clause   Another name for *rent clause*.

rental grid   In apartment management, a listing of the types of units in the building, showing for each type the number of units and the base rent. Additional columns are included to list rent adjustments for each unit type based on special features (e.g., different views, new carpeting).

rental ledger   A record of rent received, date of receipt, period covered, and other related information for each individual tenant; also called *rent ledger* or *tenant ledger.*

rental office   Space on a property used for leasing.

rental price level   An indicator that moves up or down in response to changes in the supply of and demand for rental space and reveals the economic strength of the real estate market.

rental property operations insurance   An insurance policy for income-producing properties that provides for specific kinds of coverage (e.g., fine arts, valuable papers, rental value).

rental schedule   A listing of rental rates for space in a given building (e.g., for units or suites or per square foot); also called *rent schedule.*

rent clause   A lease provision that states the amount of rent to be paid, the method of payment, and when and to whom payment is to be made; sometimes also called *rental clause.* In commercial property leases, such a clause may refer to *base rent* only, or it may include provision for rent increases, either directly or by reference to an *escalation clause.*

rent collection policy   The set of procedures needed to ensure that tenants make rental payments on the day established in the lease document. Usual practice is for rent to be due and payable on the first of the month.

rent control   State or local laws that regulate rental rates, usually to limit the amount of rent increases and their frequency.

renters by choice   People who prefer to rent, either for the freedom from home maintenance or because their need for living space is limited, even though they may be able to afford to buy a home. Renters by choice include career professionals, senior citizens, and parents of grown children (empty-nesters).

renters by circumstance   Persons and households whose current situations require them to rent on a temporary basis; also called *renters by necessity.* These are people who cannot afford to buy a home and those who are trying to save enough money for a downpayment as well as students and families with children.

renters' insurance   Insurance coverage for tenants' personal possessions, which are not covered by a landlord's insurance policies.

rent escalation clause   Another name for *escalation clause.*

rent escalator clause   Another name for *escalator clause.*

rent ledger   Another name for *rental ledger.*

rent loss   In measuring property income, the incremental deficiency resulting from vacancies, bad debts (delinquencies), and the like. The difference between projected rental income (for a given period) and actual rents collected and collectible.

rent loss insurance   Coverage that makes up for lost income when damage from a fire or other peril interrupts or terminates the flow of rental income to the property.

rent overage   Another name for *overage.*

rent roll   In residential property, a listing of each rental unit described by size and type. This also includes the following information if the unit is rented: amount of monthly rent, tenant name, lease expiration date, and any security deposit collected (or being held); also called *rent schedule.* For a residential property, the rent roll may also list rent and other payments received.

Usually at commercial properties, the rent roll does not indicate payments received; these are reported separately (e.g., a *collections summary*) because of the payments in addition to rent (e.g., pass-through charges, tenant improvement allowance reimbursement). However, it may include information about rent escalations and when they apply. In a shopping center, such a listing may be called a *tenant roster.*

rent schedule   A listing of the rental rates for each space in a property; also called *rental schedule*. See also *rent roll*.

rents insurance   Often used in real estate investments where rental income is a key factor in meeting financing commitments, a form of indirect loss coverage that indemnifies the owner (holds the owner harmless) if the rental income stream is interrupted or stopped because of an insured peril (e.g., fire).

rent step-up   Another name for rent escalation. See *escalation clause*.

rent-up budget   Another name for *lease-up budget*.

rent-up period   The time following construction, renovation, or conversion that is required for a rental property to achieve specified occupancy rates and projected income levels; also called *lease-up* or *rent-up*.

rent-up program   Another name for *lease-up program*.

repair   To restore to function by replacing a part or putting together (mending) something that is broken.

replacement cost   The estimated cost to replace or restore a building to its pre-existing condition and appearance (and in compliance with applicable current building codes); a common method of determining insurance coverage. In appraisal, the cost at current prices to replace an existing building with one of equal utility. In insurance, replacement cost coverage reimburses the total cost of rebuilding; no deductions are made for depreciation.

replacement cost coverage   Insurance to replace or restore a building or its contents to its pre-existing condition and appearance. Compare *actual cash value (ACV)*.

replacement reserves   Funds set aside for future repair and replacement of major building components (e.g., roof, HVAC system). At a condominium property, funds set aside to repair or replace common area components at some future time.

reproduction cost   The cost at current prices to construct an exact duplicate of a building using the same materials. In appraisal, a consideration in regard to historic buildings.

reputation   Esteem in which a person or organization is held by the public.

request for proposal (RFP)   Written specifications for services to be provided by a bidder, often including the scope of work and details of design and use and asking for specifics regarding materials, labor, pricing, delivery, and payment.

request for qualifications (RFQ)   A written communication sent to a large number of firms to determine the range and caliber of potential service providers. Such requests seek general information about the business, its principals and key staff members, its ability to provide the type of service that is being sought in the required time frame, and its financial condition as well as specific information about its services (e.g., previous work done or projects completed, with pictures) and a list of key clients, both former and current. Often used in contracting for architectural, space planning, and construction services.

rescind   Invalidate, annul, cancel, repeal, etc.

reserve fund   Money set aside to provide funds for anticipated future (usually capital) expenditures.

reserve replacement fund   An escrow account used to help defray the costs of replacing a property's capital items. In regard to government-assisted and/or subsidized housing, HUD and Rural Development provide guidelines on initial amounts required to establish the fund, maintenance and monitoring of the fund, and withdrawal of amounts from the fund for capital expenditures.

reserves   Funds set aside for foreseeable expenses or charges. For a condominium, funds set aside to enable the association to meet nonrecurring and/or major expenses (a requirement in most states).

resident   One who lives (or resides) in a place. Referring to residential tenants as "residents" is preferred by many real estate professionals. Compare *tenant*.

resident-based assistance   Programs under which government pays a portion of a resident's rent to the property owner. Once eligible, a resident may select any property that will accept the subsidy payment as part of the rent (e.g., Section 8 vouchers and certificates). Compare *property-based assistance*.

resident handbook   Minimally, a compilation of house rules and other information apartment occupants need for ready reference. Ideally, such a handbook will inform residents of their basic rights and responsibilities, covering basic lease provisions (e.g., when rent is due) as well as management's policies regarding use of the facilities at the site (swimming pool, exercise room, laundry room), the keeping of pets, and requests for maintenance or other services.

Residential Lead-Based Paint Hazard Reduction Act   Federal law enacted in 1992 that requires all owners of residential properties built *before* 1978 to notify new renters and potential buyers about the presence of lead-based paint. New rules regarding particulars of disclosure came into effect in December 1996. Rental applicants and residents who renew leases must be given a government pamphlet on lead paint hazards, a disclosure form detailing lead paint hazards at the property, and any reports that describe lead paint hazards at the property.

residential manager   One who manages a residential property or properties.

residential utility billing system (RUBS)   Allocation of energy costs to residents using a mathematical formula, rather than a metering system that monitors usage. See also *master meter*.

resident ledger   A record of individual residents' rent payment history, lease arrangements, and personal information (e.g., automobile registration, emergency contact numbers); a *rental ledger*.

resident manager   An employee residing in a building for the purpose of overseeing and administering the day-to-day building affairs in accordance with directions from the property manager or owner; also called *on-site manager, site manager,* and *residential manager*.

resident organization   In government-assisted or subsidized housing, a formal or informal organization of a group of residents through which residents communicate with the property owner and/or management and through which various resident services and activities can be organized and conducted.

resident profile   A study and listing of the similar and dissimilar characteristics of the present occupants of a residential property; used to assist the real estate manager in positioning the property in the market. May also be called *tenant profile.*

resident relations   See *tenant relations.*

resident retention   See *tenant retention.*

resident selection plan   In government-assisted or subsidized housing, a written plan that provides criteria for acceptance and rejection of applicants for housing.

residual analysis   A method of calculating the portion of the sales potential in a market that is available for a new store to capture.

Resource Conservation and Recovery Act (RCRA)   Enacted in 1976 and amended in 1984, the federal law that provides "cradle-to-grave" control of solid wastes.

retailing   The selling of goods and services to the ultimate consumer.

retail merchandising cart   Typically, a portable, wagon-like structure used for selling small items of merchandise, which may be positioned inside (or outside) of an enclosed shopping mall.

retail merchandising unit (RMU)   A portable sales/display structure, similar to a *kiosk,* used in selling goods in the interior common area of a mall.

retainage   Money held back from payments to a contractor, usually a percentage of the total cost of the project, until any outstanding work (e.g., punch list items) is completed satisfactorily.

retainer   The act of employing an attorney; the nature of the services to be provided are spelled out in a *retainer agreement.* Also, a fee paid to an attorney or other professional for advice or to be able to make a claim upon that person's services in case of need.

retaliatory eviction   Requirement by a landlord that a tenant vacate leased premises in response to a complaint from the tenant concerning the condition of the building or efforts to form a tenants' union. Landlord-tenant laws in many states forbid such evictions.

retention   One of four methods of *risk management.* Deliberate acceptance of a certain amount of potential economic loss rather than pay the cost of insurance premiums is called *intentional retention. Unintentional retention* occurs when an individual or business is unaware that a potential loss exists.

retention marketing   The notion that customers should be considered stakeholders in the enterprise and implementation of strategies to keep current customers happy so they will come back again and again.

retrofit   The replacement of fixtures or facilities in a building with new equipment that is more efficient, usually in terms of energy consumption, fire protection codes, or accommodations for new technology.

return   Percentage rate of profit earned in relation to the value of the capital investment required. See also *yield.*

return on equity (ROE)   A measure of return on the owner's initial investment. A ratio used in evaluating an investment, in which cash flow is divided by the equity investment. Generally, if the return on equity is less than the return on investment (ROI), leverage is said to be negative. See also *leverage.*

return on investment (ROI)   The ratio of net operating income to the total investment amount, for a given time period, which provides a measure of the financial performance of the investment. A measure of profitability expressed as a percentage and calculated by comparing periodic income to the owner's equity in the property (income ÷ equity = % ROI). A measure of cash flow against investment, it can be calculated either before or after deduction of income tax. ROI measures overall effectiveness of management in generating profits from available assets; however, it does not consider the *time value of money.*

revenue   Income of various kinds to a corporation or individual; *yield.* Also, a government's income from various sources, including taxes.

rezoning   A change in prevailing *zoning ordinances;* rezoning changes the permitted uses for the affected parcel or parcels of land. See also *downzoning; zoning.*

rider   An amendment or attachment to a contract such as a lease, a management agreement, or an insurance policy. See also *endorsement.*

rider to lease   A legal document that adds to or amends the terms of a standard lease form. See also *addendum.*

right of first refusal   A right sometimes sought by a commercial tenant (and granted by the landlord at initial leasing or lease renewal) that allows the tenant to lease previously defined additional space within a specific time period after the space becomes available for lease to another tenant or after the landlord has received a bona fide offer to lease that same space from another potential tenant (a third party). Usually the lease terms require the landlord to notify the tenant of the availability of the space or of the terms of the third-party offer, and the tenant must lease the space at market terms or under the terms of the third-party offer (if appropriate) or refuse the space so that it can be rented to the third party. This type of lease provision may also be written granting the tenant the right of first refusal to lease a particular space within a defined time period at a negotiated rent (often market rate) when that space becomes available. This may be sought by the tenant as an alternative when the landlord will not negotiate an option to expand the tenant's space. See also *option.*

right of re-entry   A right granted to the owner of leased property under landlord-tenant law so that leased premises can be inspected, maintained, or shown to others at reasonable hours; sometimes called *right of access.* Also, the right of the owner to terminate a lease and resume possession of the leased premises for nonpayment of rent or breach of any of the lease covenants by the tenant within the limits of state laws, including *abandonment* of the premises. The act of resuming possession of lands, or tenements, in pursuance of a right reserved by the owner on parting with the possession. Leases usually contain a clause providing that the owner may terminate the lease and re-enter for nonpayment of rent or breach of any of the covenants by the tenant.

right of survivorship   A distinguishing characteristic of a joint tenancy relationship between two (or more) people that, when one of the joint tenants dies, the property rights of the deceased automatically transfer to the surviving joint tenant (and not to the deceased party's heirs). See also *joint tenants.*

rings   A means of describing population concentration by referring to a series of circumferences, usually set as one mile, three miles, and five miles from a retail property. See also *trade area zones.*

risk   The likelihood of loss. In insurance, the degree of probability of loss to the insured from the peril or perils specified in an insurance policy. In finance, the probability that an investor will not receive the required or expected rate of return.

risk capital   Another name for *venture capital.*

risk-free rate of return   A return rate that has no variance. The rate of return one would earn on an investment that is virtually riskless (e.g., a U.S. Treasury bill, which offers a fixed rate of return for a defined period). Real estate investors and property managers often use T-bills as a benchmark to determine how much additional interest a real estate investment must return in order to compensate for its illiquidity and other risk factors.

risk management   Procedures to minimize the adverse effects of a (financial) loss by identifying potential sources of loss, measuring the likely impact of such losses, and implementing controls to minimize losses when they occur. In insurance, the process of controlling risks and managing losses. See also *avoidance, control, retention,* and *transfer.*

risk premium   The excess return over and above the risk-free rate, commonly established by comparing the risk of a particular investment to the risk of a standard investment portfolio (e.g., *Standard and Poor's Index of 500 Common Stocks*).

robbery   The taking of money or property from another person, against that person's will, by force or violence. (Robbery involves bodily injury or the threat of injury; because of that, it is classified as a felony.) In addition to filing a police report, instances of robbery are often documented in order to monitor the effectiveness of security at a managed property. Documenting crime is a critical component of *risk management.* All instances of robbery should be documented and, in the event of any liability exposure, such documentation would be used to report a potential claim to the insurance company.

roll-over loan   A type of mortgage loan common in Canada that amortizes principal based on a long term but establishes the interest rate for a much shorter term, after which the interest is adjusted (i.e., the mortgage is rolled over at the current market interest rate).

routine maintenance   Custodial or janitorial maintenance, basic lawn care, and completion of service requested via *work orders.*

rowhouses   Single-family dwelling units that are attached to one another by common walls and generally share a common facade.

rules and regulations   Guidelines for tenants who lease space in a building, usually outlining requirements specific to rent payment, tenant maintenance responsibilities, and the like; also called *house rules and regulations.* Specifics are usually incorporated in the lease, either as a specific provision or as a rider, and they vary by property type. As an example, rules for rental apartments may include other specific requirements, such as policies regarding the keeping of pets (use of leashes, cleaning up excreta). Those for an office building are likely to address operational issues (security requirements or after-hours access). Shopping center rules address issues of conformity (uniform shopping hours).

Rural Development   Formerly Farmer's Home Administration. The federal agency under the Secretary of Agriculture responsible for rural housing programs. See also *Farmer's Home Administration (FmHA)*.

R/U ratio   In office building leasing, the ratio of a tenant's *rentable area* (on which rent is paid) to the *usable area* of the tenant's demised premises; a type of *load factor*. See also *add-on factor*.

S

Safe Drinking Water Act (SDWA) Enacted in 1974 and amended in 1986, the law that sets federal regulations for drinking water systems and provides for their administration.

salary Fixed compensation paid on a regular schedule (weekly, monthly, quarterly) to those in executive, professional, or administrative positions. Compare *wage*.

sale-leaseback Sale of a property to investors on condition that the seller may lease the property for a specified term at a predetermined rent. A financing arrangement whereby land is sold and simultaneously leased back to the seller, usually on a long-term basis, at a rental rate that will amortize the investment and give a return to the buyer.

sales analysis A comparative evaluation of tenants' sales for specified periods (e.g., one-month or one-year intervals) to measure growth and change, commonly on a per-square-foot basis. In shopping centers, sales analysis is used to evaluate prospective tenants, compare retailers within merchandise categories, and measure the success of the center as a whole.

sales potential The total number of consumer dollars available to retailers for the entire trade area.

sales tax A tax on the transfer of personal property (as distinguished from a tax on the property itself), usually measured as a percentage of the purchase price. It is added to the selling price and collected by the seller for the governmental agency (state, local) imposing it.

sales volume The total dollar sales for a specified period, usually either a fiscal or a calendar year; may also be stated in dollars per square foot: sales volume ÷ gross leasable area (GLA) = dollars per square foot of GLA. Sales volume is often used as a measure of a retailer's success and for comparison of retailers to each other and within their merchandise categories. It is also used to compare shopping centers.

sampling In market research, a process used to determine whether the results of a study are valid—a large number of respondents permits generalizations to be made from partial results.

scheduled completion date   A term used in renting up a residential property when construction of a unit is within 30 days of completion. See also *projected completion date.*

schedule of commissions   A document that outlines the terms of a commission agreement stating how and when the fee is to be paid. See also *commission.*

S corporation   A corporation established under Subchapter S of the Internal Revenue Service Code that does not pay federal corporate income taxes, and losses as well as profits are passed to its shareholders, who report the income (or loss) on their individual income tax returns; also called *small business corporation.* S corporations have specific limitations on the number of shareholders and the type of stock (one class only) that can be offered.

searcher   A designated member of a building *emergency response team* who is responsible to make sure that all areas of the building, including rest rooms, have been evacuated. Usually one or more searchers are appointed for each floor of a commercial building.

seasonal rent   Rent that is adjusted by season, often used in resort areas. See *high season; low season; off season.*

seasonal variation   A regularly recurring pattern of change that occurs in nearly all business and economic activities owing to periodic climate changes, holidays, and other factors.

second mortgage   A mortgage loan secured by real estate that has previously been made security for a prior mortgage loan. A mortgage loan against real estate that creates a lien subordinate to the first mortgage; also called *junior mortgage* or *junior lien.*

Section 8 housing   Privately owned residential rental units that participate in the low-income rental assistance program created by the 1974 amendments to Section 8 of the 1937 Housing Act. Under this program, the U.S. Department of Housing and Urban Development (HUD) pays a rent subsidy to the landlord on behalf of qualified low-income residents so they pay a limited portion of their incomes for rent (voucher program). Alternatively, residents may receive rent subsidies for the entire rent and not pay any portion of the rent themselves (certificate program).

secured lien   A lien backed by a mortgage or pledge of collateral.

Securities and Exchange Commission (SEC)   An independent regulatory agency within the U.S. government that administers statutes designed to provide the fullest possible disclosure to the investing public. The SEC monitors and regulates corporate financial reporting and disclosure, accounting and auditing practices, and trading activities. SEC regulations apply to publicly held real estate companies such as real estate investment trusts (REITs).

securitization   The process of turning certain kinds of investments into securities. For example, real estate investment trusts (REITs) are set up to issue shares of beneficial interest (securities) based on buying and financing real estate ventures.

security   Terms or property guaranteeing the payment of a debt in case the debtor defaults (e.g., *collateral* for a mortgage loan). A share in a company's ownership normally called a *stock.* An investment in a company that obligates the company (or a governmental agency) to pay set periodic interest to the investor, usually called a *bond*. Documents proving ownership in a corporation such as stock certificates and bonds. Also, freedom from fear. The employment of personnel, policies, procedures, and devices to protect people and property from harm.

security audit A comprehensive evaluation of a property's security status that includes not only a *security survey*. but also other components of a comprehensive risk assessment (e.g., life-safety compliance issues, recommendations of specific security measures, a cost-benefit analysis) and development of a risk management program for the long term.

security deposit A preset amount of money advanced by the tenant before occupancy and held by an owner or manager for a specific period to ensure the faithful performance of the lease terms by the tenant; also called *lease deposit*. (Local or state law may require the landlord to pay the tenant interest on the security deposit during the lease term and/or hold the money in an *escrow account*.) Part or all of the deposit may be retained to pay for rent owed, miscellaneous charges owed, unpaid utility bills, and damage to the leased space that exceeds normal wear and tear. Limitations on withholding may be imposed by local and state ordinances.

security survey A critical examination and analysis of a property to ascertain the present security status, identify vulnerabilities, and make recommendations to reduce crime risks and improve overall security. Often conducted as an inspection of a facility using a checklist or series of questions to be answered. (A security survey may be performed by a local crime prevention officer or a security consultant, and it may be restricted to current shortcomings.) See also *security audit*.

seizure of assets Taking (seizure) by order of the court of the property of someone against whom a judgment has been rendered.

self-amortizing loan Another name for *direct-reduction loan*.

self-insurance The practice of a business or a property owner assuming payment responsibility for all risks, usually as a means to avoid paying insurance premiums. Also, a formal program established by an individual or a business that sets aside funds to pay losses incurred at a future date.

self-insured retention That portion of a risk or potential loss assumed by the insured party in the form of a *deductible, self-insurance,* or the lack of insurance.

self-management A plan for operating a condominium whereby the unit owners carry out policy decisions and administer the affairs of the association. An alternative to hiring third-party management.

self-service storage facility A rental property comprising individual units of space, with individual doors and locks, used for storage of personal property. Spaces may be leased by individuals or by businesses. The terminology relating to this type of property continues to evolve. At different times it has been called *miniwarehouse, ministorage* (one word or two) *facility,* and *self storage.*

Self Storage Association (SSA) A trade association whose members consist of owners, operators, and suppliers of the self storage (formerly: miniwarehouse) industry.

service contract   In real estate management generally, a formal agreement to perform certain work, as to maintain specific operating systems (e.g., preventive maintenance of HVAC, elevators) or for general upkeep (e.g., janitorial or custodial maintenance), in exchange for specific compensation. Services may be contracted for a flat fee for a designated period or on a time and cost basis (e.g., a rate per hour plus the cost of replacement parts).

service request   A resident's or tenant's request for maintenance service. Also, a form for documenting specifics of maintenance work requests; sometimes combined with a *work order* form.

sexual harassment   Unwelcome sexual advances, requests for sexual favors, and other verbal or physical conduct of a sexual nature when (1) submission to such conduct is made either explicitly or implicitly a term or condition of an individual's employment, (2) submission to or rejection of such conduct by an individual is used as the basis for employment decisions affecting such individual, or (3) such conduct has the purpose or effect of unreasonably interfering with an individual's work performance or creating an intimidating, hostile, or offensive working environment.

shadow space   Term used in referring to vacant space that is under lease but the tenant is not using it and has not made it available for sublease; sometimes also called *phantom space.* The tenant may have never occupied the space, or the space is not being used because the tenant has reduced its work force (job cuts, scaled-back hiring), but the tenant is holding onto it to accommodate possible future growth. Shadow space is not counted as vacant space because it is not available for lease or sublease, which may impact market absorption when those tenants are again looking to expand their business and begin to use space they have held onto rather than leasing additional new space.

shareholder   One who owns a share or shares in a corporation; a *stockholder.*

shares of beneficial interest   Shares sold by real estate investment trusts (REITs); they are traded on the stock markets similar to corporate common stock. See also *real estate investment trust (REIT).*

shell space   The condition of a (commercial) tenant's space before occupancy and before any tenant improvements are constructed. For retail space, the definition may vary with regional location and type of shopping center.

shock sensor   A type of alarm that signals attempted entry through glass, walls, or roof by detecting energy shocks caused by severe hammering, chopping, breaking, etc.

shopper   A consultant who "shops" rental apartment buildings, using a checklist to evaluate and comment on the appearance of signage, common areas, exterior maintenance and upkeep, and a variety of other factors, including what they see and how they are treated by on-site personnel, especially leasing personnel. "Shopping the competition"—a *benchmarking* process—helps identify strengths and weaknesses and pinpoint truly comparable properties. Shopping one's own managed property similarly identifies strengths (to be promoted) and weaknesses (to be improved). In shopping center management, such a consultant may be referred to as a "secret shopper." The term shopper is also used generally to refer to a retail customer.

shopping center   A group of commercial establishments planned, developed, owned, and managed as a unit related in location, size, and type of shops to the trade area the unit serves and providing on-site parking in definite relationship to the types and sizes of stores. A generic term applied to a collection of retail stores enclosed in one building or adjacent to each other in separate buildings. Shopping centers are categorized as either convenience, community, neighborhood, regional, super regional, or specialty centers based on their gross leasable area (GLA), type of tenancy, and the extent of their geographic trade area (customer base). Variations such as megamalls, power centers, and hypermarkets are also called shopping centers.

shrinkage In retailing, a measure of losses from theft, mispricing, and other wastage. Also used in real estate management as a euphemistic reference to losses from inventories of parts and supplies from pilferage.

sick building syndrome (SBS) Acute symptoms exhibited by building occupants that are apparently linked to time they spend in the building but dissipate when they leave it and for which no specific cause or illness can be identified.

signage A lettered board or other device placed on or in front of a building to identify the location or to advertise the business transacted there. Also, a conspicuously placed board or placard containing direction, warning, or other type of information.

signature block The section of a lease (or other contract) containing a statement that all parties have read and understand the lease (or contract), with space for signatures.

sign restriction clause A provision in a shopping center lease that limits the use of outdoor and indoor advertisements and other graphic displays. More specifically, it requires the tenant to comply with specific sign criteria regarding sign placement, size, and graphics and to submit the plans for exterior signs for the landlord's approval; such signs are installed and maintained by the tenant. Sign criteria may be governed in part by local laws that regulate size, materials, and positioning.

simple assault See *assault.*

simple interest Interest computed only on the principal (original amount) of a loan or savings deposit. Compare *compound interest.*

single-deed estate Real property covered by one title.

single-family house A detached dwelling designed for occupancy by one family.

single-room occupancy (SRO) A specialized type of rental housing that may be owned and operated by nonprofit entities.

single-tenancy floor In an office building, a floor leased exclusively by a single business.

single-wide Used in reference to the size (width) of manufactured housing. See *double-wide.*

site manager An employee who oversees and administers the day-to-day affairs of a property in accordance with directions from the property manager or the owner. A site manager may live in the building being managed *(resident manager)* or off site.

site plan   A plan, prepared to scale, showing locations of buildings, roadways, parking areas, and other improvements. A drawing of a retail site as it will look when it is completed, including individual tenant spaces, common areas, elevators, escalators, food courts, service areas, parking, and access routes.

site presentation packet   A marketing tool presented to a serious retail tenant prospect, usually during the site visit, including a site plan, demographic data, and other market- or site-related information.

slander   Speaking falsely and maliciously about another; oral defamation. See also *libel*.

slum   A residential area in a city in which overcrowding and deterioration of buildings are evident. A declining neighborhood.

slum clearance   The razing of urban residential real estate when it has deteriorated to a point at which salvage is impossible.

small business corporation   Another name for *S corporation*.

small claims court   A special court with limited jurisdiction set up to expedite handling of claims on debts of relatively small dollar value, usually on an informal basis with the parties representing themselves. Dollar limits for small claims vary. In some areas, collection of judgments awarded in evictions for nonpayment of rent may be handled in small claims court.

smart building   An office building that has a single building-wide computer system to provide data processing and telecommunications and to control the HVAC, elevator, electrical, and security systems.

social services   Any combination of services, activities, or referrals that help residents solve or prevent personal problems and allow them to live independently. These services include providing economic and social counseling, organizing and assisting resident organizations, operating day care centers, maintaining recreational facilities, and acting as a liaison between residents and various community agencies.

Society of Industrial and Office REALTORS® (SIOR)   Membership organization of real estate brokers specializing in industrial and office properties and other individuals and businesses with interests in these types of real estate; an affiliate of the National Association of REALTORS® (NAR).

soft market   Used in referring to a real estate market in which supply significantly exceeds demand, enabling potential buyers or renters to obtain lower prices or rents. Often a reason for leasing concessions related to rent.

software   A computer program.

sole proprietorship   A business enterprise carried on by one person.

Southern Building Code Congress International (SBCCI)   See *International Code Council (ICC)*.

space planning   The process of designing an office configuration for maximum functional efficiency based on a prospective tenant's space utilization needs, aesthetic requirements, and financial limitations.

special assessment   A special tax levied by a local government to fund public improvements (sidewalks, curbs, or other infrastructure) within a small area; only properties directly benefitting from the improvements are assessed the tax. In a condominium or other common interest association, monies collected from owners to fund a capital expenditure (e.g., roof replacement) when reserve funds are insufficient. This is in addition to the regular assessment for maintenance of common areas. See also *assessment*.

special damages   A type of *compensatory damages*. See also *damages*.

specialization   Narrowing the scope of a person's job responsibility or a firm's business activities.

special multiperil (SMP) insurance policy   A commercial insurance contract that provides property and liability insurance under a single policy. Crime insurance and boiler and machinery insurance are optional additions to this policy.

special property coverage   See *all risk insurance*.

specialty center   A type of shopping center often dominated by food and gift tenants and having 50,000–300,000 square feet of gross leasable area (GLA). There may be no conventional anchor tenant. Many such centers have been created by conversion of an existing old building *(adaptive use)* in a tourist-oriented area, usually perpetuating an architectural theme suggested by the site; also known as theme or festival shopping centers.

specialty leasing program   See *temporary tenant*.

special-use building   In insurance, a structure that is specifically rated according to its condition and occupancy at the time of inspection. Examples include manufacturing and mercantile buildings.

specification   A written description of construction work to be done that describes the kind and quality of materials to be used, the mode of construction (type and extent of work), and dimensions and other particulars that define the job as the basis for estimating costs. The prepared specification should allow for the job to be bid in its entirety *(standard specification),* but it should also include a line-item specification that provides for a cost per lineal foot or per square foot or square yard for additional work *(nonstandard specification).* Also used in referring to a written description of other (nonconstruction) work that describes the scope of work, materials and methods to be employed, and other specifics used as a basis for estimating project or service costs (e.g., a janitorial specification).

specifications   Written instructions to a contractor or supplier specifying all aspects of the work to be performed or the material to be supplied.

specific coverage   Insurance that covers a particular item (e.g., a valuable item of personal property such as a fur coat).

specific hazards insurance   Property coverages that, in addition to the standard fire insurance policy and extended coverage endorsement, provide protection against losses incurred from specifically named risks such as floods, earthquakes, and water damage.

specific policy   An insurance policy form written to cover a particular type of property loss exposure (e.g., damage from fire sprinkler leakage).

specific rate   A scheduled insurance rate applied to special-use buildings that reflects the condition and occupancy of the building at the time of inspection; also called *specific (or schedule) premium rate*. See also *class rate*.

speculative building Development of a single (usually commercial) building without preleasing commitments from one or more major office, retail, or industrial tenants. See also *preleasing*.

splash blocks Concrete blocks placed at the bottom of downspouts which guide water away from the building.

spot zoning A change in the use of an individual property which may be inconsistent with an area's zoning classification.

spreadsheet The ledger layout that provides for a table of numbers to be listed in columns and rows and related by formulas. Used in reference to computer software that creates such tables and automatically performs the calculations according to predetermined formulas. In office building management, a written listing that separates building standard tenant improvements from tenant-paid extras.

sprinkler leakage insurance Protection against loss caused by accidental discharge of water or other liquid from an automatic sprinkler system.

square-foot cost The cost per square foot of area to build, buy, rent, etc.

stabilization A component of the *real estate cycle,* comparable to the recovery period in the business cycle. A period when demand begins to increase and absorb the oversupply, but there is little new construction, and rental increases are asked to keep pace with inflation.

stabilized budget See *long-range budget.*

stabilized income A situation in which income projections account for rent increases the market will bear, concessions or extraordinary vacancies no longer have to be accounted, and there are no extraordinary operating expenses (i.e., income exceeds expenses; net operating income is positive and growing).

stabilized net operating income Income of a property adjusted for operating expenses but before considering debt service. See *net operating income (NOI).*

Standard and Poor's Index of 500 Common Stocks (S&P 500) A measure of changes in stock market conditions based on the average performance of 500 widely held common stocks. The S&P 500 is commonly used as a measure of market return and as a benchmark for comparing the degree of risk in real estate and other investments.

standard deviation A statistical value calculated by taking the square root of the average of the squares of the deviations from the mean.

standard form lease A basic lease form in common use in a given locale (i.e., one that is generally accepted) into which specific clauses or provisions may be written. More specifically, ownership's lease form into which clauses or provisions may be written or deleted, depending on the state of the current market and ownership's leasing objectives, as well as the unique terms negotiated with a specific tenant prospect.

Standard Industrial Classification (SIC) System A U.S. government-designed standard numbering system for identifying business entities by the type of business activity and the products or services they provide. Widely used by securities analysts, market researchers, and others who compare statistics within and across industries. The SIC was superseded in 1997 by the *North American Industry Classification System (NAICS)*.

standard lease   A lease form into which specific clauses or provisions may be written. A generic form that provides boilerplate language for the common or standard terms and conditions of a lease.

standard metropolitan statistical area (SMSA)   A designation of the U.S. Bureau of the Census for a geographic area comprising a central city with a minimum population size and all adjacent counties that are economically interdependent with it. The term is no longer in common use but may appear in older publications of census statistics. It was thought that statistics compiled for the larger SMSA were more descriptive of the area's importance than those for the political jurisdiction of the city by itself. See *metropolitan area (MA)*.

standard operating procedure   A step-by-step course of action that states exactly how a particular policy is to be carried out.

standard operating procedures (SOP) manual   A compilation that details all of the policies, procedures, and job functions concerned with the operation of a business or an investment rental property; also called *operations manual*.

standards of performance   Mutually agreed upon productivity standards determined by both manager and employee.

standard specification   See *specification*.

standard tenant improvement allowance   See *tenant improvement allowance*.

start-up fee   Level of compensation sometimes required by management upon take-over of a property. In single-family home and condominium management, a one-time fee charged when the management contract is signed. The fee is used to cover extra operating expenses involved in setting up the management account.

statement of disbursements   A detailed, usually chronological, record of all the funds spent by management on behalf of a property owner during an accounting period, usually one month. A component of the periodic (monthly) management report to the property owner.

statement of members' equity   A financial report that indicates the vested interest of condominium unit owners, or the value of their property after all liabilities have been deducted, on a specific date.

statute law   Written law that has been enacted by a governmental body. Compare *common law*.

statute of frauds   State law which requires that, in order to be enforceable, certain contracts and like instruments must be in writing.

statute of limitations   Any law, federal or state, that sets a maximum time period during which certain rights are legally enforceable.

steering   An illegal discriminatory practice that conceals vacancies from a rental prospect, shows prospects only a portion of a site or area, or encourages a prospective tenant to look at another site for housing. Under fair housing law, the illegal assignment of any person to a particular complex, building, section, floor, or unit of a building based on their membership in a *protected class.*

stepped-up rent   See *graduated rent.*

stipulated value provision   An insurance provision under which the insurer agrees that the face amount of the policy meets the insurer's standards set out in the provision.

stock   A share in the ownership of a corporation sold to investors. A *common stock* is an example of an equity security with dividends paid from company earnings. Common stocks have less of a claim on company dividends than *preferred stocks,* which have priority. In retailing, inventory of merchandise for sale.

stockholder   Another name for *shareholder.*

stock option   The right to buy a specified number of shares of a company stock at a stated price within a defined period of time.

stock turnover   The rate at which inventory is sold in a retail store, normally expressed in turns per year; also called *stockturn.* A measure of how quickly merchandise has been sold. The number of times during a year that the average inventory is sold.

store hours   A common provision in shopping center leases that specifies hours set by the landlord during which the retail tenant is required to remain open for business. Normally, these are the operating hours for the shopping center as a whole although leases for certain non-retail and/or service uses (e.g., restaurants, motor vehicle registration sites, schools) may allow variations in hours to accommodate the tenant's clientele. The landlord usually reserves the right to change the center's hours of operation as may be necessary or appropriate. An important consideration in malls and large shopping centers where uniform center-wide hours are necessary to attract and serve consumers.

store split   A method of reducing a store's gross leasable area (GLA) and releasing the newly created space to another retailer(s) as a means to increase sales potential and improve tenant mix at a shopping center.

straight deductible   An insurance plan under which the insurer pays nothing on losses that are less than a specified amount; see *deductible.*

straight-line depreciation   Part of the Internal Revenue Service income tax code that allows the value of an investment to be recovered by deducting a certain amount each year over a set span of years. See also *cost recovery; depreciation.*

strategic planning   Determination of a company's future environment and response to organizational changes. Determination of the principal products to be offered and/or services to be provided to a particular market.

strategy   The art of devising or implementing specific plans to achieve a specific goal; a careful plan.

street rent   The rental rate quoted to new prospects and that new residents will pay; also called *market rent; optimum rent;* and *street rate.*

strict performance   A lease provision stating that ownership's waiver of one default does not constitute a waiver of any other default, either of a different nature or of the same nature at a later date.

strip center   A type of shopping center designed in a single, unenclosed strip of stores set in a row facing the street. See also *convenience center.*

studio apartment   Commonly used term to describe an efficiency or bed-roomless apartment. In certain areas, the term refers to a small apartment with two levels. See also *efficiency apartment.*

subchapter C corporation   See *corporation.*

subchapter S corporation   See *S corporation.*

subcontractor   A (usually) specialized contractor who performs part of the general contractor's responsibility under a contract for construction or other work. People skilled in the building trades (carpentry, plumbing, etc.) are often enlisted as subcontractors.

subdivision   A tract of land divided by the owner into blocks, building lots, and streets by a recorded subdivision *plat;* compliance with local regulations is required. In mobile home parks, a tract of land divided into parcels that are each suitable for a mobile home; lots are sold to individual mobile home owners.

sublease   A lease given by a tenant or lessee to another entity to use or oc-cupy part or all of the tenant's leased premises for the duration (remainder) of the original tenant's lease term. The original tenant may retain some rights or obligations under the original lease and remains liable to the owner in case of default by the subtenant. See also *assignment.*

sublet   The leasing of part or all of the premises by a tenant to a third party for part or all of the tenant's remaining term. Under a *subletting agreement,* the original tenant is responsible for rent not paid or damages committed by the subtenant regardless of his/her agreement with the subtenant. Compare *as-signment.*

sublet clause   A lease provision that prohibits the subleasing of leased prem-ises by the tenant without the property owner's written permission; also called *subleasing clause.* Often combined with assignment in a single clause; see also *assignment clause.*

submarket   A segment or portion of the market comprising entities that share certain characteristics to which the seller attempts to appeal.

submeter   An energy-consumption monitoring device used in conjunction with a *master meter.* A submeter is installed in individual leased premises and owned by the property (or a private service) rather than the utility company, and the property manager is responsible for operating and maintaining the submeters and for billing tenants for the energy they consume.

subordinated ground lease   See *ground lease.*

subordinate loan   Secondary financing. In the event of default, it is junior to any previously recorded mortgage lien against the property.

subordination   The process of lowering the rank of a legal claim; for ex-ample, giving a lease a lower priority than a mortgage lien, which then sub-ordinates the lease to the mortgage lien. The condition whereby a tenant's lease is transferred to the mortgagee in the event of a foreclosure on the owner's mortgage.

subordination clause A lease covenant in which the tenant agrees to take any action required to subordinate his/her claims against the property to the rights of the lender under a first mortgage or deed of trust, so long as it does not affect his/her right to possession.

subrogation The substitution of one creditor for another such that the substituted person succeeds to the legal rights and claims of the original claimant. In insurance, the right of an insurer to attempt to recover amounts from an at-fault third party for claims paid to the insured party. See also *waiver of subrogation.*

subsidized housing Usually privately owned rental property for which a portion of the return on the owner's investment may result from additional tax advantages granted for development, for leasing part of the property to residents who are eligible for housing subsidies, or for leasing to a local housing authority. The National Housing Act, which has been amended substantially over time, includes provisions for subsidies to landlords via low mortgage rate loans and for payment of rent on behalf of qualified individuals. Compare *government-assisted housing; public housing.*

substitution of premises A lease provision reserving the owner's right to relocate the tenant to comparable space in the building.

suburban office building A usually low-rise office building set in a landscaped area located in an outlying suburb rather than in or near a city's central business district (CBD).

suburban office park See *office park.*

summation approach Another name for *cost approach.*

sundry income Another name for *miscellaneous income;* also called *unscheduled income* or *ancillary income.*

Superfund The name commonly given to the laws encompassed in CERCLA and SARA. See *Comprehensive Environmental Response, Compensation, and Liability Act (CERCLA).*

Superfund Amendments and Reauthorization Act (SARA) See *Comprehensive Environmental Response, Compensation, and Liability Act (CERCLA).*

super regional center A shopping center anchored by three or more full-line department stores and having 500,000–1,500,000 square feet of gross leasable area (GLA).

suppliers Vendors who provide goods and services to a property.

supply The amount of a good or service that is available for sale or use. In marketing terms, the quantity or amount of a specific commodity at a given price available to meet a demand. Compare *demand.*

supply bond A guarantee or assurance by a third party (surety) that a supplier will furnish the quantity and quality of material according to the contract as protection for the general contractor in a construction project.

surety See *fidelity bond; surety bond.*

surety bond A three-way contract between a bonding company (surety), the contractor (principal), and the property owner (beneficiary) designed to protect the owner from construction risks related to nonpayment of suppliers by the general contractor or failure of the contractor to complete the project as contracted.

suretyship   A contract (or bond) that states that one party will answer to another party for the acts or omissions of a third party. Suretyship, like insurance, is regulated by the states. Unlike insurance, it is a three-party agreement.

survey   The use of linear and angular measures and applied principles of geometry and trigonometry to determine the size, shape, and location of a tract of land or a specific feature of land, such as a harbor or coastline. In marketing and market research, to conduct a generalized examination and study of the market, especially to identify characteristics of likely consumers of a product or service.

suspended loss   An income tax term for a passive loss that can be carried forward until it can be offset by future passive income or applied to a gain at sale of the real estate.

syndicate   Individuals or companies who join together to pool their capital and talents and invest in a project on a scale they are unable or unwilling to pursue alone. *Syndication* enables very large projects to be undertaken and spreads the risk among many investors. One who organizes a syndicate and oversees its operation is called a *syndicator.* Also, a type of professionally managed limited partnership formed to invest in different types of real estate.

syndication   A form of partnership that permits investment in very large projects by spreading risk among a larger number of investors. A form of real estate ownership in which a *syndicator* sells equity interests to investors.

systematic risk   A concept derived from covariance and involving the statistical analysis of an asset's returns as compared to the market's average returns.

T

take back clause A lease article giving the owner the right to take back sub-leased space in order to rent it to a new tenant.

takeout commitment An agreement by a lender providing permanent (long-term) financing for a real estate project that it will pay back previously arranged construction (short-term) financing as part of the permanent loan arrangements. A takeout commitment is required by construction loan providers to ensure that short-term financing will be paid back (taken out) when the construction work is completed. See also *loan commitment*.

takeout loan Permanent financing that is funded at the completion of construction, with the funds being used to pay off (take out) the construction lender.

take-over checklist A form, ideally tailored to the specific property, used as a means of assuring that all appropriate steps have been taken to effectively transfer management from the owner or the prior management to the new managing agent and that all requisite documentation is identified and transferred.

tangible asset Any asset that has physical existence, such as cash, real estate, or machinery. *Fixed assets* are an example of tangible assets. Compare *intangible asset*.

target market The specific group of consumers whom a retailer wishes to attract. A group of people or type of business to whom the management of a rental property directs its promotion in order to interest those people or businesses in leasing space.

target marketing A sales program designed to attract specific tenant prospects.

tax An amount assessed by a government body for public purposes, usually based on income or the relative value of real or personal property. Taxes take many forms, including *real estate tax* (an operating expense before NOI), *sales tax* (paid on goods and equipment needed to run the property), and *personal income tax* (paid by the owner from the proceeds or cash flow generated by a property).

taxable income   Income for a given period of time against which there is an income tax liability to a municipal, state, or federal income tax agency. Under federal tax law, taxable income is what remains after gross income is reduced by adjustments and allowable deductions.

tax deduction   An expenditure that legally may be deducted from gross income to arrive at taxable income.

tax exempt   Certain kinds of income (e.g., interest on state or municipal bonds) which are not subject to federal income tax. Also, property used for educational, religious, or charitable purposes that is ordinarily exempted by law from assessment for taxes.

tax exemption   Immunity from the obligation of paying taxes that apply to others, whether in whole or in part. See also *exemption.*

tax lien   A monetary lien placed by federal, state, or local tax authorities for unpaid taxes.

Tax Reform Act of 1986   Legislation that restructured the federal income tax and its associated deductions. Of primary importance in real estate are its definitions of *passive activity income (and loss),* which include real property income, and its restrictions against using passive losses to offset active income — i.e., salary. (The Technical and Miscellaneous Revenue Act of 1988 delineated technical corrections to the Tax Reform Act of 1986.)

tax shelter   A device whereby a taxpayer may reinvest earnings on capital without paying income tax on them. Any device used by a taxpayer to reduce tax liability (e.g., via deductions or credits) or to defer payment of taxes. Also, a tax code provision that reduces tax liability. Under the *Tax Reform Act of 1980,* the ability to invest in real estate that generated little or no income and still make a profit because the real estate loss could be used to offset wages and other income. The incentives created in the 1980 Act were greatly reduced under the *Tax Reform Act of 1986.*

T-bill   Short for (U.S.) Treasury bill.

technical oversupply   A condition arising when there is more rental space available than there are potential tenants to occupy it.

technical shortage   A situation that arises when there are more potential tenants than there is rental space to accommodate them.

telecommuting   A work strategy in which employees connect to their employers' offices directly via telephone lines; compare *home-officing.*

telephone survey   A type of market research in which consumers in a predefined geographic area (often selected on the basis of zip codes) are contacted by telephone and asked to answer questions regarding their shopping preferences and habits. See also *market research.*

temporary tenant   A retail tenant that rents for a short period of time, often on a seasonal or month-to-month basis, usually occupying a *kiosk* or cart in the common area of a shopping center. A temporary tenant program may also be called a *specialty leasing program.* See also *retail merchandising cart.*

tenancy   The estate or interest held by a tenant. Occupying or holding land or other real estate on a rental basis, with or without a written lease. Also, the period for which a tenant has the right of possession, as under a specific lease.

tenant   A legal term for one who pays rent to occupy or gain possession of real estate; the lessee in a lease. Real estate managers often limit the use of the term tenant to commercial tenants and refer to residential tenants as residents. See also *lessee; resident.*

tenant charges   Another name for *pass-through charges.*

tenant contact   In commercial property management, an individual named by the tenant as a liaison with building management.

tenant coordinator   In an office building or shopping center, a member of the property management team who functions as the management liaison with tenants, often working with and approving tenant construction or alterations to the tenant's leased space.

tenant directory   A signboard in a building lobby that lists the names of tenants in the building. In an office building, there may be a tenant directory on each floor, and sometimes the names of the principals of the businesses are listed as well.

tenant improvement allowance   In commercial leasing, an amount a landlord agrees to spend (office) or grants to the tenant (retail) to improve the leased space before tenant move-in or as a condition of lease renewal. The exact amount, if any, is negotiable. A *standard tenant improvement allowance* is a fixed dollar amount allowed by the owner for items that may be installed in the leased premises at no charge to the tenant. Payment for tenant improvements is part of the lease negotiations. See also *building standard.*

tenant improvements   Fixed improvements made to tenants' office space, usually based on specific building standards determined in advance by ownership; specifics are often negotiable, especially in a slow market. In apartment rentals, additions or alterations to the leased premises for the use of the tenant, made at the cost and expense of the tenant and becoming a part of the realty unless otherwise agreed to in writing.

tenant ledger   A written record of rent payments and any other charges paid by a commercial tenant, usually also including details of the financial terms of the lease. At a residential property, this record may be called a *resident ledger.*

tenant manual   A compilation of management policies and procedures that relate to commercial tenants and the use of their leased space.

tenant mix   The combination (or types) of businesses and services that lease space in a shopping center or office building or (sometimes) industrial park.

tenant organization   Usually formed at residential properties, a group of tenants who join together to use their collective powers against an owner to achieve certain goals such as improved conditions, expanded facilities, and lower rent.

tenant profile   A study and listing of the similar and dissimilar characteristics of the present tenants in a property; for a residential property, a *resident profile.*

tenant relations   All of the interactions between tenants and building management personnel; at residential properties, *resident relations.*

tenant rent   In government-assisted and/or subsidized housing, the amount the tenant must pay the owner. If there is no utility allowance, *total tenant pay-*

ment (TTP) equals tenant rent. If the utility allowance is greater than the TTP, the tenant pays no rent. Instead, the tenant receives a utility reimbursement from the owner. (This reimbursement is often called *negative rent.*)

tenant retention   A defined program that attempts to maintain harmony between tenants and management, often related to sound maintenance procedures; at a residential property, *resident retention.* In actual practice, a tenant retention program includes measurement of tenant satisfaction, often via written surveys, and efforts to encourage lease renewals by providing exceptional service.

tenant roster   Compiled from the lease summaries at a retail property, a list of each tenant's square footage, the rental rate per month and per square foot, the percentage rate, and the amount of any security deposit along with the lease term (often including commencement and expiration dates). Usually this record does not show any payments made by the tenant. Compare *rent roll.*

tenant selectivity   An established set of standards used in the selection of tenants for a particular (usually residential) property.

tenant union   An organization formed by tenants to represent their interests; also called *tenant organization.*

term   A limited or defined period of time. The duration of a tenant's lease; the duration of a mortgage (e.g., a thirty-year term); the duration of a contract for services.

terminal value   The price a property is expected to sell for at the end of a specified holding period.

termination   The ending of a contract, usually when the conditions of the agreement have been carried out. Ending of an employee's employment; firing. Also used in referring to the process of voluntarily leaving a job.

termination checklist   A form, ideally tailored to the specific property, used as a means of assuring that all appropriate steps have been taken to effectively transfer management of a property, including necessary documents and records, back to the owner or to the successor managing agent.

term lease   A binding landlord-tenant agreement for a specified time period.

term life insurance   See *life insurance.*

term rent   A type of rent sometimes collected in resort areas for a specified term, usually the high season, and payable in full in advance. Also, the total amount of rent due over the period (term) of the lease.

terrace apartments   Another name for *garden apartment building.*

theft insurance   A policy that provides for the repayment of individuals and businesses victimized by burglars, robbers, embezzlers, and thieves.

theme   A concept for a property or development upon which all marketing efforts will be based.

therm   An amount of heat equal to 100,000 Btu.

third-party insurance   Another name for *liability insurance.*

tickler file   A record-keeping system that serves as a reminder of important dates.

time-and-material method   Another name for *cost-plus pricing.*

time clock   A device used to record arrival and departure of employees, who insert a time card into the device to punch in and punch out; applicable to hourly wage earners only.

timer   A device used to control the on/off functions of electrical devices automatically. In real estate management, timers are used to control outdoor lighting in parking lots and other areas around the property.

timeshare   A form of divided ownership of real estate, usually at resort properties, whereby ownership is segregated over a stated period of time. For example, a resort unit may be divided into two-week or one-month time shares, under which each owner has the right to use the unit for a specified two-week or one-month period each year.

timeshare ownership   A form of condominium ownership, usually in resort or vacation developments, in which owners buy a specific period of time to occupy a particular unit.

time value of money   The concept that a dollar in hand today is worth more than a dollar that has been promised at a future date. The basis of compounding to determine future value or discounting to determine present value. Growth of an investment over the years, especially as measured using such concepts as *compounding, discounting, present value,* and *future value.*

title   Ownership of property. Also, the instrument that is evidence of the right that a person has to the ownership and possession of land.

title abstract   See *abstract of title.*

title insurance   A policy insuring an owner or mortgagee against loss by reason of defects in the title to a parcel of real estate, other than encumbrances, defects, and matters that are specifically excluded by the policy.

title theory   Lending practice in some states in which the title to mortgaged property transfers to the lender or to a third party to hold for the lender by means of a *deed of trust.*

tort   Wrongful conduct by one party, either an act or failure to act, which violates the common law or statutory personal or property rights of another and for which the victim may elect to bring a civil suit (distinct from a contract or criminal action) to obtain judicial relief.

tort action   Legal filing of a civil suit arising out of a wrongful act, property damage, or injury involving liability.

total tenant payment (TTP)   The total amount the HUD rent formula requires the tenant to pay toward the gross rent. In public housing, TTP is defined as the monthly amount a household must pay toward shelter and a reasonable amount toward utilities. This does not include charges for excess utility consumption or other miscellaneous additional charges agreed to between the owner and the tenant (e.g., charges for the use of a garage).

townhouse   A type of single-family home built as attached or semi-detached row houses. A one-, two-, or three-story dwelling with a separate outside entryway sharing common or partitioning walls with other similar dwellings.

townhouse condominium A multifamily dwelling under condominium ownership that utilizes an arrangement of units attached side by side, often as *rowhouses* with individual entrances; also called *zero lot line housing.*

toxicity The quality or state of being toxic or poisonous. the degree of danger posed by a substance to living organisms through exposure by ingestion, absorption through the skin, or otherwise.

Toxic Substances Control Act (TSCA) Enacted in 1976, the law that authorizes the U.S. Environmental Protection Agency (EPA) to require testing of chemical substances and to regulate hazardous substances.

trade area The geographic area from which a shopping center obtains most of its customers. A trade area is generally divided into primary, secondary, and tertiary zones based on distance from the center, travel time, and other factors. The size of the trade area depends on the type of center, location of competition, and other factors. See also *demographics.*

trade area zones A way of subdividing the trade area on the basis of distance, travel time, and other factors; usually classified as primary, secondary, and tertiary. See also *rings.*

trade association An organization formed by companies in a particular industry or field of endeavor for mutual protection and to promote their common interests, including interchange of ideas and statistics and establishment and maintenance of industry standards. Compare *professional association.*

trade fixture See *fixture.*

trading A communication technique used in interviewing. The process of gaining information by asking a question in return for each piece of information given.

traffic The number of prospects seen by a leasing agent in reference to a particular property or rental space within a given time.

traffic control The regulation of people and materials entering and leaving a building to ensure such movement is orderly and safe.

traffic count The number of automobiles passing an intersection or point along a street within a given period of time. In shopping center development, these counts are used by market researchers to determine whether a site will support a proposed center. Also used in referring to the number of pedestrians entering a shopping center or mall within a defined period.

traffic report A record of the number of prospects who visit or make inquiries at a property and the factors that attracted them to it, often used to measure the effectiveness of advertisements and other marketing vehicles.

transceiver See *ultrasonic motion detector.*

transfer One of four methods of *risk management.* Shifting the burden of risk to a third party, usually an insurance provider who assumes the risk in return for payment of a premium.

transfer of mortgage A situation in which a lender transfers to another its rights to the mortgage and the mortgage debt. The security for a debt (mortgage) cannot be transferred without the debt it secures also being transferred. A loan document may include a restrictive transfer of mortgage clause that prohibits the lender (mortgagee) from transferring the rights to the mortgage or the mortgage debt to another.

transit advertising   All types of advertising signs on or in trains, subways, taxis, buses, and other public transportation vehicles and the stations from which they operate.

travel trailer   A dwelling that is not intended for year-round use (although some are so used). Travel trailers are designed for use by vacationers; because travel trailers are not motorized, they must be towed from site to site.

trespass   Unauthorized entry of private property of another with no apparent intent to commit a separate crime—otherwise such entry to commit a crime would be *burglary.* (*Loitering* may be considered a form of trespass. If the trespasser remains on the property knowing such presence is unauthorized, or in defiance of an order to leave, the offense would be a form of *criminal trespass.*)

triple-net lease   Also called net-net-net lease. See *net lease.*

trust   A right or interest in real estate or other property separate and distinct from ownership of that property. An interest in property held by one person for the benefit of another person.

trust account   A fiduciary account established by one person to hold funds that belong to another person. A separate bank account, segregated from an agent's own funds, in which the agent is required to deposit monies collected for the client; in some states called an *escrow account.*

trust company   A corporation created to act as trustee, fiduciary, or agent for individuals or firms, often associated or combined with a commercial bank.

trust deed   The document by which a trust is created. An instrument given to a trustee by a borrower, thereby vesting title to a property in the trustee as security for repayment of borrowed money. See also *deed of trust.*

trustee   The person or entity to whom property is transferred in order to hold it for the benefit of another person or entity (the beneficiary), to whom the trustee owes a fiduciary duty.

trustor   One who creates a trust by transferring legal title to real or personal property to a trustee under an agreement that the trustee will administer the item in trust for the benefit of another (the beneficiary of the trust).

tuckpointing   The cement repair of mortar joints on brick and stone walls.

turnaround investment   Short-term investment in real property that usually includes renovating the property, raising rents, and reselling the property for a profit within a small amount of time.

turnkey operation   A concession whereby the owner agrees to provide a completely finished space for a commercial tenant.

turnover   The number of units vacated during a specific period of time. Also used in referring to the rate at which tenants move in and out of leased premises. See also *economic turnover* and *lateral turnover.*

turnover rate   The number of units vacated during a specific period of time, usually one year, typically expressed as the ratio between the number of move-outs (or the number of new tenancies) and the total number of units in a property.

U

ultrasonic motion detector A device for detecting movement that emits high-frequency sound waves from a transmitter into the detection area and back to a receiver. The most common type is a *transceiver,* which combines both transmitter and receiver in one unit.

umbrella association Another name for condominium *master association.*

umbrella liability insurance A policy that provides liability coverage above and beyond the limits of a basic liability policy.

unconscionability Gross unfairness. Under landlord-tenant law, a lease may be struck down if it is found in court to contain an unconscionable clause. Alternatively, only the offending clause may be found unenforceable.

underground storage tank (UST) A large container located partially or completely underground that is designed to hold petroleum products, chemical solutions, etc. A *leaking underground storage tank (LUST)* can be an environmental hazard.

underwriter In insurance, the party who assumes a risk in return for a premium payment; the *insurer.* Also, one who assesses the potential risk of various casualties and liabilities and assigns a dollar value (premium) to be paid for insurance coverage.

underwriting Financial backing; an agreement to contribute to a financial venture. In insurance, the process of evaluating an applicant against pre-established criteria of insurability to determine whether the applicant will be accepted for coverage (or rejected) and whether the premiums will be set at standard or modified rates.

undivided interest Ownership that is inseparable and cannot be divided or severed, such as a condominium unit and its share of common areas.

unemployment compensation A government program that provides cash benefits to workers who are involuntarily unemployed. The program is funded through a payroll tax paid by employers and administered by the states.

Uniform Commercial Code (UCC) A collection of laws established to standardize the state laws that apply to commercial transactions. Few such laws apply to real estate; specifically, the UCC applies to *chattel mortgages,* securities, commercial paper, and the like.

Uniform Residential Landlord and Tenant Act   Legislation designed to regulate and standardize the relationship between residential landlords and tenants. Drafted by the National Conference of Commissioners on Uniform State Laws, the most widely accepted source regarding the rights and responsibilities of landlords and residential tenants. Many states have adopted this law or some version of it.

uninterruptible power supply (UPS)   A special power source (battery backup or auxiliary generator) used to reduce the risk of computer memory loss or damage due to a sudden power outage. The UPS is connected to the mainframe computer or network and to the AC power source and is constantly in standby mode. In the event of an outage, the electrical load is transferred to the UPS.

union   An organization of workers formed for the purpose of collective bargaining with employers concerning wages and conditions of employment.

unit   A single, distinct part of the whole; a single apartment.

unit deed   A document that legally transfers the title of a condominium unit and its undivided portion of the common areas from one owner to another.

U.S. Department of Housing and Urban Development (HUD)   A federal department created to supervise the Federal Housing Administration (FHA) and other government agencies charged with administering various housing programs.

unit make-ready report   A maintenance checklist used during inspection of a newly vacated apartment unit for defects and needed repairs in order to prepare it for the next occupant.

unit mix   The combination of apartment types within a property. The number or percentage of the total of each unit size or type contained in a particular property.

unit owner   A person or persons, corporation, partnership, or other legal entity that holds title to a condominium unit and its undivided interest in common areas; also called *co-owner.*

unit owner insurance policy   A policy specifically designed to provide property and liability coverage to meet needs of owners of condominium units.

unit size   A listing of the number of bedrooms and bathrooms an apartment contains; the square footage of an apartment.

unlawful detainer   Failure of a tenant to move out at the end of a tenancy or following lawful eviction.

unscheduled income   Income a property produces from sources other than rent, such as coin-operated laundry equipment, vending machines, late fees, etc.; also called *miscellaneous* or *sundry income.*

unsecured loan   A loan that is not backed by specific collateral, one that is not secured by a mortgage on a particular property; *unsecured debt.*

unsubordinated ground lease   See *ground lease.*

upcoming inventory Used in referring to units nearing completion in apartment properties that are under construction.

upside potential An estimation of the ability of a real estate investment to appreciate in value.

upward budgeting The practice of allotting more money in the budget than will probably be needed.

Urban Development Action Grant (UDAG) A federal or state government grant given to a city which, in turn, lends the funds to developers at low interest rates to finance urban improvements.

urbanized area A densely populated urban area and its surrounding suburbs.

Urban Land Institute (ULI) An independent nonprofit research and educational organization dedicated to improving the quality and standards of land use and development.

urban renewal A complete program for clearing *slum* areas and designing redevelopment projects. The process of redeveloping a deteriorated section of a city through demolition and new construction. Any of various programs undertaken by government and private business to redevelop and improve portions of cities.

usable area The area in an office building that is available for the exclusive use of a tenant; compare *rentable area*. On a multitenant floor, the area remaining after the area devoted to core facilities (public corridors, elevators, washrooms, stairwells, electrical closets) is subtracted from the gross area of the floor. On a single-tenant floor, usable area excludes ducts, stairwells, elevators, and the building elevator lobby on the floor if such exists, but includes washrooms and electrical closets.

use clause A lease provision that restricts the use of the rental space. In an apartment lease, the stated use would be a private dwelling. In an office lease, the type of business operation would be cited. In a retail lease, the use clause restricts the tenant's use of the rented space by indicating what types of goods can and cannot be sold.

use factor The number of hours a building operates in relation to the total number of hours in a given time period. The term is generally applied in office building operation and management.

useful life The period of time during which a building is expected to yield a competitive return. For purposes of cost recovery under U.S. tax code, useful life is based on property type (e.g., residential or commercial building) and does not necessarily coincide with the building's actual physical or economic life.

use restrictions In a condominium or other common interest development, rules and regulations, often prohibitive in nature, that regulate the behavior of unit owners and others in common areas and govern relations between neighbors.

use value A building's special value for a certain owner, based on that person's use of it. Use value often applies to the classification of a "special purpose" building or property. Also referred to as *user value* or *value in use*.

usury   The practice of lending money at an exorbitant or illegal rate of interest.

utilities and services clause   A lease provision detailing any and all utilities and services that the owner is to provide to the tenant.

utility   A public service such as gas, water, or electricity. Telephone service is often considered a utility as well.

utility allowance   In government-assisted or subsidized housing, HUD's or the contract administrator's estimate of the average monthly utility bills (except telephone) for an energy-conscious household. This includes only utility bills paid directly by the tenant.

V

vacancy An area in a building that is unoccupied and available for rent or could be made ready for occupancy.

vacancy rate The ratio of vacant space to total rentable area, expressed as a percentage; see also *occupancy level*. On a larger scale, the amount of vacant rental space available in the market expressed as a percentage of the total supply of rental space. For rental housing, the vacancy rate includes vacant units in existing stock plus vacancies in new construction (the unrented inventory of newly built apartments) but excludes vacancies that are, for any reason, not available for occupancy—i.e., units unoccupied because of seasonal occupancy or because they are awaiting demolition, rehabilitation, or conversion. (The numbers of single-family homes, condominiums, and other owner-occupied units, as well as their respective vacancy rates, would also have to be analyzed to determine the total supply of housing and the overall vacancy rate in a particular market area.) For commercial space, the ratio is expressed in rentable square feet (office space) or gross leasable area (retail space).

valuable papers insurance Insurance that provides for reimbursement of the costs incurred by the insured to reconstruct or replace important documents in order to operate normally following damage to or destruction of property.

valuation An estimation or calculation of the worth of an object; the process of determining an object's worth. The result of the process of appraising property for tax and other purposes. See also *appraisal*. Market value is the price at which a willing seller would sell and a willing buyer would buy—the most likely price that an asset on the open, competitive market will fetch. Investment value is the value of the property according to the specific requirements of the investor and is measured by capitalizing the cash flow. See also *market value; investment value.*

value The worth or usefulness of a good or service expressed in terms of a specific sum of money.

value enhancement To increase the worth and the potential selling price of a property, usually as a goal of real estate management.

value in use   Another name for *use value.*

vandalism   Any willful or malicious act intended to damage or destroy property without regard for the rights of others. See also *malicious mischief.*

vandalism and malicious mischief (VMM) insurance   A policy that covers losses caused intentionally by vandals, including graffiti art.

vanilla shell   Used in referring to the condition of the interior of a retail *shell space* that has been partially improved by the landlord. The improvements include only the drop ceiling, *demising walls* ready for paint, finished handicapped-accessible washrooms (ADA requirement), floor covering, water heater, and basic electrical outlets. Compare *gray shell.*

variable-rate mortgage   A mortgage in which the lending institution can raise or lower the interest rate of an existing loan depending on prevailing loan rates or a prescribed index; compare *adjustable-rate mortgage.*

variance   See *budget variance; zoning variance.*

venture capital   An important source of financing for start-up companies and others embarking on new entrepreneurial activities where there is some investment risk but also the potential to yield above-average profits in the future; also called *risk capital.*

venture capitalist   An investor particularly interested in participating in new undertakings.

very-low-income household   A household whose income is 50 percent or less of median income as defined by HUD and adjusted for household size.

Veterans Administration (VA)   Former name for the U.S. *Department of Veterans Affairs (VA).*

visitor   In apartments, condominiums, and mobile/manufactured home parks, a nonresident who spends time at the home of a resident (with that resident's consent) but does not stay overnight. Compare *guest.*

volatile organic compound (VOC)   Any organic compound that can be emitted into the air as a vapor; a sometime component of air or water pollution.

W

wage Compensation paid for labor or services (skilled or unskilled) on an hourly, daily, or piecework basis.

Wage and Hour Law See *Fair Labor Standards Act (FLSA)*.

wage-hour laws Federal laws and state statutes that govern the number of hours that may be worked and the compensation earned. Minimum wage rates are governed by the federal *Fair Labor Standards Act (FLSA);* states may enact higher minimum wage rates.

waiting list A list of people who are interested in renting an apartment at a specific property. In assisted housing, site managers are required to maintain a waiting list of rental applicants who are qualified to lease an apartment at the property and willing to wait for an apartment to become available.

waiver Surrender or giving up of a right or privilege. See also *lien waiver; waiver of subrogation.*

waiver of subrogation In a lease, a clause whereby tenant and owner both agree not to file insurance claims against each other for any damage to the property. In insurance, a relinquishment of the insurer's right of subrogation, usually stated in a specific provision of the insurance policy. See also *subrogation.*

walk-up An apartment building of two or more floors in which the only access to the upper floors is by means of stairways.

want ads Another name for *classified advertising.*

warranty A guarantee, usually in writing, given to a buyer by a seller stating that the goods (or services) purchased are free of defects and will perform as promised or the seller will repair any defect at no charge or replace the item or refund the purchase price. Warranties are usually effective from the date of purchase (or when a manufacturer receives a notice of purchase or other application for warranty from the buyer). Often they include specific limitations as to time (e.g., 90 days, 3 years, 10 years), depending on the item and its anticipated use life, and they usually exclude defects not caused by the manufacturer.

warranty deed A deed that warrants or guarantees clear title to a property. See also *general warranty deed.*

watercraft liability insurance   Protection against loss from bodily injury or damage to others' property arising out of ownership, operation, and mainte-nance of boats or other watercraft.

water damage insurance   Protection against direct property loss or damage caused by water, usually with specific exclusions.

watt-hour meter   A device that measures the power a building actually uses in kilowatts per hour of electricity consumed. The meter whose periodic read-ings are the basis of electrical billing.

weighted mean   A statistical term meaning the average of a set of values, with certain values given greater weight to reflect their actual importance. Weighting involves the use of multipliers and division of the sum by the num-ber of weights. See also *mean.*

whole life insurance   See *life insurance.*

Worker Adjustment and Retraining Notification (WARN) Act   Federal law that requires employers of large numbers of workers to give affected work-ers 60 days' notice if a mass layoff or business closure is planned. The number of workers employed by the company determines whether the WARN Act applies.

workers' compensation insurance   Insurance which, by law, must be car-ried by an employer to cover the expenses that arise from employee sicknesses and injuries that occur in the course of employment, usually including medical and disability benefits and lost wages.

working capital   The amount of money a company has on hand to conduct business over the short term (thirty to ninety days).

working drawings   Drawings (architectural and mechanical specifications) that contain the information needed to construct a building or a component of a building. Part of the contract documents, they are used by the architect, the contractor, subcontractors, and others. Sometimes also called *construction drawings.*

workletter   An addendum to the tenant improvement clause of an office or re-tail lease that lists in detail all the work to be done for the tenant by the owner; sometimes called a *construction rider.*

work order   A written form, letter, or other instrument for authorizing work to be performed; sometimes combined with a *service request* form. A means of controlling and recording work ordered. More specifically, a record of mainte-nance work initiated by the property manager as a result of a building inspec-tion or at the request of the owner or a tenant or resident for maintenance ser-vice. The completed form documents the nature of the work, where it was done, who performed it, and the materials used and time required to complete it.

workstation   Strategically positioned panels configured as a free-standing group in place used to create individual work spaces for employees; also called *cubicle.*

world-class   Something considered of the highest caliber in the world. A broader meaning would be outstanding or first-rate.

wraparound loan   An all-inclusive secondary loan that permits the borrower to incorporate the balance due on an existing debt with additional new financing under a single debt-service payment to the wraparound lender. (The lender then undertakes to amortize the senior mortgage.) Also called *wraparound mortgage.*

writ of execution   A statement issued by a court ordering the enforcement of a judgment.

wrongful discharge   A cause of action against an at-will employee's former employer alleging that the discharge was discriminatory under federal or state statutes or in violation of an implied employment contract or an implied covenant of fair dealing and good faith; sometimes also called *wrongful termination.*

Y

yard That portion of a building lot not occupied by the structure. Usually used in connection with private residences (e.g., single-family homes, townhouses) in referring to the space between the lot (property) line and the front, either side, or the rear of the building. Yard requirements may be included in zoning ordinances, especially in regard to placement of structures on lots (e.g., setbacks). Commercial properties developed in suburban areas may be similarly required to comply with zoning ordinances regarding building placement.

yield The total economic return to an investor. The rate of return on a financial investment usually expressed as a percentage of the original amount invested. From a lender's perspective, the amount of money paid back on a loan over a certain period of time. See also *rate of return; return; revenue*.

yield maintenance Another name for *maintenance yield*.

Z

zero-base budgeting   A method of budgeting for private businesses and government agencies that requires justification of all expenditures, not just those that exceed their allocation for the prior year. In this practice, all budget line items begin at a zero base and are funded for the upcoming period according to their individual merits.

zero lot line housing   A type of residential development in which individual dwelling units are placed on separately defined lots, but the units are physically attached to one another. The term applies to both *rowhouses* and *cluster housing* when a single building has clusters of individual units on its sides. See also *townhouse condominium*.

zoning   A public regulation to control the character and intensity of land use by areas or zones. A legal mechanism whereby local (municipal) governments regulate the use of privately owned real property to prevent conflicting land uses, promote orderly development, and regulate such conditions as noise, safety, and density. Zoning regulations are specified in *zoning ordinances*. See also *downzoning; rezoning*. Establishment of independently controlled sections within an HVAC system such that the temperature and other conditions in each zone (space or group of spaces) are regulated by a separate control.

zoning ordinance   A type of law passed by a municipality to regulate and control the character and use of property.

zoning variance   An exception made to a prevailing zoning ordinance that does not constitute a change in the legally applicable zoning.

Appendices

Acronyms and Abbreviations

The following list comprises acronyms, abbreviations, and short forms cited within this *Glossary* accompanied by the full name of the term with occasional clarifications. Duplicate acronym entries are presented so that common or more-widely used terminology precedes abbreviations unique to real estate and its management.

ACM   asbestos-containing material

ACV   actual cash value

ADA   Americans with Disabilities Act

ADEA   Age Discrimination in Employment Act

AED   automatic external defibrillator

AFDC   Aid to Families with Dependent Children

AFHMP   Affirmative Fair Housing Marketing Plan

AI   Appraisal Institute

AIP   additional interest provision (in a loan)

AIR   American Industrial Real Estate Association

ALTA   American Land Title Association

AMO®   ACCREDITED MANAGEMENT ORGANIZATION®

ARM   adjustable-rate mortgage

ARM®   ACCREDITED RESIDENTIAL MANAGER®

ASHRAE   American Society of Heating, Refrigerating, and Air-Conditioning Engineers

BMIR   below market interest rate

BOCA   Building Officials and Code Administrators International

BOMA   Building Owners and Managers Association International

BOMI   Building Owners and Managers Institute International (former name of BOMI Institute)

Btu   British thermal unit

CAA   Clean Air Act

CAD   computer-aided design

CAI   Community Associations Institute

CAM   common area maintenance

CAM   Certified Apartment Manager

CBD   central business district

CCIM   Certified Commercial Investment Member

CC&Rs   Covenants, Conditions, and Restrictions

CCTV   closed-circuit television

CDBG   Community Development Block Grant

CERCLA   Comprehensive Environmental Response, Compensation, and Liability Act

CFC   chlorofluorocarbon

CFM   Certified Facility Manager

CGL   comprehensive general liability (insurance)

CID   common interest development

CIRA   common interest realty association

CIREI   Commercial Investment Real Estate Institute (former name of CCIM Institute)

CLS   Certified Leasing Specialist

CMBS   commercial mortgage backed security

CMCA   Certified Manager of Community Associations

CMD   Certified Marketing Director

CMO   collateralized mortgage obligation

CMSA   consolidated metropolitan statistical area

COBRA   Consolidated Omnibus Budget Reconciliation Act

COS   Certified Occupancy Specialist

CPA   Certified Public Accountant

CPCU   Chartered Property Casualty Underwriter

CPI   Consumer Price Index

CPM®   CERTIFIED PROPERTY MANAGER®

CPR   cardiopulmonary resuscitation

CPTED   crime prevention through environmental design

CRE   Counselor of Real Estate

CSM   Certified Shopping Center Manager

CWA   Clean Water Act

dba; d/b/a   doing business as

DCF   discounted cash flow

E&O   errors and omissions (insurance)

EC   extended coverage (insurance)

EDP   electronic data processing

EEOC   Equal Employment Opportunity Commission

EER   energy efficiency ratio

EIS   environmental impact statement

EPA   Environmental Protection Agency

EPPA   Employee Polygraph Protection Act

ERISA   Employee Retirement Income Security Act

Fannie Mae   Federal National Mortgage Association (FNMA)

FCRA   Fair Credit Reporting Act

FDCPA   Fair Debt Collection Practices Act

FDIC   Federal Deposit Insurance Corporation

FEPCA   Federal Environmental Pesticide Control Act

FFO   funds from operations

FHA   Federal Housing Administration

FHLMC   Federal Home Loan Mortgage Corporation

FICA   Federal Insurance Contributions Act

FIFRA   Federal Insecticide, Fungicide, and Rodenticide Act

FLSA   Fair Labor Standards Act

FmHA   Farmer's Home Administration (former name for Rural Development)

FMLA   Family and Medical Leave Act

FMRR   financial management rate of return

FNMA   Federal National Mortgage Association

FOB   free on board

Freddie Mac   Federal Home Loan Mortgage Corporation (FHLMC)

FTC   Federal Trade Commission

FUTA   Federal Unemployment Tax Act

FV   future value

FWPCA   Federal Water Pollution Control Act

G&A   general and administrative (costs)

GAFO   General merchandise, Apparel, Furniture, and Other (categories of merchandise)

GDP   gross domestic product

Ginnie Mae   Government National Mortgage Association (GNMA)

GLA   gross leasable area

GNMA   Government National Mortgage Association

GNP   gross national product

GPI   gross potential income

GRI   Graduate, REALTOR® Institute

GRM   gross rent multiplier

HAP   Housing Assistance Payment

HOA   homeowners' association

HQS   Housing Quality Standards

HUD   Housing and Urban Development, U.S. Department of

HVAC   heating, ventilating, and air-conditioning (system)

IAQ   indoor air quality

ICBO   International Conference of Building Officials

ICC   International Code Council

ICSC   International Council of Shopping Centers
IFMA   International Facility Management Association
INS   Immigration and Naturalization Service
IRCA   Immigration Reform and Control Act
IREM®   Institute of Real Estate Management
IRR   internal rate of return
IRS   Internal Revenue Service
IRV formula   Income divided by Rate equals Value

k   loan constant
kwh   kilowatt-hour

LIBOR   London Inter-Bank Offering Rate
LLC   limited liability company
LLGP   limited liability general partnership
LLLP   limited liability limited partnership
LLP   limited liability partnership
LP   limited partnership
LTV   loan-to-value (ratio)
LUST   leaking underground storage tank

MA   metropolitan area
MACRS   Modified Accelerated Cost Recovery System
MAI   Member of the Appraisal Institute
MGIC   Mortgage Guarantee Insurance Company
MIRR   modified internal rate of return
MSA   metropolitan statistical area
MSDS   material safety data sheet
MXD   mixed-use development

NAA   National Apartment Association
NAHB   National Association of Home Builders
NAICS   North American Industry Classification System
NAIOP   National Association of Industrial and Office Properties
NAR   National Association of REALTORS®
NAREIT   National Association of Real Estate Investment Trusts
NCHM   National Center for Housing Management
NEPA   National Environmental Policy Act
NOI   net operating income
NPDS   net prior to debt service
NPV   net present value
NSF   nonsufficient funds

OAR   overall capitalization rate
OLT   owners', landlords', and tenants' (liability insurance)
OSHA   Occupational Safety and Health Act; Occupational Safety and
Health Administration

PCAM   Professional Community Association Manager
PCB   polychlorinated biphenyl
PHA   public housing agency
PIN   personal identification number
PIN   property (or parcel) identification (or index) number
PIR   passive infrared (motion detector)
PMI   private mortgage insurance
PMSA   primary metropolitan statistical area
P.O.   purchase order
PPI   Producer Price Index
PUD   planned unit development
PV   present value

RAM   Registered in Apartment Management
RCRA   Resource Conservation and Recovery Act
REA   reciprocal easement agreement
REIT   real estate investment trust
REMIC   real estate mortgage investment conduit
REO   real estate owned (bank-held property)
RFP   request for proposal
RFQ   request for qualifications
RMU   retail merchandising unit
Rn   radon
ROE   return on equity
ROI   return on investment
ROR   rate of return
RPA   Real Property Administrator
RUBS   residential utility billing system
RV   recreational vehicle

S&P 500   Standard and Poor's Index of 500 Common Stocks
SARA   Superfund Amendments and Reauthorization Act
SBCCI   Southern Building Code Congress International
SBS   sick-building syndrome
SDWA   Safe Drinking Water Act
SEC   Securities and Exchange Commission
SIC   Standard Industrial Classification System
SIOR   Society of Industrial and Office REALTORS®
SMP   special multiperil (insurance policy)
SMSA   standard metropolitan statistical area
SOP   standard operating procedures
SRO   single-room occupancy
SSA   Self Storage Association

T-bill   Treasury bill (U.S.)
TSCA   Toxic Substances Control Act

TTP   total tenant payment

UCC   Uniform Commercial Code

UDAG   Urban Development Action Grant

ULI   Urban Land Institute

UPS   uninterruptible power supply

USDA   United States Department of Agriculture

UST   underground storage tank

VA   Veterans Affairs, U.S. Department of (formerly Veterans Administration)

VMM   vandalism and malicious mischief (insurance)

VOC   volatile organic compound

WARN   Worker Adjustment and Retraining Notification (Act)

Mathematical Formulas
and Equations

breakpoint = sales volume × percentage rate

capitalization rate = net operating income (NOI) ÷
 property value (or sales price)

cash-on-cash return = cash flow ÷ initial investment base

coverage ratio = building area (square feet) ÷ land area (square feet)

current ratio = current assets ÷ current liabilities

debt-coverage ratio = annual net operating income ÷
 annual debt service payment

efficiency factor = net rentable area ÷ gross building area

efficiency ratio = net rentable area ÷ gross area

employee turnover = number of employees who leave employment ÷
 total number of employees

equity dividend ratio = cash flow ÷ initial investment base

free-and-clear return = net operating income (NOI) ÷ property cost

IRV formula: income ÷ (cap) rate = value

load factor (electrical) = kilowatt-hours ÷ kilowatts of demand

load factor (R/U ratio) = rentable area ÷ usable area

loan constant (k) = annual debt service ÷ loan amount

loan-to-value (LTV) ratio = loan amount ÷ property value

margin of safety = net operating income (NOI) – annual debt service (ADS)

natural breakpoint = annual base rent ÷ percentage rate

occupancy level/rate = leased units (or square feet) ÷
 total units (or square feet)

operating expense ratio = operating expenses ÷ gross potential income operating ratio = operating expenses ÷ effective gross income

return on equity (ROE) = cash flow ÷ equity

return on investment (ROI) = income ÷ equity

sales volume per square foot = sales volume ÷ gross leasable area (GLA)

turnover rate (per period) = number of move-outs ÷
total number of (residential) units

use factor = hours of building operation ÷ total hours (in a given period)

vacancy rate = vacant rental space (units or square feet) ÷ total rental
space (units or square feet)

Other Publications Available from IREM

Text and Reference Books
Principles of Real Estate Management
Practical Apartment Management
Office Building Management
Business Strategies for Real Estate Management Companies
Spotlight on Security for Real Estate Managers
The Real Estate Manager's Technical Glossary

Research Reports
Income/Expense Analysis®: Conventionally Financed Apartments
Income/Expense Analysis®: Federally Assisted Apartments
Income/Expense Analysis®: Office Buildings
Income/Expense Analysis®: Shopping Centers
Expense Analysis®: Condominiums, Cooperatives, and Planned Unit Developments